A Web of Fantasies

Gaze, Image, and Gender in Ovid's *Metamorphoses*

PATRICIA B. SALZMAN-MITCHELL

The Ohio State University Press
Columbus

Library of Congress Cataloging-in-Publication Data

Salzman-Mitchell, Patricia B.
    A web of fantasies : gaze, image, and gender in Ovid's *Metamorphoses* /
Patricia B. Salzman-Mitchell.
        p. cm.
Includes bibliographical references and index.
    ISBN 0–8142–0999–8 (alk. paper)—ISBN 0–8142–9077–9 (cd-rom)
    1. Ovid, 43 B.C.–17 or 18 A.D. Metamorphoses. 2. Fables, Latin—History and
criticism. 3. Mythology, Classical, in literature. 4. Feminism and literature—Rome.
5. Metamorphosis in literature. 6. Sex role in literature. 7. Women in literature.
8. Gaze in literature. I. Title.
    PA6519.M9S24 2005
    873.'01—dc22
                                        2005012352

Cover design by Laurence Nozik.
Typeset in Goudy.
Printed by Thompson Shore, Inc.

9 8 7 6 5 4 3 2 1

To Ken and Alex Mitchell,
in our shared search for vision

Contents

ACKNOWLEDGMENTS

T his book could not have been written without the guidance and support of my doctoral supervisor, Alison Sharrock. She directed my
thesis at Oxford University, which gave birth to this study of the gaze in
Metamorphoses. I deeply thank her for her friendship, for her efforts and
input, and for her unfailing encouragement at pivotal and uncertain
moments. Don Fowler was my teacher and supervisor for over three years,
and I am grateful and feel privileged to have had the opportunity to work
with such an outstanding, generous, and inspiring man. He is and will
always be dearly missed. Much of our conversations and work are present
in the pages that follow. Don was especially interested in alternative
forms of expression for women and encouraged me to explore the meanings of weaving, movement, and color in relation to gender.

John Henderson and Denis Feeney kindly read and commented on
chapters 1 and 2. Philip Hardie read chapter 3, Gianpiero Rosati chapter
4, and Maria Wyke chapter 5. Christina Kraus and María Zulema Abreu
Crespo gave me insightful ideas on an early version of the Arachne section
in chapter 4. Ronnie Ancona provided stimulating comments on some
sections of Book 3. Stephen Heyworth and Duncan Kennedy were my
DPhil examiners and offered valuable feedback. I thank them all for taking the time to read my work and for their suggestions and discussions.
Finally, I am indebted to Professor Elisabeth Caballero de Del Sastre at
the University of Buenos Aires for introducing me to Arachne, Orpheus,
Narcissus, and other Ovidian personages.

I also thank The British Council and Fundación Antorchas, the Over-
seas Research Scheme, Oxford University, St. Hugh's College, and the

British Federation of Women Graduates for funding my DPhil at Oxford where research for this project began. I am likewise indebted to St. Peter's College for their support of my research in the form of summer and travel grants. I am indebted to Dean Mary Papazian and William Rosa, from the College of Humanities and Social Sciences at Montclair State University, for their financial support for this book. I would like to thank Timothy Renner and the Department of Classics and General Humanities at Montclair State University for their interest and encouragement of my work, for their financial contribution to my project, and for giving me the opportunity to join them. I am grateful as well to Prudence Jones, my colleague at Montclair, for many discussions on Latin literature, publishing, and academic life. My editor, Eugene O'Connor, and the anonymous readers at The Ohio State University Press provided insightful and thought-provoking comments. However, all errors and omissions are mine. A revised version of the discussions on the myths of Perseus and Atalanta in chapter 3 has been published in R. Ancona and E. Greene, eds., *Gender Dynamics in Latin Love Poetry* (Johns Hopkins University Press). I thank the readers and editors for their comments and the publisher for permission to reprint. The Bodleian Library, Oxford, provided the image for the cover and Mr. Michael Paley, from Holkham Hall, where the manuscript with the illumination is housed, provided permission to use it. I am very thankful to them. Translation from the *Iliad* and *Odyssey* are adapted from the Loeb translation by A. T. Murray (1924; rev 1995, 1999). The translation of Lucian, *Amores* 14, is from the Loeb edition (trans. A M. Harmon, 1993). All other Greek and Latin translations are my own.

I am deeply grateful to my family in Argentina for supporting my work and for their unbending love and understanding. I would also like to thank friends and family in California, New Jersey, Argentina, and England for their company and encouragement. Good friends like Neil Graves, Effie Spentzou, Sonja Marzinzik, Eugenio Frongia, Gabriela Fairstein, Eleonora Tola, Mario Pecheny, and Gary Scott made the writing experience more enjoyable. Finally, I am profoundly grateful to my husband, Kenneth Mitchell, whose unfailing support, patience, and confidence in me made this project possible. This book is also dedicated to my son, Alexander Mitchell, whose joy, energy, and love of life are a constant inspiration in this search for seeing.

CHAPTER ONE

❦

Gaze, Image, and Reading
Metamorphoses

R eading *Metamorphoses* is a constant challenge to our imagination. As readers we try to imagine and figure in our minds myriad transformations and fantastic chains of changing forms. In particular, imagining *Metamorphoses* is a process of visualization, and the visual component of the stories has often been recognized by the critic.[1] Visual imagery is such a powerful component of the poem that even when Ovid presents abstract concepts like Hunger and Envy, he does so fundamentally through visual description. No wonder, then, that Ovid's episodes have constituted favorite models for the visual arts. This quality of the Ovidian text has led critics to search for a direct connection between the text and contemporary pictures or sculptures.[2] Ovid's stories stimulate us to create visual representations and incite us to transform text into image.[3] *Metamorphoses* is a visually charged text where the acts of seeing and representing images are widely exploited in the internal stories, in the relationship between characters, and in the effect that the text produces in the reader. Further, visualization is an intrinsic aspect of metamorphosis as not only are the changes impregnated with visual imagery, but also looking is often the trigger of transformation and is deeply entrenched in its meanings.

This study examines the complexities, symbolisms, and interactions between gaze and image in Ovid's hexameter poem from a gender-sensitive perspective. It proposes as a methodology of reading to envisage the poem as a mosaic of pictures woven in text. To do this, our reading resembles the viewing of a film that, often from text, brings images alive before the spectator's eyes. It will not be surprising, then, that film studies and the visual arts considerably inform my theoretical approach. One of the great insights of feminist film studies is the production of gender-aware readings of images. My work points in this direction. It is a feminist study of *Metamorphoses*, where discussions of viewers, viewing, and imagery strive to illuminate Ovidian constructions of the male and the female. However, I am more concerned with representations of femininity and thus the focus will lie primarily on images of women.

Visual imagery has been discussed by critics of *Metamorphoses* like Gianpiero Rosati or Nicolae Laslo who assume the position of viewers but without taking gender as a primary component of analysis.[4] On the other hand, modern readers have addressed questions of gaze and looking as gender-connoted activities, but centering only on a few standard episodes, especially Pygmalion and Narcissus. This book combines both trends; it looks at gaze and visual imagery in the poem as a 'whole,' and at the same time it explores the gender implications of looking. The aim is, in particular, to expand the analysis of gaze and viewing to less commonly studied stories (like the tale of Aglauros and Envy and the love triangle of the Sun, Leucothoe, and Clytie) and to approach the poem through this theoretical prism in its totality rather than through 'morselization'— a common critical fate suffered by Ovid's "epic."[5] Though every single verse cannot be examined in detail,[6] I will constantly "keep an eye" on the context from where the selected episodes are taken.[7]

Ovidian studies have been greatly enriched by a recent wave of books on *Metamorphoses*.[8] The present book follows and is inspired by this movement but wishes to add another feminist viewpoint. It hopes as well to encourage further debate on the subject, to stimulate future readings of the author, and to show how a new theoretical perspective can open the doors to productive and alternative readings of well-known and often visited episodes as well as of some more obscure, less studied passages.

The book also contributes to putting Latin literature on the map of gaze studies, against its common omission in comparison with Greece and early Christianity. This endeavor has recently been undertaken in a collection entirely dedicated to the Roman gaze.[9] Of course, valuable work has been done in the area, but, as David Fredrick in the introduction to *The Roman Gaze* explains, historians of Western sexuality, like Michel Foucault and philosophers from Henri Bergson to Luce Irigaray, have tended to assimilate Rome to Greece, leaving the question of Roman differences unheeded.[10] *The Roman Gaze* (2002) has opened an important area of research; my book owes a great deal to it and places itself in its line of inquiry. I hope that my study of the gaze and visual imagery in Ovid will encourage similar readings of other Roman authors.

In a broader sense, this approach to *Metamorphoses* offers another way to look at the meanings of myth, classical and beyond, and contributes to larger contemporary discussions on the vicissitudes of the act of looking in literature, art, the media, and popular culture. Ultimately, this book has a place in feminist studies, as understanding how the gaze works from a gender perspective raises further awareness of the complexities of gender.

Earlier I described *Metamorphoses* as a mosaic of pictures woven in text. While the text is the 'material' substance that we have, images are mental constructions, first of the author and then of the reader. Initially, the author forges visual images in her imagination and in the process of reading the reader creates her own imagined representations. The textual process that most explicitly reflects on this interaction between author and reader is *description*. We are facing the difficulty of how to reconcile text and image, for we are discussing with words an experience that has non-verbal aspects. The problem also involves thinking about both similarities and differences between the acts of viewing and reading. Ancient and modern theorists have debated these questions, focusing specifically on the multifaceted phenomenon of ekphrasis. While in modern terms we tend to understand ekphrasis as a textual description of a work of art, like Aeneas' shield, for example, ancient writers understood the term as description in general. These ideas offer clues on how to approach issues of text and image, as it is said that ekphrasis bestows a voice on a mute picture.[11] In the *Progymnasmata* (exercise manuals), Hermogenes, a second-century CE Greek rhetorician and a very influential rhetorical writer in imperial Rome, explains:

> Ekphrasis is a descriptive account; it is visible—so to speak—and brings before the eyes the sight which is to be shown. Ekphrases are of people, actions, times, places, seasons and many other things. An example of people is Homer's "he was bandy-legged and lame in one foot" [*Iliad* 2.217]; of actions, the description of a land or sea battle; of times, peace and war; of places, harbors, sea-shores, and cities; of seasons, spring, summer, and festival. You could also have a mixed ekphrasis—such as the night battle in Thucydides, for night is time and battle is an action. . . .
>
> The special virtues of ekphrasis are clarity and visibility; the style should contrive to bring about seeing through hearing. (*Progymnasmata* 10, trans. Elsner [1995])

Although, as John Elsner notes, there are no descriptions of paintings
in the rhetors' examples of ekphrasis, there is, however, a strong emphasis
on clarity (σαφήνεια) and visibility (ἐνάργεια), which constitute the
"special virtues of ekphrasis." "Ekphrasis is a description—which is to say,
a reading—of a particular object or event so as to 'bring it to sight,' to
make it visible. It is therefore a reading that is also a viewing. . . . To hear
an ekphrasis is also to see what was described, and to write an ekphrasis is
to make the description visible."[12] It is in this fashion that Ovid introduces visual imagery. One can make an ekphrasis out of a "real" image or
work of art, but, as in Hermogenes' passage, what the writer describes is a
picture that he creates with his "mind's eyes." Even if one were describing
a real, external, and tangible picture (say the images in the *Ara Pacis
Augustae*), in the process of transforming image into text through description the author is always working on his own mental image of the work of
art.

Technically, this 'mental image' is what the Stoics called *phantasia*,
which is deeply linked with the idea of ekphrasis.[13] *Phantasia* means "visualization" or "presentation," and for the Stoics it came to mean "visualization" or "presentation" from an object. It is, by extension, "the situation in
which enthusiasm and emotion make the speaker see what he is saying
and bring it visually before the audience" (Longinus, *De Sublimitate* 15.1).
As Elsner states:

> It was explicitly both a vision seen through the mind's eyes which had
> been evoked and communicated in language and a mental vision which
> in its turn gave rise to language. In the context of descriptions of art . . .
> *phantasia* was the vision which gave rise to ekphrasis as well as being the
> vision which ekphrasis communicated to those who listened.[14]

We thus see various levels of *phantasia*. The artist, whether a sculptor,
painter, or writer, has a mental vision before creating his work. The writer,
from the *phantasia* that he has created in his mind, constructs a text. The
text in its turn stimulates the reader or listener to form her own *phantasia*
and see the description with her "mind's eyes." In the case of a plastic work
of art, the viewer sees the image with her own eyes. Even in this type of
direct visual impression, although the concept is not applied specifically to
this kind of viewing, we could talk of *phantasia*, as each viewer forms a particular image of the same object, which is transformed according to individual perceptions. *Phantasia* as a working concept of interpretation belongs
to a reader/viewer-response-oriented approach, which relies on constructionism rather than essentialism.[15]

From the previous discussions on gaze and *phantasia* one recognizes at least three types of gazes that will play out in the reading of the poem. First, there is the gaze of the characters who literally look. Second, when internal and external readers construct a *phantasia* from a narrative they hear or read, they are endowed with a mental gaze. Third, there is the gaze of the internal and external authors that is previous to the creation of visual images whether in art or text. These gazes are not to be taken only as physical, concrete ways of looking; they also involve metaphoric conceptions of seeing like knowing, realizing, and understanding.

But the concept of *phantasia* has larger implications for the ways in which we look at art. *Phantasia* is a more 'idealistic' way of viewing, based on the 'idea,' which gradually replaced, in Hellenistic times, the classical concept of mimesis, a representation of nature that aspires to realism.[16] *Phantasia*, then, is a more creative and subjective process than imitation. As Garth Tissol states, "descriptions of *phantasia* depend on a metaphor of visual perception for an imaginative activity of the audience."[17] According to Rosati, it seems unlikely that Ovid would have consciously adhered to the aesthetic principles of *phantasia*; it is, however, possible to establish a connection with Ovid's anti-naturalistic and anti-mimetic taste, which leads him to envision an autonomous space for literature, transcending the realistic mode.[18] In this reader-response-oriented study of *Metamorphoses*, the concept of *phantasia* will be a key in defining what we understand by visual imagery.

There is, however, a problem that will pervade much of the present discussions. Although critics have used the postulate of the reader as a viewer, and so will I, it must be recognized that the reader's approach to the text is essentially an act of reading and not viewing (despite the paradox that to read we need to 'see' the letters on the page), while viewing is an imaginary process that both critics and readers construct and undergo. I will, like many other critics, use terms like 'reading' and 'viewing' or 'reader' and 'viewer' as closely identified. Nonetheless, one should be aware that for all the similarities between reading and viewing there are still differences which one needs to be conscious of, especially when we apply theoretical strategies created with visual and not textual media in mind. The most obvious difference between reading and viewing is that viewing is a synchronic experience that perceives things *all at once*. Reading, on the contrary, is a diachronic process performed *in time* and which is carried out by appreciating one element after another.[19] Some may find this distinction rather reductive, but it is still generally true, for while it is possible to view images or details of images *one at a time*, this would be a second step in the appreciation of a picture.

Feminism and the Gaze

The gaze has been at the center of feminist approaches to text and art for at least thirty years, and the role of looking in power issues is well established. The question sprang from gender concerns in film studies. Several critics were faced with the problem of how women viewed and were viewed on the big screen and in what ways power and gender ingrained themselves in the gaze. Laura Mulvey published a seminal article in 1975, in which she drew on Freudian and Lacanian psychoanalytical theory to analyze the erotic pleasure of viewing in film. One of the many pleasures of film is scopophilia, which Freud in *Three Essays on Sexuality* identified as one of the components of sexuality. In the pleasure of looking, Freud recognizes subjects and objects. Scopophilia begins with a pre-genital autoeroticism (narcissistic scopophilia) but afterwards, the look is transferred to others. Cinema uses the scopophilic instinct and turns the (male) spectator into a voyeur. Lacan gave theoretical entity to the "gaze" (*le regard*) and largely influenced film theory with his account of the mirror stage as a fundamental step in the formation of the subject. With this influence of Lacan's theory of the mirror stage—which is closely linked to narcissism—screen theory suggests that self-recognition in the images projected is an important function of the gaze.[20] Cinema explores the narcissistic type of visual pleasure by centering on the human body and thus offers two contradictory (yet overlapping) forms of pleasurable visual modes: As Mulvey states, "The first, scopophilic, arises from pleasure in using another person as an object of sexual stimulation through sight. The second, developed through narcissism and the construction of the ego, comes from identification with the image seen."[21] In the process of reading *Metamorphoses* as a web of visual images, these two modes, which we can dub 'objectification' and 'identification,' will prove instrumental.

One of Mulvey's greatest steps was to expand the psychoanalytic ideas about the objectifying power of the gaze to viewing Woman as object and Man as bearer of the look. Woman as visual object will have various positions in film and in narrative. She is an eroticized image for the characters within the screen or story, but she is also an erotic and visual object for the spectators (and readers in this case) within the audience. Woman thus becomes spectacle, a spectacle controlled by the power of the male gaze. In the narcissistic or ego-building mode, the spectator "identifies with the main male protagonist, '*he*' [my emphasis] projects his look on to that of his like, his screen surrogate, so that the power of the male protagonist as he controls events coincides with the active power of the erotic look."[22] In simplifying terms, this is what happens in the Apollo-Daphne story of

Metamorphoses 1. The external male viewer/reader projects his gaze on Apollo's and by seeing through his eyes, he gains the power of objectification and control over Daphne. However, the story is more complex than it seems because the god is at some level de-masculinized in his elegiac stance and cannot 'actually' rape. In every act of male visual control, as Mulvey explains, this reification of Woman as icon has a provocative side. If, following Freud's ideas, Woman is an emblem of "what is missing" in Man's body and embodies the threat of castration by her very appearance, her entrapment as visual object adds some sense of discomfort to Man's visual pleasure.

Mulvey's ideas of Man and Woman should be taken as gender categories and not as strictly biological, in accordance with the distinction of sex as biological and gender as a social construction. Although usually 'female gender' coincides with the biological entity 'woman,' there is no obligatory correlation between biology and gender. Gender, of course, is in direct relationship with power.[23] In the same way, talking about 'male gaze' or 'female gaze' does not imply that the actual eyes belong to a man or a woman, but they are rather positions of power from where the act of looking is performed. Some would say, for example, that phallic women like Salmacis assume a 'male gaze' or that the girl in the mirror, making herself pretty for a male viewer, looks at herself with a 'male gaze' while the eyes are still female. Conversely, a woman who has a powerful gaze is still not in the same position as a man, as she cannot stop being a woman and, like Salmacis, loses even her own identity.

Illuminating as Mulvey's article was, it still left central issues of gender and viewing unresolved, in part because they discomfited her neatly shaped model. What she left unexplored was what happens when the viewer, spectator (or reader) is a woman and what the outcome is when the creator (i.e., the film director in her case) and the main characters are women. Mulvey is aware of the last question, but does not answer it; instead, she quickly, in a footnote, directs the attention of the inquisitive reader to other texts. The other two questions she leaves untouched at this moment.

Mulvey's ideas were seminal and incited further contributions that critiqued her and attempted to fill in gaps. Kaplan, among others, asked some crucial questions. She starts by stressing that objectification in itself may not be a serious problem, as the capacity to reify may be a component of both men and women who look. The problem is that

> men do not simply look; their gaze carries with it the power of action and
> of possession that is lacking in the female gaze. Women receive and

return the gaze but cannot act on it. Second, the sexualisation and objectification of women is not simply for the purposes of eroticism; from a psychoanalytic point of view, it is designed to annihilate the threat that woman (as castrated, and possessing a sinister genital organ) poses.[24]

This statement, which agrees fairly well with Mulvey's views, is rather reductive, for it precludes any possibility of women acting upon their gazes. While it is true that women cannot respond with violence to the penetrative male gaze, they can still find alternative ways to act upon what they see, especially by narrating and becoming witnesses, as in the cases of Iole, Alcmene, and Arethusa, among others. Further, Kaplan questions whether the gaze is *necessarily* masculine, or whether it would be possible to structure things so that women may own a gaze. She also inquires if women would want to own a gaze, were it possible, and what it would mean to be a woman spectator.[25] Kaplan does not answer all these questions successfully, but in this case and for such a complex issue, which cannot have a monolithic answer, formulating them might be almost as productive as answering and in fact, a straightforward answer would even be self-defeating.

To some of the criticism of her earlier arguments, especially to her assumption of the spectator as *he*, Mulvey responded with a new article in 1989.[26] To the question "What about the woman in the audience?" she envisions two possible female spectators. The first does not partake at all in the pleasure that is on offer and thus the "spell of fascination is broken." The second finds "herself secretly, unconsciously almost, enjoying the freedom of action and control over the diegetic world that the identification with the hero provides."[27] This is what Mulvey calls trans-sex identification; she recognizes that the process in popular cinema is inherited from traditional forms of storytelling. But this is still problematic. If one follows Mulvey, the female spectator is either assimilated to the gaze of the male or if not, she is simply deprived of all pleasure and participation in the aesthetic process. Furthermore, the model of trans-sex identification seems to confirm rather than challenge the system where the male is the only possible position for power. So, to return to the example of *Metamorphoses*, the only possibility for a woman reader/viewer to gain power and enjoyment would be to identify with Apollo's desire, which in itself is not only restrictive but also problematic.

Instead, various situations may be recognized for the woman viewer. She may well identify with the woman in the film or narrative, and thus locate herself as erotic fantasy and erotic recipient in a somewhat masochistic stance. But she is also often encouraged by Hollywood to identify with the star and then buy associated merchandise. An alternative would be to identify with the male gaze, in which case the woman would be placed in a slightly askew position. This enjoying and identification with the male allows the female spectator to revert, at least imaginatively, to the active independence of what Freud termed the female child's early masculine phase.[28] But she could also position herself as a woman watching a woman who is a passive recipient of male sexual activity. She can even be a woman watching a man who is looking at a woman, or in fact, she can place herself as an observer of the whole process that takes place between male gaze and female visual object without focalizing[29] with any of the participants in particular. This capacity of the gaze of women to serve as 'witness' is, this study suggests, an important element in the search for a female gaze, which will be discussed in depth for the cases of Iole, Cyane, Philomela, and others. In brief, the possibilities for the gaze of a woman are more complex than Mulvey suggests.

An important question that Kaplan raises is "when women are in the dominant position, are they in the *masculine* position? Can we envisage a female dominant position that would differ qualitatively from the male form of dominance? Or is there merely the possibility for both sex genders to occupy the positions we now know as masculine and feminine?"[30] (original emphasis). All these questions are extremely important for any gendered discussion of the gaze and are specifically crucial for *Metamorphoses*. We will encounter these problems in several women who possess a gaze in the poem, Medea, Scylla, and Salmacis being clear examples. Does the fact that women hold the gaze necessarily mean that there is a 'gender reversal'? What femininity is left in their gazes? While much 'masculinization' is seen in the ideology of these episodes, this study will show how these cases are problematic, as women can never stop being women, even when they occupy the position of men. No human female viewer of a man triumphs completely in *Metamorphoses*; on the contrary, they are normally punished and abandoned and their gazes are not as paralyzing and controlling as those of men. The exception, however, could be made for women who witness events that happen to others or themselves and can, in some way, triumph by telling the stories.

Kaplan ends her article with an attempt at suggesting an alternative gaze for women. Though not completely convincing, her example of the mother and child exchanging gazes is a promising effort, for in this bond there appears to be a mutual gazing not based on a subject-object relationship.[31] It is in this exchange of looks that Kaplan challenges us to search for a different path in the power struggle of looking. This study of *Metamorphoses* assumes this enterprise, if not specifically focusing on the

mother-child bond. But despite the strong patriarchal weight of the subject-object implications of looking, Ovid's poem offers fissures from where
unconventional possibilities for the gaze, especially among women, can
emerge. In Book 13, for example, Scylla shares Galatea's story while combing her hair, in an intimate situation where neither gaze is dominating or
paralyzing.

Reaction to Mulvey from male viewers and critics was also construc-
tive. Edward Snow objected to the apparent narrowness of the subject-
object, male-female dichotomy. As a sympathizer with feminism Snow
felt that the power relations in the gaze as established by critics like Mulvey might undermine the very project of exposure of patriarchal strictures. Snow worried that

> such a theory can—and in practice often does—become an unwitting
> agent of the very forces of surveillance it wishes to oppose. Crucial as the
> unmasking of patriarchal/ideological/pornographic motives may be, the
> demystifying project runs the risk of occluding whatever in the gaze
> *resists* being understood in those terms. . . . Nothing could better serve the
> paternal superego than to reduce masculine vision completely to the
> terms of power, violence, and control, to make disappear whatever in the
> male gaze remains outside the patriarchal, and pronounce outlawed,
> guilty, damaging and illicitly possessive every male view of woman.[32]
> (original emphasis)

Snow examines several paintings, especially Velazquez's *The Toilet of
Venus,* and explores images of women and the power of reflections in mirrors. He concludes that, at least in these particular paintings, there are
more nuances to the gaze at play and that there is a downplaying of nudity and the female body that precludes a view of woman as object.
Likewise, through the reflection of Venus in the mirror we may well see
an interior and introspective image rather than a framed spectacle for the
male eye, although he admits that other, conventionally feminist readings
are possible.[33] The value of Snow's discussion is that it puts the hegemo-
ny of the male gaze under suspicion and opens up the spectrum of possibilities for a gendered conception of the gaze.

Approaching the issue from the philosophical viewpoint of aesthetics,
Mary Devereaux reminds us that the gaze can never be neutral and that
every act of seeing involves a "way of seeing." She also notes that talking
about the "male" gaze does not necessarily imply a man looking. For
example, a woman beautifying herself and spending great amounts of
time, money, and energy "making herself pretty" for a man, is looking at

herself with a male gaze, as an object of desire and not a subject. "In this sense, the eyes are female but the gaze is male."[34] While this statement is interesting as it gives another dimension to the male gaze, placing it beyond the male eyes, it is still rather reductive, as women are still women even when they look with a somewhat 'masculine' gaze—or rather a masculine perspective. The problem is that *Metamorphoses* also features males in the mirror like Narcissus and Polyphemus. So how does the Cyclops look at himself? Is he adopting a male gaze to objectify himself when the prospective viewer is actually a female?

Another of Devereaux's points which will be of use in this analysis of *Metamorphoses* is the recognition that even when films feature women characters who are alternative and depart from societal norms, their independence is somewhat limited and they need to (and usually do) undergo a process of re-education into 'proper' femininity, otherwise they end up dead or outcast.[35] This is mostly true for Ovid's epic, where characters like Scylla, Arachne, or Salmacis lose themselves through transformation, which is a metaphoric—yet paradoxical—form of death of their identity as women. But perhaps the most emblematic example of a female that needs to be 'domesticated' in *Metamorphoses* is the wild and independent goddess Thetis, who is finally forced into passivity by Peleus, who has the support of Jupiter. Another observation about film, which applies quite well to *Metamorphoses*, is the idea that when men are positioned as objects of the gaze one normally sees them in action, chasing the enemy, fighting, riding horses, and so on. Women, instead, are pictured as static.[36] Finally, Devereaux observes that the audience is not a uniform entity and that it entails multiple audiences. Talking about "male spectator" or "female spectator" is in itself reductive, as perceptions and readings may well vary according to whether the viewer is a black, white, poor, rich, conservative, liberal, homosexual, heterosexual, man, or woman, and as many varieties of readership that this world has to offer.[37] This is one criticism to be raised to Wheeler's illuminating recent thesis on *Metamorphoses*, namely, that he treats the audience as a fairly homogeneous whole, a criticism that has already been raised by reviewers.[38] Nonetheless, we cannot do without some generalization, or we would be talking about individual experience only and criticism, being a "communal activity"—as Stanley Fish recognizes—wishes to go beyond the purely personal.[39]

While much of the feminist critique has tried to '(re?)appropriate' the act of looking for women in more positive and meaningful ways, Alison Sharrock wonders whether significant advances have been made. Commenting on her interest in Burgin's experiment to coalesce and blur the distinctions between object and subject (the male photographer appears also as object in the photos), she sees that there is still a difference between women looked at and men looked at. Men in pictures are viewed as exhibitionist, while women are objects of the gaze; their exhibitionism becomes spectacle and men seem to hold a more powerful position nevertheless. Likewise, Sharrock agrees with Devereaux in that there is a "tendency for men as-viewed-as-objects (whether overtly erotic or not) to be portrayed as *doing something*, and men who are portrayed not 'doing something' to be read as 'feminine' (depowered, deviant)."[40] Finally, to Caws's question, "Is there some way of looking that is not the look of an intruder, some interpretation from which we would exempt ourselves as consumers?" Sharrock responds negatively.[41] For even when the pattern male as active viewer and woman as passive object is destabilized as in the Narcissus story, it seems that "the dominant mode of reading is enhanced by the very awareness that these cases involve such a paradigm shift" and that "there is no way of presenting women . . . that is not at least partly repressive."[42]

Nonetheless, some feminists seem to have been successful in discovering an alternative to the monolithic male gaze. A good example of its deconstruction is Eva Stehle, who argues for a non-possessive gaze in Sappho. She does this by avoiding or breaking down the sharp opposition between the viewer and the object of the gaze. In poem 31 (Voigt), for example, the focus is placed on the effects of love on the viewer rather than on the viewed. Likewise, Sappho achieves a blurring of the distinction of viewer and object by unspecific description. In other poems, the beauty of the woman viewed is displaced onto the surroundings like songs, scents, flowers, rich cloths, and enclosed places that reflect the woman's sexual attractiveness. This dilution of the boundaries between self and other brings forth a blurring of the traditional male/female visual hierarchies and precludes a specific place for the phallus.[43]

While some of their most useful points for my reading of *Metamorphoses* have already been outlined, critics of the monolithic 'male gaze' are too numerous for a full account of the debate in this introduction.[44] Approaching *Metamorphoses* from this complex framework of theories is a challenging task. In accordance with its protean nature, the poem cannot be framed in only one way of understanding the gaze. While, in principle, the male gaze seems to be an overarching concept which matches the patriarchal ideology of Rome, there is much room for alternatives. On the one hand, in the episodes of Daphne and Pygmalion the woman appears as visual object. But many women do the looking, too, for example, Scylla or Medea, who may appear to appropriate the male gaze. Yet this gaze is not entirely male, as it lacks the power to control and win that a male viewer holds. Women with penetrative and performative eyes seem to be punished or destroyed in the poem. However, there are certain episodes where the concepts of male gaze and female object cannot be applied in the same way. When Arachne weaves her beautiful tapestry, for example, a crowd of women looks. The viewers do not objectify or control the image (Arachne) and the weaver is in full action rather than the usual immobility of the object. Yet the viewers gain pleasure and enrichment from the act of looking.

Metamorphoses *and the Gaze*

Adding to the traditional literature on *Metamorphoses* by critics like L. P. Wilkinson, Hermann Fränkel, Karl Galinsky, Otto Due, Brooks Otis, and Joseph Solodow, among others, a more recent burgeoning interest in the poem is reflected in studies that strive to apply modern literary theories and tools. Most illuminating are those of Stephen Hinds, Leonard Barkan, Garth Tissol, Sara Myers, and, more recently, Stephen Wheeler's study on audience and performance and the collection of essays on *Ovidian Transformations* edited by Philip Hardie, Stephen Hinds, and Alessandro Barchiesi.[45] All these books touch at some point on issues of visual imagery and some of them make specific allusions to power relations and gender. Additionally, many revealing articles deal directly with these matters. Indeed, scholars of a previous generation who did so much to begin the modern studies of Ovid were already remarking on the power of images and the gaze. As is always the case, however, they make gender(ed) assumptions, often taking them as objective truths. Otis, for example, referring to the Apollo-Daphne episode, notes that "we watch the lover's eye devouring the girl" and comments on Apollo's "undignified desire to see more." Piquant as well is Otis's recognition that "Daphne is really nothing but the determined virgin whose single role is to thwart the infatuated lover. It is on him that our attention is focused: his thoughts and words that we share."[46] Otis is here focalizing. He embodies the stereotype of a male voyeuristic reader who identifies with Apollo's male intrusive gaze, who shares the god's "thoughts and words" and even probably his desire.

Attention to the meanings of art was raised particularly by Rosati in his *Narcisso e Pigmalione,* and earlier on by others like Laslo.[47] But while these critics focus on questions of art, nature, and representation, providing insightful comments on specific episodes, neither uses feminist approaches nor are they particularly interested in gender/power relationships in the act of looking. I shall here re-address the material that these critics examine with the tools provided by gaze theory and feminist film studies.

One of the most stimulating early studies is Charles Segal's discussion of landscape in *Metamorphoses*.[48] Although Segal does not position himself consciously as viewer and despite the fact that he does not attempt to write a gender-sensitive piece, landscape is inseparable from viewing. Since many of my discussions deal with description, and especially with descriptions of landscape from a gender perspective, Segal's book has definitely been thought-provoking.[49] Segal's main thesis is that landscape conveys a sexual metaphor and that its intrusion and disruption can tell us much about the symbolism of sexual violence in the poem. Further, Segal observes how Ovid innovates in the use of landscape with respect to his predecessors in pastoral poetry, Theocritus and Virgil. While the bucolic landscape is in general pleasant in these authors, Ovid makes it the theater of sexual violence. Finally, Segal even proposes that landscape is a unifying leitmotif of many books of *Metamorphoses* and that it stages an insecure world which points to the lack of a clearly defined order of nature and reveals no reliable moral structure.

Barkan also offers a particularly interesting insight into some highly visual episodes. Although his is not an explicit gender-directed analysis, he recognizes that metamorphosis is a particularly female experience and that to believe in characters like Arachne and Europa is to believe "in an antiheroic upside-down world of flux characterized by a reaction against the masculine-dominated world of stability. It is to believe in an aesthetic that is personal, non linear and fluid."[50] More specifically, he analyzes the episodes of Tiresias, Cadmus, and Actaeon—with further references to Pentheus and Narcissus—and concludes that "metamorphosis is, at the deepest level, a transfiguration of the self," exercised in these episodes through the eyes. All these characters reach a point in their stories where they gaze at something sacred and in it they perceive a mirror image of themselves. The encounter with their own identity through viewing produces such a deep impact that the only possible outcome seems to be transformation; thus physical metamorphosis is a literalized symbol of inner change. Yet, unlike these characters, Perseus seems to be a master of both mirror and the sacred being, which Barkan identifies with the serpent. He never looks at his own image, but instead learns to look at the Gorgon only through her reflection on his shield. Perseus, according to Barkan, has a special ability with shadow and reflection.[51] Barkan's ideas are relevant because he explores the act of looking and its links to power and transformation. However, he does not place the accent on the female; the characters he is interested in are mainly men, including problematic males like Narcissus. Even when he discusses Actaeon or Pentheus his eyes are aligned with those of the male characters while the females who are vital actors in these stories are left somewhat in the dark.

Tissol, in his study of wit and narrative in *Metamorphoses*, makes some acute observations about *phantasia* and visualization. He analyzes the process of bringing abstract concepts "before the reader's eyes" in the *prosopopeiae* of Invidia, Fames, Somnus, and the house of Fama. He recognizes that Ovid "took this form of imaginative actualization far beyond its origins, making it a thematic principle, an embodiment of transformation itself. . . . Personification embodies the transformative nature of Ovidian language in an especially extreme form, and nothing could be more closely bound up with Ovidian metamorphosis."[52] Again, change is tightly entwined with visual imagery.

Sharrock's *Womanufacture* offers an illuminating analogy between Pygmalion's creation of his own object of love and the elegiac poet who construes a fictitious *puella* to fall in love with her, a reading that takes into account the identification of woman as visual object and text and the artist as poet and reader.[53] In 1991, Elsner and Sharrock offered some interesting reflections on the myth of Pygmalion from two different yet complementary viewpoints. Traditional criticism tended to view Pygmalion as an alter-ego for the poet Ovid, where Pygmalion's "success" as artist serves as a "most celebrated exemplar of the potentialities belonging to the fine arts."[54] But Pygmalion had also been seen as an episode of artistic failure.[55] Elsner's new perspective does not take Pygmalion as a myth of the artist but rather sees the sculptor as viewer. This has important repercussions for reading *Metamorphoses*. Pygmalion the artist is suggestive of the writer (whether this implies Ovid or Orpheus or both); Pygmalion as viewer can function as a myth of the ideal reader. The ivory statue, which can be taken as a metaphor for the poem, was created by Pygmalion the sculptor but turned him into viewer-lover. Elsner's juxtaposition of viewer and reader, which extends in much of this study to internal and external viewers, is compelling. Elsner shows that Pygmalion's supremacy as an artist has to do with his preponderance as viewer—he is actually the only one who ever sees his statue. Pygmalion as viewer embodies a metaphor for the reader as creator of his own narrative.[56] Sharrock also sees Pygmalion as reader and the ivory statue as art-text, but she focuses on the male creative activity as erotic. She believes that "like Ovid in *Amores* 1.2, Pygmalion is in love with love rather than with a love-object: he is in love with his own creative and erotic process. Such are the erotics of the art-text. As 'reader' of his own art-text, Pygmalion is seduced by it and enticed to penetrate its meaning."[57] However, unlike Genevieve Liveley, Sharrock assigns no subjectivity or self-agency to the statue.[58]

In his article on Narcissus in *Sexuality in Ancient Art*, Elsner focuses on the late antique interpretations of pictures of Narcissus in Roman art by Philostratus and Callistratus. But while doing so, he investigates the articulation of the viewer's desire with the object of the gaze.[59] Although Elsner does not analyze Ovid's episode directly, his comments on the myth of Narcissus are enlightening for readers of *Metamorphoses*. He explores issues of objectification through the gaze of the viewer and applies it specifically to the effects of self-objectification. He concludes that Narcissus is a perfect viewer of art in the mode of naturalism and offers some cogent remarks about gender issues and the gaze. He suggests that Narcissus looks at his image as a man would look at his *eromenos* or at a woman; but he also looks at himself as a woman in a male-dominated society would look at herself or as a boy in a homosexual culture. That is, he looks at himself as one who is being looked at. From subject, Narcissus has turned himself into a kind of object.[60]

Georgia Nugent re-appraises the story of Hermaphroditus from a feminist perspective. In her analysis she makes acute observations on the gaze and the use of mainly Freudian but also Lacanian psychoanalytical approaches. Nugent understands that while in appearance this is a story of blurring and inversion of sexual differences, the text refuses to upset in any fundamental way the axis of masculine and feminine. She sees that Salmacis' relation to herself is specular and her nymphomania can be linked to psychoanalytic views of female narcissism where the woman knows herself as the image others perceive. Nugent seems to suggest a gender inversion in Salmacis' gaze and she also relates her ocular desire to possess Hermaphroditus to the fantasy of penis envy.[61]

Amy Richlin's article on Ovid's rapes also addresses issues of gaze, pornography, and problems of gender and reading.[62] Richlin focuses on the spectacle of violence in rape and shows how characters like Daphne and Philomela are turned into visual objects. Against critics who see the stories as sympathetic pictures of rape, Richlin shows that the text conveys a sense of pleasure in violence.

But one of the most direct applications of gaze theory to *Metamorphoses* is seen in Segal's 1994 article on Philomela, which raises some of the same issues as Richlin. Segal observes that in the case of Tereus the "'tyrannical' assertion of male domination over the female body"—which later culminates in rape and mutilation—is enacted "symbolically through the aggressive penetration of the male gaze," which combines fetishistic scopophilia and sadism.[63] Segal not only recognizes Tereus as a tyrant who holds a powerful male gaze in the terms of Mulvey, but he also sees a female reader in Procne when she decodes her sister's weaving. Segal also adopts a reader-response approach when he inquires about the possible reactions of the external reader to Philomela's cloth: it may invite the male reader to voyeuristic complicity in the crime or the female reader to complicity in the vengeance.[64] Issues of gaze, gender, art, and power are also discussed in his 1998 analysis of Pygmalion, Andromeda, and Philomela: "If the female body in the *Metamorphoses* is characterized by its status as a visual object, its passivity, its appropriation by the male libidinal imagination, and its role as vessel to be 'filled' by male seed to continue a heroic lineage, the ideal of the male body is impenetrability."[65] While there is much truth in Segal's statement, such gender pigeon-holing runs the risk, as Snow warns us, of undermining the very project of patriarchal exposure that it tries to carry out by limiting the options for men and women.

Ways of Reading

The focus of this study is deeply linked with issues of readership and narrative. The viewer will be frequently identified with the reader and the image with the text. But the author as 'plastic' artist, through the use of *phantasia* to construct visual images, is also a reader and a viewer. The range of reading strategies that most suits inquiries about the reader is that of reader-response criticism, though concerns about the role of the audience and their response to a text are already present in the works of ancient literary critics like Plato, Aristotle, Horace, and Longinus. Reader-response theory is broad and by no means uniform, but its common aim is to ask about the reader's role. It gives pre-eminence to the eyes of the reader rather than to the text as sacrosanct voice.[66] In essence, "reader-response critics would argue that a poem cannot be understood apart from its results. Its 'effects,' psychological and otherwise, are essential to any accurate description of its meaning, since that meaning has no effective existence outside of its realization in the mind of the reader."[67] In this sense, reader-response criticism questions the status of the text and its objectivity and poses for the reader an active role whereby he participates in the production of meaning.[68] For many reader-response theorists like W. Iser, this does not imply the death of the text, but "the range of interpretations that arise as a result of the reader's creative activity is seen rather as proof of the text's 'inexhaustibility.'"[69] Furthermore, Iser states that it is precisely "the convergence of the text and the reader" that "brings the literary work into existence."[70] This kind of approach opens up to a multiplicity of readings and viewings, which is more appropriate to the nature of *Metamorphoses*.[71] While the reader holds some independence and participates actively in the creation of meaning, the text still stands. For Stanley Fish, the act of literary criticism becomes the description of the act of reading. This redefines literature, not as an object but as an experience, because it makes the responses of the reader, rather than the contents of the text, the focus of critical attention.[72] For reader-response critics, then, talking about reading is also part of the act of reading and this forms part of the present project. As a general caveat, then, whenever I refer to "Ovid," the "author," or the "text," what I am implying is the reader's perceptions of them. But Fish's definition of interpretation removes the text from the center of attention almost completely.[73] I want to stay somewhere in the middle, for I recognize that through interaction between the properties of the texts and readers, different meanings can be uncovered for and by different readers. I also combine reader-response approaches with gaze theory, a task that has been successfully undertaken for readings of classical antiquity by Helen Elsom, Segal, and Sharrock.[74]

But if one is describing the experience of the reader, how is it possible to approach this mainly individual experience in a meaningful way without falling into indiscriminate generalizations? Following Devereaux (above), in strict terms there is no general reader and there are as many readings as readers. This said, generalization is at some level necessary.[75] Here, the concept of 'interpretative communities,' which plays a crucial role in recent theories of reading, is relevant. Stanley Fish first insinuated it in 1980 with "Literature in the Reader" and then fully developed it in "Interpreting the *Variorum*." He implied that since sign systems are basically social constructions that individuals share, a reader's perceptions and judgments are a function of the assumptions shared by the communities he belongs to.[76] This same problem was faced by Due in his study of *Metamorphoses*, where he attempted to read the poem "through the eyes of ancient readers" and to expose "why and how" ancient readers understood *Metamorphoses*.[77] While it may be questionable to what extent this enterprise is feasible or useful, Due argues the problem of readership in a convincing way. He believes that only when a reading can be shared by others does it have some objective value and that the experience of the audience has points in common even when we cannot agree on the analysis of a work.[78] However, Fish's concept of interpretive communities is not without its problems, for the response of the reader may be seen to be unpredictable at some level and 'like-mindedness' is not sufficient to account for the experience of each individual reader.[79] Thus, the following readings of *Metamorphoses* do not claim to be common to the whole Ovidian audience; rather my hope is to present some features that readers will recognize that they share and to stimulate them to create new, ever-changing readings of this ever-changing poem.

I have previously discussed the question of female viewers and female creators of film. The same question must be addressed for the reader: In what ways do a female and a male reading differ and how can a woman read a text?[80] This issue has a long history in the scholarly debate, which exceeds the limits of this introduction.[81] Nonetheless we may begin with two modes of reading that are particularly useful: *resisting* and *releasing* Reading as resistance began with Judith Fetterly's *The Resisting Reader*, where the author attempts to appropriate a feminine reading by questioning the authority of the male author and critic and by exposing the patriarchal strategies of the texts.[82] Fetterly also recognizes that the woman reader is forced to adopt a male point of view for male-biased texts and that readings of texts tend to present the masculine experience as universal. This 'immasculation' of the female reader can be equated with the visual experience of the woman viewer who is forced to adopt a masculine gaze in Mulvey's model. Thus Fetterly's strategy seems complementary to Mulvey's in the field of reading.

To escape this bind, critics like Devereaux—who also claims for "reading against the grain, re-reading or revision" of traditional male texts—remark that to react against patriarchal conceptions of art and art products, two solutions are possible. On the one hand, feminists have created 'counter-cinema,' a strategy that strives to create a 'female voice.' On the other hand, one can develop methods of dealing with existing texts by 'resisting' them. Or, as Richlin puts it, there are three things that one can do with male-authored/biased texts: "throw them out, take them apart, find female-based ones instead."[83] The strategies of the resisting reader have the aim both of critique and re-appropriation, thus providing an alternative to the male gaze. But this mode of reading, as sympathetic to feminism as it appears, is not entirely unproblematic. Criticisms were raised because Fetterly's project risks replacing one monoview with another and does not give "sufficient credit to the multiplicity of perspective in the act of reading."[84]

An alternative way of reading would be releasing. This strategy essentially allows women's voices to speak despite the author. It is a reading of the female voice in male-authored texts as independent from the voice of the male authorial intention. This is a more recuperative method that subordinates the authority of the author to that of female characters,

which is well exemplified by Efrossini Spentzou's reading of the *Heroides* as
women writers and critics who awaken from their literary lethargy and
assume their own artistic voices. Releasing is, in essence, a shift of focus
away from the author that allows agency to the female (and male) characters.[85]

Students of *Metamorphoses* have gone in both directions. Richlin is an
obvious resisting reader and so is Leslie Cahoon; but while Richlin sees an
intrinsic misogyny in Ovid, Cahoon takes the richness and multiplicity of
voices and female characters in *Metamorphoses* as a sign that the poem is
open to multiple perspectives, including that of a female reader.[86] Clara
Shaw Hardy's piece on Arachne also follows this critical direction.[87] She
maintains that although Ovid is being sympathetic to women and female
victims, we actually see an erasure of them in favor of the transformed
gods. Therefore, Arachne's voice is somewhat silenced even before metamorphosis. A fine reading, but does this mean that Ovid or "the author" is
suppressing Arachne's voice? How does this fit with the common identification of the girl with the poet himself, later silenced by a "god"? Finally,
Patricia Joplin resists the "misogyny" of psychoanalysis and sees in Ovid
and some of his interpreters a "silencing" of women in the tale of
Philomela that feminists must fight and expose.[88]

Liveley's approach to Pygmalion and the Propoetides is both resisting
and releasing.[89] While at first she unmasks the male bias in the apparent
authorial (of Ovid, Orpheus, and Pygmalion) judgment of them in the
poem, she proceeds to analyze the episode from a feminine perspective.
She allows the ivory maiden some subjectivity and female agency. Also, a
rather recuperative approach can be found in Elissa Marder's work on
Philomela. Marder sees that in the silence of Procne and Philomela and
their vengeance there are a refusal to speak the language of the father and
a violation of his laws. Likewise, she likens the women in the tale striving
for an alternative, "disarticulated" language with the struggles of feminism "to find a discursive vocabulary for experiences both produced and
silenced by patriarchy."[90]

This study will not adopt a one-way reading strategy for *Metamorphoses*. There is indeed a powerful male pen behind the poem, but I still
want to let the female voice and image speak for themselves. In a poem
that is in constant flux and where the voices of characters and author(s)
are in constant movement and cannot (are not meant to) be sharply distinguished, a unique critical positioning will only lead to the impoverish-
ment of the reading. I am then consciously opting for eclecticism, because
the very nature of the poem claims it and deserves it. Although I try to
bear in mind that the visual images are constructed by a male viewer/

artist and that they are intended—for the most part—for a masculine viewer/reader (this would fit quite nicely with Mulvey's model), if this were the only perspective, it would simplify the wealth of meanings and possibilities that *Metamorphoses* offers to a modern reader. I also intend, to some extent, to de-historicize the poem and read it as a work open to modern audiences, which include women readers. Likewise, while I discuss the possible male authorial "intentions" (or rather the reader's perceptions of what the "authorial intentions" are) and gaze behind the construction of a certain episode, I also allow agency to female characters, because *Metamorphoses* lets women act and become central actors in the stories, even when their achievements are restricted. My method is therefore not entirely resisting but also not only recuperative, and in many episodes I try to explore the outcomes of examining a story from both perspectives.

CHAPTER TWO

❧

The Intrusive Gaze

Gaze, Desire, and Penetration

That the 'male gaze' is active and penetrative is a well-established tenet of feminism. This performative power is stressed in Kaplan's observation that men's gazes carry the power of action and possession, while women can return the gaze but cannot act upon it. Her contention is particularly relevant for the discussion of the present chapter and to Roman conceptions of seeing and sexuality.[1] Latin views on the gaze transpire clearly in a poignant entry of Varro's *De Lingua Latina*:

> *video* a visu, <id a vi>: qui<n>que enim sensuum maximus in oculis: nam cum sensus nullus quod abest mille passus sentire possit, oculorum sensus vis usque pervenit ad stellas. Hinc:
>> visenda vigilant, vigilium invident.
> et Acci:
>> cum illud o<c>uli<s> violavit <is>, qui invidit invidendum
> a quo etiam violavit virginem pro vit<i>avit dicebant; aeque eadem modestia potius cum muliere fuisse quam concubuisse dicebant.

> "*I see*" from "vision," that is, from *vis* "force," for the greatest of the five senses is in the eyes. For while no sense can perceive what is a thousand paces away, the strength of the eyes' perception reaches up to the stars. Hence:
>> They watch what must be watched, and hate the vigil
> And in Accius:
>> When he [Actaeon], who looked upon what must not be seen, violated [her/Diana] with his eyes,

From which they even said "he violated the virgin" instead of "he ruined
her," and with the same modesty they said that someone "was" with his
wife rather than "he lay together" with her. (*De Lingua Latina* 6.80)

Varro's false derivation of *video* from *vis* can be taken nonetheless as a
reflection of Roman ideology about the gaze and can be linked with
Western *phallogocularcentrism*.[2] *Vis* is sometimes associated with sexual
violence and thus Varro connects seeing with the male power to violate
the female body. This link between vision and sexual potency points to
the performative power of the male gaze. The very word for man in Latin,
vir, has also been connected in a mistaken etymological derivation with
the word for strength, *vis*.[3] A similar relation is latent in the Latin word
acies which means at the same time a sharp edge or point, vision, and
sharpness or keenness of the sight, thus implying a penetrative power in
the gaze.[4] The fact that *acies* is used in the semantic field of battle may
also be relevant for Roman ideas about the gaze, as it also involves an
active advancement of a military troop or line. Finally, one may also consider here that "the eye is a tactile creature, an agent of human contact,"
as Claude Gandelman states, and that in a more *haptic* (and eroticized?)
form of vision the gaze "touches" the surface of an image.[5] In a simplifying way, one could say, for example, that in the erotic look of Jupiter on
Callisto, there is always an implicit yearning for touch. This chapter,
then, will explore these connotations of seeing, namely, the penetrative
and intrusive aspects of looking, in Ovid's *Metamorphoses*, and will also
investigate its variations, destabilizations, and deconstructions.

RE-VIEWING RAPE

Rape is a pervasive theme in Ovid's epic and a situation where the male
gaze is acting, controlling, and penetrating.[6] Jupiter is the most prominent
rapist in the poem, who in his various adventures maintains a pattern: he
sees, he falls in love, he chases and deceives and finally ravishes the
woman. The first victim of the lord of the thunderbolt—and the first
'true' rape victim in the poem—is Io in Book 1, whose father, Inachus,
laments her loss, not knowing what has happened. Soon her fate is
known.

The first contact of Jupiter with the girl is achieved through the eyes:
viderat a patrio redeuntem Iuppiter illam/ flumine/ "Jupiter had seen her
returning from her father's stream" (*Met*.1.588–89).[7] Then the god woos
her with words, but the girl escapes (*Met*.1.597). As usual with gods, and

Jupiter in particular, there is a display of masculinity in the speech of the wooer. Here, Jupiter remarks that he holds the scepter and throws the thunderbolts ("*sed qui caelestia magna/ sceptra manu teneo, sed qui vaga fulmina mitto*"/ "'But I am the one who holds the celestial scepter in his mighty hand, I am the one who hurls the wandering thunderbolts,'" Met.1. 595–96). Both elements are well-recognized phallic symbols. The girl tries to escape but soon after, Jupiter catches up and rapes her (*tenuitque fugam rapuitque pudorem/* "He held her flight and raped her," Met.1.600). What began as a penetrative gaze is followed by a grasp/detention of the victim by the aggressor implicit in *tenuit* and concludes with an act of penetration. The power of action involved in the male gaze is fairly obvious, but there are aspects of the story which have been disregarded, perhaps because the feminist efforts to dismantle and expose patriarchal strictures have led critics to focus almost solely on Jupiter and Io. What is missing in much of the discussions is Juno. To rape Io, Jupiter needs to blind his divine sister and consort. He covers the scene with a thick dark cloud (*cum deus inducta latas caligine terras/ occuluit* . . . / "When the god covered the wide land with a dark mist spread over it," Met.1.599–600).[8] In contrast with her husband, Juno's gaze cannot penetrate the darkness, and she cannot see. Nonetheless, she senses that she is being wronged. Juno's gaze, like that of most gods, is vertical. She looks downward from the sky (*Interea medios Iuno despexit in Argos* "Meanwhile Juno looked down upon the middle of Argos," Met.1.601; *atque suus coniunx ubi sit circumspicit* . . . *quem postquam caelo non repperit/* "And when his wife looked around to see where her husband was . . . after she did not find him in the sky," Met.1.605 and 607; *ait delapsaque ab aethere summo/* "She said so sliding down from the top of heaven," Met.1.608). The vertical gaze pertains to deities and males but is felt as devious in women.

A witty twist operates in the passage. While Jupiter changes Io into a white heifer to disguise her, Juno can still 'see' who she is. Juno asks for the heifer as a present and Jupiter feels that *non dare suspectum est/* "Not to give it to her would be suspicious," (Met.1.618) and that if he did not give it to her *poterat non vacca videri!/* "She could seem not to be a cow!" (Met.1.621). *Suspicere* points precisely at the idea of seeing what is underneath the appearances, and this is exactly what the cow-eyed goddess does, which also represents a more feminine and alternative way of seeing and reading. Perhaps, the askance position of Juno's gaze may hint at the way females read and look at/in *Metamorphoses*, placed in an oblique spot, not being able to read like men, yet not having a clearly constructed place as women. But perhaps this very oblique positioning opens up to more and different readings for women than a straightforward gaze. Juno's "suspicion" can be then taken as meta-literary and programmatic.

Interestingly, the play on eyes goes on, as the girl is put under the custody of Argus, the monster with one hundred eyes. Argus' eyes are, however, surrogates for Juno's and in this sense the oblique quality of her gaze is developed further. While the goddess has certain power to control the girl with the gaze, she has no rule against males, neither Jupiter, nor Mercury, who puts all of Argus' watchful eyes to sleep with the story and *phantasia* of Pan and Syrinx. Mercury finally cuts off Argus' head, but Juno, in an effort to preserve the power of her surrogate's gaze, collects Argus' eyes and places them in the feathers of her bird, the peacock (*Met.*1.722–23). Later in Book 2 she flies across the skies in her chariot borne by peacocks (*habili Saturnia curru,/ ingreditur liquidum pavonibus aethera pictis,/ tam nuper pictis caeso pavonibus Argo/* "The daughter of Saturn advances through the flowing air in her swift chariot drawn by decorated peacocks, decorated only recently after the death of Argus," *Met.* 2.531–33). This symbolic decapitation of Argus is also a form of castration. Juno as a female cannot control her gaze and is overwhelmed by masculine *vis*. Not only is her own gaze easily obstructed, but she also ends up in a sadly mocking and fetishistic gesture of carrying Argus' eyes as decorative blind spots on her peacocks. The hundred eyes of Argus have become, from being powerful and controlling, passive articles of visual enhancement of the birds. Juno then represents an intersection in the axes divine/human and male/female. As goddess she manages to possess a gaze, which can have some effective power over humans; but against the divine male, her eyes become disarmed and nonperformative. Yet the eyes of Argus on the peacock may recapture the power of the female gaze even after decapitation by keeping the idea that the *matrona* has eyes out everywhere for the security of the *domus*. Thus Juno is not so easily defeated as she can seem, for, like a *matrona*, she wins by the appearance of submission.

It can also be added that Juno's jealousy (*in-vidia*) is based on a desire to regain Jove's gaze, which had been placed on Io, for herself. It is significant that Juno punishes Io by throwing the horrifying image of a fury before the girl's eyes and blinding her from knowledge and sense of reality:

> horriferamque oculis animoque obiecit Erinyn
> paelicis Argolicae stimulosque in pectore caecos
> condidit et profugam per totum exercuit orbem.

> She cast the image of the horrifying Erinys before the eyes and mind of
> the Argive concubine, placed hidden goads in her heart and pestered her
> in flight throughout the whole world. (*Met.*1.725–27)

There is here an interesting struggle for the possession of the gaze. While
Juno has been striving to see and to regain Jupiter's gaze for herself, she now
imposes *stimulos caecos* on her rival. This is an interesting phrase because
although it means "hidden goads," *caecos* can also allude to the blindness
of madness imposed on Io. The fact that Juno throws a dreadful *phantasia*
to terrify and destroy the girl preannounces, and is in tune with, the interactions between Minerva, Envy, and Aglauros in Book 2. It is curious here
that one of the epithets for Juno in Homer and elsewhere is βοῶπις, the
"cow-eyed." This is a rather odd, even unflattering epithet which indicates
some quality both of the goddess's gaze, probably that she has wide and
powerful eyes, and of her visual appearance. It is said that this attribute of
Hera in Homer may be a relic of the time when the goddess was theri-
omorphic, but according to Kirk this is doubtful. Instead, Kirk suggests
that βοῶπις may mean "with placid gaze," like that of a cow. However,
given the restlessness of Juno's soul and gaze, this seems doubtful.[9]

There is a curious coincidence in the episode. Juno is the jealous
matron who has been deprived of her husband's attention and through
the Homeric epithet she is in some way assimilated to a cow. It is most
interesting in this respect that out of all possible creatures on earth,
Jupiter decides to transform Io into a heifer, who is not only called a *vacca*
(*Met.* 1.612 and 621) or *iuvenca* (*Met.* 611, 652, 745), but also a *bos*
(*Met.*1.612 and 743). Io's transformed shape offends Juno in the very
locus of her sight, as Jupiter seems to have replaced one *bos* with another
and the "informed reader," to borrow Fish's term, will be delighted at the
recollection of the Homeric name.[10] Likewise, it is probably because of
Juno's "cow-ish" quality that she can recognize that Io is not a true *bos* and
see beyond appearances.

In Book 2, Jupiter chances to see Callisto, a nymph of Diana's cohort, in
a deep forest (*Iuppiter ut vidit fessam et custode vacantem . . .* / "When
Jupiter saw her tired and unguarded . . . ," *Met.* 2.422).[11] He soon decides
to approach her. Ovidian wit and humor are displayed in the clever
sound-play of *vacantem* and *vacca*, the name to identify Io in the previous
rape episode.[12] One could suppose that he does not only see Callisto
"without a *custos*," but that he also sees her as a "cow." Thus, despite the
promises to Juno that Io would not be a cause for her care ever again, he

has done it one more time, and the play on *vacca* and *vacantem* points to Callisto being another Io. The *hoc certe furtum* ("for sure *this* deceit") of line 423 tells the reader to think back and reflect on the connections between the episodes of Io and Callisto. Jupiter's penetrative gaze at the beginning translates into action and Callisto is ravished:

> illa quidem contra, quantum modo femina posset
> (adspiceres utinam, Saturnia, mitior esses),
> illa quidem pugnat, sed quem superare puella,
> quisve Iovem poterat? . . .

> She indeed fights back, indeed she does, as much as a woman can (if only you had seen her, Saturnia, you would be kinder), but whom could a girl overcome? Or who could overcome Jupiter? (*Met.* 2.434–37)

He is here again concerned with Juno seeing and knowing about his adventures. What Jupiter does is something that the goddess cannot see. But what would happen if she were actually allowed to see? The text assumes that she would align with the rape victim. If this were the case, then Jupiter is here preventing sisterhood and asserting the power of the phallus over feminine alliances. Furthermore, this prevention of sisterhood is seen in Diana's rejection of Callisto at the discovery of her pregnancy. The narrative delay in the uncovering of Callisto's rape displays Ovid's sense of humor and his anti-mimetic and anti-realistic taste, as it is absurd that the goddess had not recognized a nine-month pregnancy before. While it is true that the nymphs and goddess do not know whether Callisto had been raped or consented to sex, Diana never even gives her the opportunity to explain and rejects her immediately. Instead, the text accuses her with the ideological weight of words like *culpa* (*Met.*1.452) and *crimen* (*Met.* 2.462). Finally, the pool acts as a mirror that discloses truth (even though Callisto doesn't look directly into it), for it is the locus where Callisto is exposed, a crucial moment that will change her life and conclude in transformation. Interestingly, while Juno struggles to destroy the girl's *forma* by turning her into an awful bear, Callisto and her son end up as very visible stars in the sky.[13] Then again Juno is mocked and humiliated, and the final prohibition to the stars not to "bathe" in the waters of the seas seems mild and insufficient for Juno's wrath.[14]

In the same book, Jupiter has another adventure, Europa. There is no specific mention of the god's gaze in this story. He transforms himself into a bull to seduce her on the shores, but it is actually the girl who does the looking:

> . . . miratur Agenore nata,
> quod tam formosus, quod proelia nulla minetur

> The daughter of Agenor looks at him with admiration because he is so
> beautiful, because he threatens no battles. (Met. 2.858–59)

Her gaze, however, is powerless and nonperformative while he is actually
shown in action. Likewise, her gaze cannot penetrate the meanings
behind the aspect of the bull, that is, that he is a fake bull. Europa does
the looking over Jupiter, yet her gaze is not 'male,' as it does not control.
In fact, it is the god who acts upon it, runs away with her, and finally rapes
her. Is Europa's a 'feminine' gaze? or rather what would a 'feminine' gaze
entail? If one understands feminine as the opposite of masculine, then if
the male gaze is performative, penetrative, controlling, and objectifying,
Europa's gaze is feminine as it is the contrary. The interesting thing about
this story is that the male, not even looking, and by his very image seems
to control and be able to penetrate the girl later. Although the reader does
not see Jupiter directly looking, we could—based on what we already know
about how gods fall in love—suppose that he has previously seen her and
loved her. In the three episodes discussed up to now, Io, Callisto, and
Europa, the standard view of the monolithic male gaze seems to work quite
well. The three girls have no power over the gaze of a male god.
Conversely, in Juno there is an attempt to possess an active gaze, though
askew, which, although it does not achieve its purposes completely successfully, provides the story with the twists and spice necessary to entice
the interest of the reader and seduce him. Thus, while the author still
maintains the supremacy of the male gaze and in the end preserves the gender balance of power relations, the narrative needs women and women's
gazes. Ovid then exploits the possibility of women looking to turn the
world of Metamorphoses into a more complex and multifaceted one.

Finally, regarding the role of the reader, critics have proposed a very
stimulating audience-oriented interpretation of Argus, where his fate
reflects on the dangers for the audience of falling asleep during the performance of the poem. Says Wheeler, "The fate of Argus tells us that contin-
uing participation in the narrative transaction is, figuratively speaking, a
matter of life and death."[15] But what are the gender assumptions for the
reader? On the one hand, one can say that the male reader—or the female
reader in a trans-sex identification—aligns his/her gaze with Jupiter's as
dominating and controlling force. But on the woman's side, there are various other possibilities. One is to identify with Juno as offended matrona,
who, as it is common, sees the rape victim as guilty of her misfortune; the

other is to sympathize with Io, Callisto, and Europa. The interesting design of the episodes is that Ovid seems to split the female audience, which inhibits the possibility of sisterhood—that is, the possibility to be with Juno and the maidens at the same time and understand that in the end they are all victims of patriarchy. Furthermore, for a woman reader and viewer, the embedded *phantasia* of Syrinx and Pan and the consequences for Argus, the internal audience, constitute a warning that they need to be witnesses of rape and keep their eyes open.[16] Io being the first actual rape of the poem (Daphne avoids physical rape) is an exemplary instance of how one should read sexual violation. If a woman reader does not want to be decapitated and lose her gaze, she must keep awake and listen to the stories. In this sense, the two critical movements of interpretation dealing with women in Ovid may be applied. If we see a defender of patriarchal hierarchies in Ovid, we (I am assuming a collective female *we* here) may think that he wants us to see so that we "learn the lesson." If, on the contrary, we see in *Metamorphoses* a text that is sympathetic to women, we may take these stories as exposure and denunciation of what women must be aware of.

Apollo's first love affair is Daphne.[17] Once Cupid has pierced him with an erotic arrow, his attraction to Daphne is envisioned as visual: *Phoebus amat visaeque cupit conubia Daphnes/* "Phoebus loves her and desires marriage with Daphne when he sees her" (*Met*.1.490). Further, Cupid takes revenge over Apollo with two shafts of opposite effect: a golden one provokes love; the other, made of lead, produces the rejection of love in Daphne (*Met*.1.468–71), golden being a particularly erotic color related to the fire of passion.[18] The lover is here someone who has been previously penetrated by Cupid, which adds complexity to the sexual balance between penetrator and penetrated and aligns Apollo with the elegiac lover. There is a battle over masculinity where Apollo and Cupid dispute over who is more penetrative, whose arrows have greater power (*Met*.1.456–65). Cupid wounding Apollo stages the complexity of the standard pattern applied by historians of sexuality to the ancient world. That is, the active and penetrative partner holding power and preponderance over the passive or receptive partner:[19]

> spectat inornatos collo pendere capillos
> et "quid, si comantur?" ait. videt igne micantes
> sideribus similes oculos, videt oscula, quae non
> est vidisse satis. . . .

> He watches her unarranged hair hanging over her neck and "what if they
> were combed?" he says. He sees her eyes shining with fire like stars, he
> sees her lips and it is not enough for him to look at them.
> (Met.1.497–500)

Apollo desires what he sees and Daphne becomes a pleasurable spectacle
for his eyes. Verbs of seeing like *specto* and *video* (as in *visa decens* followed
by her description in Met.1.527) act as initiators of the narration, focal-
izers and boundary markers of visual images. Trespassing these boundaries
implies an act of visual penetration that intrudes into the picture and the
text. They act in a similar way as phrases with *est* plus a locative word in
ekphrastic description. The visual construction of Daphne that we see
here is focalized through Apollo's eyes. It is worth noting that the above
verses present a mixture of actual seeing and *phantasia*. While Apollo definitely sees the girl, and her flowing hair could be an 'actual' aspect of the
running virgin, her glittering eyes and her kisses are more a product of his
'phantasy.' Because he desires, he imagines that she desires as well. The
phrase *micantes oculos* recalls the erotic-attractive eyes of Cynthia in
Propertius 1.1 and may even convey a hint of orgasm, as in *Ars Amatoria*
2.721. But Daphne never looks back and this points to the image being a
product of Apollo's lust.[20] Likewise, the use of *oscula* is provocative
because, while the reader could understand the word as simply "mouth,"
as some translators do, the meaning "kisses" is also possible. This duality
endows the text with typical Ovidian humor and ambiguity and if one
reads *oscula* as kisses, Apollo obviously does not see them with his eyes but
with his mind, whether these kisses are his, hers, or mutual. However, by
wondering what Daphne would look like if her hair were combed, Apollo
shows a desire to change her, to modify her rather than to respect the
image that she has chosen for herself.[21]

But seeing is not enough and his gaze needs to become action. Apollo's active gaze results in Daphne's flight. It is true, however, that actual
penetration is not manifest in the story because the girl changes into a
tree and thus escapes imminent rape. Nevertheless, the laurel finally
'consents' to become the tree of Apollo, upon which he exerts control
and power and which will always, with its presence, be a symbol of
Daphne's absence.[22] The transformation into a tree bears further metaliterary connotations, for Daphne is finally enclosed by the bark of the laurel (*libro*, Met.1.549), which, as has been amply shown by the critics,
involves a word play with "book." Daphne transformed into a tree is thus
included in the book of *Metamorphoses* and identifies with the *dura/scrip-
ta puella* of Latin elegy, while Apollo the lover becomes the elegiac *ama-*

tor.[23] So what began with Apollo's act of looking and his visual focalization of Daphne's image is now transformed into text. Daphne's episode thus embodies the transformation of image into text that is so pervasive in *Metamorphoses*.

Of the love affairs of Apollo in *Metamorphoses*, two are young boys: Cyparissus (*Met*.10.106ff) and Hyacinthus (10.162ff). Yet in neither episode is Apollo's gaze mentioned as a possessive and penetrative force. Both boys are transformed, Cyparissus into a tree and Hyacinthus into a flower. It is noteworthy, however, that in the one moment in these episodes that Apollo's gaze is mentioned, it does not objectify but rather produces an introspective effect in the god:

> Phoebus ait "videoque tuum, mea crimina, vulnus.
> tu dolor es facinusque meum: mea dextera leto
> inscribenda tuo est. ego sum tibi funeris auctor."

> Phoebus said, "I see your wound, which is my crime; you are my sorrow and guilt and my right hand should be branded with your death. I am the cause of your funeral." (*Met*.10.197–99)

Likewise, the loves of Apollo with boys are never envisioned as rapes but rather as scenes of mutual love and camaraderie. Though there is a power relation between the active dominant partner and the passive or submissive one, in the homosexual relation the boy is not visually objectified in the same way as women are. The narrator, Orpheus, who has rejected the company of women and is a strong advocate of homosexual love, carefully chooses these two stories. Thus the positive, nonviolent relationship between gods and boys is obviously biased and tinted by Orpheus's agenda.

But what happens when goddesses have affairs with boys? Venus loves Adonis, in a story where her son's arrows (*Met*.10.526) pierce her. But the relationship shows more signs of camaraderie than overmastering and Adonis does not appear as a spectacle until his death when Venus sees him from the sky (*Met*.10.720–22). Similar is the case of Galatea and Acis, where the lovers enjoy peacefully each other's company without visual violent domination from the woman.[24] The boy is a spectacle, but one that does not provoke a violent desire (*Met*.13.753–54). In neither case is there violence between the lovers as with Apollo and Jupiter.

WOMEN'S INTRUSIVE GAZES

But can a woman possess a penetrative gaze? Would she want to? What would this entail? Women are normally 'nonpenetrative' in sex, thus their active sexuality needs to be defined with a different parameter. The closest we get to penetrative sexuality by a woman in *Metamorphoses* is probably Salmacis.[25] The nymph does not follow her sisters in the virginal tasks of Diana. Instead she concentrates on her toilet, using her pool as mirror (*quid se deceat, spectatas consulit undas/* "She checks her image in the mirror-like waters to see what may become her," *Met.* 4.312). Salmacis looking at her image in a pool cheats expectations of readers who imagine that they will find another Narcissus-like story of self-absorption. Instead, Salmacis falls in love with the boy Hermaphroditus when he comes to bathe in her pool. The fact that she is picking flowers right before she sees Hermaphroditus also implies an innovation, for scenes of girls picking flowers often symbolize the innocence of the virgin who will soon be "deflowered." Instead, Salmacis is the sexual aggressor here. These two details can again be taken as narrative challenges of Alcithoe, the daughter of Minyas who narrates the story, to the general narrator's motifs to prove her originality. This, of course, would work only if one reads Alcithoe's story in a releasing way.[26] Salmacis' desire commences with the eyes. She sees the boy and longs to possess him: *cum puerum vidit, visumque optavit habere* (*Met.* 4.316), and Hermaphroditus becomes a spectacle henceforth.[27] Georgia Nugent, as mentioned before, observes that Salmacis' desire could be thought of in the Freudian terms of the "fantasy of the penis in the little girl."[28] Yet in a subtle play of desire and gaze, Ovid relates that Hermaphroditus saw the pool (*videt hic stagnum lucentis ad imum/ usque solum lymphae/* "Here he sees a pool of crystal-clear water all the way to the bottom," *Met.* 4.297–98) and, as his playing in its margins later on shows (340–45), he was attracted to it. But in a witty Ovidian twist the pool and nymph are really the same thing. So, while Hermaphoditus rejects Salmacis, he is attracted to her (pool).[29] Her initial gaze becomes performative in her wooing speech, which in other cases is taken up by the male. Salmacis' desire is materialized in her kisses and embraces. In the following scene, she is the desiring subject that takes pleasure in the image of the boy. The boy undresses, jumps in the pool, and swims; but the readers, as spectators, perceive the scene through the eyes of Salmacis and, with her, readers are affected in their "eyes" by the *phantasia* they construct: *tum vero placuit, nudaeque cupidine formae/ Salmacis exarsit; flagrant quoque lumina nymphae/* "Then indeed he pleased her, and Salmacis caught the fire of love with the desire of his naked body; the eyes of the nymph also burn" (*Met.* 4.346–47). The question is: is this a female gaze or is there a simple gender "reversal," where the eyes are female and the gaze is male? In other words, does Salmacis' gaze offer the male and female reader a feminine perspective from where to look at the poem? In principle, one is inclined to answer negatively, as the control and objectification of Hermaphroditus assimilate to the power of the male gaze and, like the male rapists, Salmacis cannot contain herself and jumps to his embrace. But, unlike male rapists, whose *vis* seems logical and appropriate to their gender, though not unproblematically of course, women who desire are viewed as out of their mind. In the episode of Clytie it is said of her, *dementer amoribus usa/* "madly consumed with love" (*Met.* 4.259) and Salmacis is *amens*, or "insane" (*Met.* 4.351). The links to the previous episode of the book are even more extensive. Her desire is viewed in her dazzling eyes, which are compared, in an arresting simile, to the sun reflected on a mirror:

> flagrant quoque lumina nymphae,
> non aliter quam cum puro nitidissimus orbe
> opposita speculi referitur imagine Phoebus.

> The eyes of the nymph kindled, no different than when the full face of the most dazzling Phoebus is reflected in the image of a mirror placed opposite to it. (*Met.* 4.347–79)

This very simile implies the specularity and self-reflection of Salmacis' desire, which is not reflected by Hermaphroditus.[30] Yet she is not aware of this specularity and still nourishes the hope of joining the boy in love. She jumps in the pool and wraps around him like a serpent (*Met.* 4.362–67). But the image of the serpent is itself problematic and discloses the complexities of gender definitions for Salmacis' gaze. Unlike thunderbolts, for example, which seem to be 'unproblematic' signifiers of masculine *vis*, while on the one hand serpents are analogized to the penis, on the other hand, they pertain mainly to terrifying/phallic women like the harpies or Medusa. Here, the usefulness of the concept of gender 'inversion' or 'reversal,' which has come to be a common phrase in the vocabulary of gender(ed) readings, must be placed under suspicion. A woman who appropriates male patterns is not the same as a man, for not only is she less successfully endowed with agency and subjectivity than males, but also there is a constant sense of transgression that colors every action of

women in power. Thus Salmacis' gaze is not entirely 'male,' but she is
rather a problematic female and the symbol of the serpent exemplifies it,
as an icon of gender instability.

But how successful is Salmacis? It is partly true that she succeeds in
some sort of penetration of the *puer*'s body, as both bodies merge in one
and she manages to inject some of her femininity and *mollitia* into the boy.
But she does this at the cost of self-annulment. Nugent has shown that,
although on the surface Hermaphroditus is a mixture of male and female,
it is the masculine that the story preserves:

> ergo ubi se liquidas, quo vir descenderat, undas
> semimarem fecisse videt mollitaque in illis
> membra, manus tendens, sed iam non voce virili
> Hermaphroditus ait: "nato date munera vestro,
> et pater et genetrix, amborum nomen habenti:
> quisquis in hos fontes vir venerit, exeat inde
> semivir et tactis subito mollescat in undis!"
> motus uterque parens nati rata verba biformis
> fecit et incesto fontem medicamine tinxit.

> Thus when he saw that the flowing waters in which he had plunged as a
> male had made him half-male and his softened limbs in them, stretching
> his arms to the sky, but not with virile voice any more, Hermaphroditus
> said: "Mother and father, grant this wish to your son, who has both your
> names: let any male who comes into this spring leave from here a semi-
> male and let him suddenly soften in these silent waters!" Both parents
> were moved; they fulfilled the request of their bi-formed son and tinged
> the spring with a polluting substance. (*Met.* 4.380–88)

Although the body may be a hybrid of male and female, the mind is still
masculine.[31] Lines 380–81 tell us that when "he" saw that the water had
changed him, who had previously entered as a male, into a half-male, he
did not have his virile voice any more. The address to the parents is also
an address to "his" progenitors, and the words *vestro nato* and *nati* make
apparent that the speaker of the new body is masculine. In fact, after the
union of Salmacis and Hermaphroditus in one body, Salmacis disappears
and only a *semi-marem* (note that it is not a *semi-mulier*) is left, a boy who
is *mollis*, but still a boy in the end. While Nugent's view of Salmacis' anni-
hilation has some truth in it, the fact that the pool, which is a feminine
landscape par excellence, is still a pool hints at the preservation of something feminine. It is, however, interesting that Ovid uses the word *fons*

(385, 388), which is masculine at the moment of transformation, but combined with the feminine *unda* (380).[32] This could show that while the masculine seems to dominate, the feminine still stands and adds major aspects to the hermaphrodite result of transformation.

Echo parallels the fate of Salmacis. Questions of viewing and the penetrative gaze are essential to the story of Narcissus. But the focus here shall be Echo, who normally suffers from being a sort of appendix or "echo" of Narcissus and who is first connected with Narcissus in Ovid.[33] She was a nymph who had lost her power of speech and could only repeat what others said. This was the work of Juno, who punished her for entertaining her with talk while Jupiter enjoyed the company of the nymphs. When Echo first saw Narcissus she still had a body:

> adspicit hunc trepidos agitantem in retia cervos
> vocalis nymphe, quae nec reticere loquenti
> nec prior ipsa loqui didicit, resonabilis Echo.

> The nymph Echo, with her resounding voice, who knew neither to be silent after someone had spoken nor to speak first herself, saw him driving frightened deer into hunting nets. (*Met.* 3.356–58)

The phrase *adspicit hunc* acts as a semantic unit with a stinging effect, which may convey the idea of a quick glance rather than a prolonged look. Her gaze could be taken, as Nugent supposes for Salmacis, as a locus of desire involving the fantasy of penis envy (although this might not be a productive way to approach the episode). But hers is, nonetheless, a furtive look. It is rather intriguing that both in the case of Salmacis and in Echo, this fantasy is directed to undeveloped *pueri*, whose masculinity has not been completely achieved yet. In any case, the instant passion of Echo is similar to Salmacis' desire:

> vidit et incaluit, sequitur vestigia furtim,
> quodque magis sequitur, flamma propiore calescit,
> non aliter quam cum summis circumlita taedis
> admotas rapiunt vivacia sulphura flammas.

She saw him, burnt with passion, and secretly followed his footsteps. The more she follows, with stronger flame she burns, no different than when burning sulphur smeared all around the top of torches catches the flames that have been drawn near. (*Met.* 3.371–76)

The resemblance with Salmacis is obvious, but the parallel with the Apollo-Daphne episode will be emphasized here. There is a re-enactment of the first affair of Apollo, but with a gender destabilization. Let us bring back Apollo's erotic conflagration into the scene:

Phoebus amat visaeque cupit conubia Daphnes,
quodque cupit sperat, suaque illum oracula fallunt,
utque leves stipulae demptis adolentur aristis,
ut facibus saepes ardent, quas forte viator
vel nimis admovit vel iam sub luce reliquit,
sic deus in flammas abiit, sic pectore toto
uritur et sterilem sperando nutrit amorem.

Phoebus loves her and desires to marry Daphne when he sees her. He hopes to achieve what he desires, and his own oracles fail him, and as the soft stalks are kindled once the ears are removed, as the hedges burn with torches, which by chance a traveler either draws too close or leaves behind at daybreak, thus the god catches the fire of love, thus the god burns in his heart and nourishes his fruitless love by hoping. (*Met.* 1.490–95)

Apollo and Echo suffer the same infatuation through the gaze, which leads them to an erotic chase for the beloved. But while Apollo strenuously runs after Daphne's steps (*admisso sequitur vestigia passu*/ "He follows her footsteps at full speed," *Met.* 1.532) and the text insists on his chase in the constant use of the verb *sequor* and its compounds (*Met.* 1.504, 507, 511, 532, 540), Echo only follows Narcissus's steps secretly (*sequitur vestigia furtim*). The furtiveness makes her action weaker (note that Apollo acts rapidly and openly instead), probably reflecting the patriarchal mandate that women do not pursue men. However, although Echo is the erotic initiator of the action, she has really very little agency. Echo can only reproduce Apollo's wooing discourse by repeating other people's speech:

o quotiens voluit blandis accedere dictis
et mollis adhibere preces! natura repugnat

nec sinit, incipiat, sed, quod sinit, illa parata est
exspectare sonos, ad quos sua verba remittat.

Oh, how many times did she wish to approach him with sweet words and
to add soft prayers! But her nature forbids it and does not allow her to initiate speech, but what it allows, she is ready to do: to wait for the sounds,
which her words could return. (*Met.* 3.375–78)

Liveley suggests that Echo's "re-appropriation" of Narcissus's words may be
taken as a sign of female agency and subjectivity.[34] But hers is a very
restricted form of verbal agency and even if Echo finds expression through
the cracks of her verbal constrictions, her speech and the results of the
story give her very little power. Echo's sad desire to re-enact Apollo's wooing is only achieved later as a pale repetition of Narcissus's words.
Likewise, while Daphne remains silent during her chase and neither looks
back nor speaks to Apollo, Narcissus not only looks but also responds:

respicit et rursus nullo veniente "quid" inquit
"me fugis?" et totidem, quot dixit, verba recepit.

He looks back and seeing no one coming behind he responds: "Why do
you flee from me?" and hears in reply the words he has said again. (*Met.*
3.383–84)

It is only then that Echo can express her desire as a coda to Narcissus's
speech. Only after the boy flees like Daphne (*ille fugit fugiensque . . . Met.*
3.390). Unlike Daphne, he can articulate a speech of rejection which is
in fact effective, as Echo recedes and physically disintegrates. Like
Salmacis, her attempt to possess an intrusive gaze has led her to self-
annulment. But while Salmacis has at least instilled her "feminine
aspects" in Hermaphroditus, Echo has virtually disappeared. She has no
body any more and although the text conveys that she is now "only a
voice" (*omnibus auditur: sonus est, qui vivit in illa/* "She is heard by all. It is
a sound that lives in her," *Met.* 3.401), the reality is that she is an empty
voice with no self-agency.[35]

Previous episodes could more easily be understood by identification of
the male reader with the internal male viewer, controller, and intruder.
Yet in the story of Salmacis and Hermaphroditus the scene is focalized
through a woman and the object of the gaze is a boy. Within ancient conceptions of sexuality this should not represent a problem, because the
male reader would still play an active part in the game of viewing, and the

images of boys as erotic objects are acceptable and extended.[36] The case of Narcissus would work in a similar way. Homosexuality was not entirely without its problems, however, and these boys may put the masculine reader in an awkward position. But the tales are also strange for women readers. In the case of Salmacis, they get to identify with a powerful woman, but Salmacis' character is not entirely edifying for women either, being herself a stereotype of the dreadful female in power. She represents a sort of abomination and, in this sense, the woman reader finds herself trapped in this 'perverse' position and in the end assumes the gaze of a man but only to look at a *puer*. While some episodes of *Metamorphoses* allow positive and alternative possibilities to the female gaze that can be nonobjectifying yet creative, the story of Hermaphroditus and Salmacis does not do great wonders for the female reader.

A different case of female intrusive gaze, which does not involve sexuality directly, claims notice. Minerva has entrusted a box containing the baby Erichthonios to Aglauros and her sisters Herse and Pandrosos, daughters of Cecrops, mythical founder of Athens. But the goddess expressly commands them not to look upon her secret (*sua ne secreta viderent*, *Met.* 2.556). Aglauros cannot resist the temptation and opens the box:

> timidas vocat una sorores
> Aglauros nodosque manu diducit, et intus
> infantemque vident adporrectumque draconem.

> Only Aglauros calls her sisters timid and undoes the knots with her hand. Inside they see an infant and a snake stretched next to him. (*Met.* 2.559–61)

Erichthonios was a child who then grew to be an Attic foundation hero and king of Athens. It is said that he was begotten by Hephaestus. For when Athena went to him one time to request weapons, Hephaestus embraced her and tried to possess her. The goddess successfully rejected him, but his seed fell to the ground. A child was born from it and the baby was handed over by Gaia to Athena for her to look after. Thus this is the closest Athena ever got to having a child of her own. This story is most meaningful for understanding the opening of the box, which may well be taken as a metaphor for the goddess's (repressed) motherly instincts and even her fantasy and fears of pregnancy. This is an awkward thing for a virgin goddess, and opening the box is seen, metaphorically, as an opening of

Woman's uterus.[37] Aglauros is another version of Pandora, the 'curious' woman who opens and looks inside, triggering disaster and pollution. When she removes the lid, the 'insides' and secrets of female sexuality and the female body are released. Laura Mulvey observes that the myth of Pandora foregrounds the topography of surface/secret and interior/exterior in women.[38] Minerva constantly strives to preserve an external image of quasi-masculine power. Aglauros' curiosity threatens to disclose the goddess's hidden female interior and to expose a forbidden knowledge. Perhaps Aglauros' intrusion offends Minerva because it mimics her own curiosity and epistemic and visual desire, as the goddess of wisdom, to see and know. Minerva, by turning against Aglauros, wishes to teach her a lesson about the dangers involved in visual curiosity for women.[39]

Women who open things up with the gaze are dangerous and devious, as they appropriate the penetrative power of the male. It is now necessary to extend the meanings of the penetrative metaphor here, for while women do not penetrate sexually, they still have minds and if seeing is also knowing, realizing, and understanding, women can be penetrative with their minds. However, this type of penetrative power is still problematic from the point of view of gender and involves some appropriation of male prerogatives.

Aglauros is allowed only a glance and her gaze has no power to control. The physical position of the intrusive eye is here relevant. Not only are the sisters glancing at the forbidden, but they are observing from above. This vertical disposition is hinted at by the perspective of the bird who narrates the story placed on an elm (*abdita fronde levi densa speculabar ab ulmo,/ quid facerent/* "Hidden in the light leaves that grew densely on an elm, I watched what they would do," *Met.* 2.557–58). The positioning of the onlooker from above is in *Metamorphoses* characteristic of gods who control the human world from Olympus, as seen with Juno.[40] More specifically, it is what male gods do before raping a girl. In the same book Mercury spots Herse while flying over the Munychian fields: *hinc se sustulerat paribus caducifer alis/ Munychiosque volans agros gratamque Minervae/ despectabat humum cultique arbusta Lycei/* "From this place Mercury had lifted himself up with his twin wings and in his flight he saw the Munychian fields, the land beloved by Minerva and the groves of the Lyceum" (*Met.* 2.708–10). This vertical gaze is almost exclusive to male gods. While goddesses have the power to look down and control, mortal women are banned from this and their intrusive gazes are punished. Aglauros not only breaks the prohibition of not looking, but she probably looks down on the forbidden, just as the crow that is punished by Minerva for talking too much (*Met.* 2.557–58 and 563–64), and then she symbolically appropriates a 'right' of the gods.[41] Perhaps, behind this issue of verticality and power lies a very simple principle. Power and the body are physically identified, and it is normally the taller person who holds power. This is the case commonly between men and women, where men are normally taller and control the gaze from above. In a way, the awkwardness of a taller woman produces discomfort partly due perhaps to this question of the gaze. Women should 'look up' to their masters. Interestingly, this story pre-empts Actaeon's tragedy. The bird that saw the forbidden and divulged it is an example of what in the next book Diana will fear that Actaeon will do. But also, it is not only the sin of telling the story that damns the crow, but the fact that the bird has seen the secret.[42]

It is Aglauros who in-videt inside the box, a witty pun on the cause of her destruction: Invidia.[43] In Metamorphoses Minerva is a goddess connected with Envy and seeing. It is the rage at the disrespect to her commands that infuriates her. It is peculiar that when Aglauros seems to have it all—gold and the honor of a divine family—Minerva "looks at her with angry eyes":

> vertit ad hanc torvi dea bellica luminis orbem
> et tanto penitus traxit suspiria motu,
> ut pariter pectus positamque in pectore forti
> aegida concuteret. . . .

> The warrior goddess turned her fierce stare toward her and she heaved a
> deep sigh with such emotion that it shook both her breast and the aegis
> placed on her brave breast. (Met. 2.752–55)

This description most clearly recalls the personification of Envy later in the book, which suggests that Minerva is an envious deity; Envy's direct connection with Livor is significant as she really acts as a surrogate for the warrior deity. Envy is displayed in an interesting narrative circle. Aglauros in-videt (looks into), Minerva looks with eyes askance (a typical gesture of envy), and then looks into the dwelling of Envy. Finally, Envy attacks Aglauros, who envies her sister.

The OED tells us that "envy" may refer to any malignant or hostile feelings, but the more restricted definition as "the feeling of mortification and ill-will occasioned by the contemplation of superior advantages possessed by another" seems more appropriate for a reading of Metamorphoses.[44] When Minerva wishes to exert vengeance over Aglauros, who has dishonored her, she goes in search of Envy (Met. 2.760–61). The passage is freighted with overtones of pollution and darkness. When Minerva arrives she finds Envy eating snakes:

> . . . videt intus edentem
> vipereas carnes, vitiorum alimenta suorum,
> Invidiam visaque oculos avertit. . . .

> She sees Envy inside eating the flesh of vipers, nourishment of her vices,
> and as soon as she sees her she turns her eyes away. (*Met.* 2.768–70)

The insistence and repetition of the syllable *vi-* is crucial in the passage. It is central in the concept of seeing which is prominent here as envy itself is an act of *in-videre* and, curiously, it is Minerva who first "sees into" (*videt in-tus*). But *vi-* is also part of the concept *viper* on which envy feeds her vices (*vi-tiorum*) and it is also the ablative of *vis*. Once Minerva has seen Envy she has to *oculos avertere*. Finally the sounds *-v-* and *-vi-* are present in the root of Livor. She finally reaches Aglauros and infests her with a *venenum* that fills her with jealousy as Minerva had bid (*Met.* 2.784).

Envy is the desire of what somebody else possesses, which excites in the envious person a need to intrude and destroy, to see into, to 'poison' and pollute the person who causes the feeling of envy. In this sense, envy conveys in itself thanatic implications: it can destroy, it can kill, and it is notable in this respect that the Fury Megaera is another personification of Livor. In Nonnus's *Dionysiaca* she is the personification of the Evil Eye of Envy, and Claudian in *in Rufinum* invests her with the characteristics of an envious person: she drinks the blood from the strife within a family (1.77–79) and she has *oculis liventibus* (1.139).[45]

Envy is a particularly feminine concept in *Metamorphoses* and thus its personification in Book 2 is most significant.[46] Not all the characters who envy are female; some examples are Vulcan (*Met.* 4.167ff.), Lyncus (*Met.* 5.657), and Daedalus (*Met.* 8.250). But the overwhelming majority of envious figures are female. Not only are they more numerous, but their envy leads them to crueler action in the poem. Of course, the most envious goddess is Juno, whose *invidia* is normally expressed in its erotic variant, jealousy. She feels envy for Io in Book 1, for Callisto in Book 2; she punishes Echo for hiding Jupiter's affairs with the nymphs; she destroys Semele and her sister Ino in Books 3 and 4; she tries to prevent Alcmene's childbirth in Book 9, and in Book 10 she is jealous of Ganymede. But another goddess envies in *Metamorphoses* and not only Aglauros and Envy are envious in the episode of Book 2. Minerva is a goddess of revenge and the punishment she wishes to exert here can only be achieved through the power of Livor; thus Envy becomes a sort of alter ego for the goddess. Most interesting, however, is the combination of Minerva and Livor in the episode of Arachne, in which the goddess is clearly envious of Arachne's work. The text reads: *non illud Pallas, non illud carpere Livor/ possit opus: doluit successu flava virago/* "Neither Pallas nor Envy could carp at that work: the golden-haired goddess of war was hurt by Arachne's success" (*Met.* 6.129–30); *carpere* is a typical verb for Envy in the episode of Book 2 (781, 792). The reader here recalls the metapoetic and self-conscious allusions to the poet that envy involves.[47] Arachne is the embodiment of the artist, destroyed by a deity's wrath (or Envy if we follow this possibility).

Envy is 'materialized' in the form of visions. Aglauros' envy toward Herse is provoked by a *phantasia* of her sister enjoying the love, wealth, and honor of a divine marriage.[48] Aglauros 'sees' these things:

> germanam ante oculos fortunatumque sororis
> coniugium pulchraque deum sub imagine ponit.

> She places before her eyes her sister and her fortunate marriage, and the god under a beautiful image. (*Met.* 2.803–4)[49]

Aglauros' envy is somehow pre-announced by her ambitious reaction to Mercury when he comes to beg her help in wooing Herse: *adspicit hunc oculis isdem, quibus abdita nuper/ viderat Aglauros flavae secreta Minervae/* "Aglauros looked at him with the same eyes with which recently she had seen the hidden secrets of golden-haired Minerva" (*Met.* 2.748–49). Aglauros already possesses a gaze that looks into things and in these lines it is almost as if she were already seeing into the luck of her sister. But a woman who dares to look into things can only be heading for transformation. Mercury, taking advantage of a pun on movement and immobility (*motura, Met.* 2.817), turns her into a stone.[50]

In principle, with the sisters, the reader is allowed to look into the box and remain unscathed, unlike Aglauros. However, we do not get to know much about what we see, and in a way we are not permitted to see much, while the emphasis is laid on the act of seeing. One way of understanding the episode is to see that women readers are being warned that they should not open up secret boxes with the gaze, but at the same time, it awakens our curiosity and furnishes our desire to see.

Ekphrasis and the Intrusive Gaze

BREAKING THE PICTURE'S FRAME

Ekphrasis always evokes a set-piece description, normally within a larger narrative, that intends to bring the object vividly before the mind's eye of the reader or listener.[51] The word ekphrasis has been understood in two fundamental ways. There are descriptions of works of art like Aeneas' shield in *Aeneid* 8 or Arachne's tapestry in *Metamorphoses* 6, and descriptions of natural features and events. Still, this sharp distinction needs some deconstruction, especially in application to Ovid, who sprinkles his 'natural' ekphrases with comments like "it was so real it seemed painted" and his artistic ekphrases with remarks like "the painted image was so good it seemed real." There is, at least in Ovid, a fudging of the boundaries between descriptions of art and nature because this common methodological distinction does not seem very fruitful; a framed description of the 'natural' type can often be read as a reflection on art and the craft of the poet. The undercurrent of this is perhaps that there *is* no 'nature' in poetry but that everything is, at some level, constructed as *ars*.

Part of this study's contention is that much of the erotics of reading are meaningful for ekphrasis and that penetration is a valid metaphor for reading. We will mostly assume a masculine reader/viewer or a woman reader experiencing trans-sex identification. The text-image seduces the reader and provokes desire, a desire to keep on reading, to penetrate it. The reader/viewer exerts some sort of symbolic violence while penetrating the image with the gaze. Critics have often written about the act of reading in sexual terms (it is a way of knowing a body, a corpus, etc.) and the female body is commonly identified with textuality.[52] Writing has also been envisioned as a penetration: "the seed or semen of the author's mind brooding in the repository of the page that bodies its meaning forth" (Gubar, 77). Another common analogy is that of the pen-penis that writes on the virgin page and joins in a long tradition that identifies the author as male and his passive creation as female.[53] A parallel assumption may be drawn for the relationship between text and reader. The book with its covers (or edges of the roll) presents boundaries that the reader needs to trespass in order to read.[54] When we read we penetrate the text with our mind and eyes.[55] When we look at a picture we penetrate it with our gaze. When we read an ekphrasis we perform both simultaneously. The acts of reading and viewing art can be thought of in erotic terms.

The description of the doors of the palace of the Sun in Book 2 is a standard ekphrasis, which recalls Aeneas' viewings of the doors of the temple of Apollo at the beginning of *Aeneid* 6.[56] When Phaethon arrives at the palace of his father, the text offers a description of the carvings on the doors. The doors were radiant, but the workmanship surpassed the material (*materiam superabat opus*, *Met.* 2.5). There is no precise delineation of the borders here, but it is explicit that the designs are carved on doors (*bifores valvae*, *Met.* 2.4), which are themselves boundary markers. One needs to read and look inside the borders of the door to appreciate the images. For the designs engraved in it, much has been propounded. Yet again, one can think of a miniature *Metamorphoses* that treats the facts of the sky, the lands, and the waters with their inhabitants. What is more, some of the characters depicted on the door will appear later in the epic, like Doris and Proteus, and there are even stories of characters transformed into stars. For this ekphrasis, the internal viewer Phaethon and the external reader at a secondary level perform the same exercise of visual penetration. This act of penetration of text and work of art can be found in different degrees in all ekphrases and forms part of the erotics of reading as well as conveying important gender implications for the reader. The penetrative metaphor, however, will be obviously more useful for some ekphrases than for others.

Metamorphoses is also loaded with descriptions of natural events or scenes, and their connections with art should not be overlooked. An ekphrasis of this type also possesses a symbolic border, usually expressed with introductory phrases like "*est via . . .*" , "*est locus . . .* ," where the verb *sum* with a locative word marks the limits of the description to come. [57] The male gaze as penetrative, intrusive, and controlling wields power to "open things up" and to break up a certain enclosure, particularly of female spaces.[58] In various episodes men look into forbidden spaces and earn chastisement. But this spatial intrusion is also a narrative and visual intrusion, whereby both male internal viewer and external viewers and readers need to break visual boundaries to see and to grasp knowledge of what is going on in a scene.

A paradigmatic example where Mulvey's terms could be justified is the tale of Thetis and Peleus in Book 11, where an ekphrastic description of Thetis bathing precedes Peleus' (visual) intrusion and her rape. At first sight, the reader believes herself in the presence of an ekphrasis of the natural type, whose limits are drawn by the habitual *est* plus place formula (*Est sinus*, *Met.* 11.229). Nevertheless, the text surprises us with a second internal frame:

myrtea silva subest bicoloribus obsita bacis,
est specus in medio, natura factus an arte,
ambiguum, magis arte tamen. . . .

There is a myrtle wood near by, filled with two-colored berries. There is
a cave in the middle—it is unclear whether made by nature or art, but
rather by art. (*Met.* 11.234–36)

The illusion of a 'natural' ekphrasis is soon dismantled and lines 235–36
hint at the artistry involved in the visual image to follow. The object of
the reader's gaze inside the ekphrasis is a woman, the goddess Thetis who
will change forms to evade the embrace of Peleus. Even more poignant is
that Thetis metamorphoses *ad solitas artes* (*Met.*11.242). This detail is
curious, because Thetis becomes not only the visual object of the description, but also the artist who creates the image. Unlike the women who
passively suffer transformation by gods, Thetis has the power to transform
herself, yet to no avail, as a god will lead Peleus to subdue her.[59] But the
interesting aspect of this is that Thetis here identifies with both author
and character, with creative object and subject, and in the bigger picture,
with both Ovid and his characters.

The episode claims comparison with Actaeon, for there is here also a
goddess surprised naked in the water (*quo saepe venire/ frenato delphine
sedens, Theti nuda solebas/* "Where you, Thetis, used to come naked, riding
on a bridled dolphin," *Met.*11.236–37). The male intrusion in this scene
is, however, much more violent and forward than in the Actaeon story.
Peleus jumps at Thetis to rape her (*illic te Peleus, ut somno vincta iacebas,/
occupat, et quoniam precibus temptata repugnas,/ vim parat, innectens
ambobus colla lacertis/* "There Peleus takes hold of you when you are lying
conquered by sleep, and though entreated by his prayers you reject him, he
prepares to offer violence, entwining both arms around your neck,"
*Met.*11.238–40). Although we do not see him looking, the reader, used to
accompanying the character in his visual intrusion, presupposes that
Peleus has seen the goddess before his attack. Yet compared with Diana,
Thetis is inoffensive and seems to have no more power but that of escaping, which soon becomes annulled when Peleus keeps firm hold of her
and successfully exerts penetration.[60]

FROM VIEWER TO VIEWED: PARADOXES OF THE THEBAN CYCLE

Influenced by the mythical tradition and in particular Callimachus's *Bath of Pallas*, Ovid rewrites the story of Actaeon.[61] In comparison with Callimachus's *Hymn*, instead of the boy Tiresias and Athena, we find Actaeon the hunter and Diana. There are sexual implications and erotic desire in Actaeon's gaze and, thus, another less obvious intertext in the passage is the *Homeric Hymn to Aphrodite*, which stages the complex outcomes of seeing a goddess and having sex with her.[62]

Actaeon is the grandson of Cadmus, the founder of Thebes, whose story is significant for the boy's fate. Before Actaeon's story, Ovid tells us how an enormous serpent killed Cadmus's companions and was finally destroyed by him. Cadmus first sees his slain companions on entering a wood: *ut nemus intravit letataque corpora vidit* (*Met.* 3.55). This visual and physical intrusion will also be a central motif in the fate of his grandchild and, as Andrew Feldherr notes, one appreciates a change from viewer to viewed in the episode.[63] Once he has killed the giant serpent, he looks with pride at his achievement: *Dum spatium victor victi considerat hostis/* "While the conqueror surveys the bulk of his defeated enemy" (*Met.* 3.95). But soon he hears a voice that foretells his doom: " *serpentem spectas? et tu spectabere serpens*"/ "Are you looking at the serpent? You too will be a serpent and looked at" (*Met.* 3.98).[64] Barkan acutely observes that here Cadmus is forced to look at a reflection of himself, as if in a mirror, an image entrenched in the chiastic structure of line 98.[65] Cadmus foreshadows Actaeon's tragedy.

Actaeon has been hunting with his dogs and companions all morning and at the end separates from his crowd and looks "by chance" into a pool where Diana is bathing. Sight is important for hunting and its acuteness is essential to the successfulness of the hunt. As Leonard Shlain explains, the activity of hunting involves visual sharpness and requires the use of the 'cones' in the retina, which provide a more tubular, focalizing, and detailed vision that can be linked to penetration.[66] Actaeon's intrusion in the woods is represented almost in the same terms as Cadmus's intrusion: *per nemus ignotum non certis passibus errans/ pervenit in lucum: sic illum fata ferebant./ qui simul intravit rorantia fontibus antra/* "Wandering through unknown woods with uncertain steps he came to the grove: thus his fate would have it. As soon as he entered the grotto besprinkled with fountain spray," (*Met.* 3.175–77).[67] These fates are more than the protagonist's fates, they also carry the familial doom. Ovid introduces the scene of the bathing goddess as follows:

vallis erat piceis et acuta densa cupressu,
nomine Gargaphie succinctae sacra Dianae,
cuius in extremo est antrum nemorale recessu
arte laboratum nulla: simulaverat artem
ingenio natura suo.

There was a vale dense with sharp-needled cypress, Gargaphie by name,
sacred to high-girt Diana, in whose extreme corner is a shadowy cave,
made by no art, but nature had imitated art with its talent. (*Met.*
3.155–59)

The phrase *vallis erat* introduces an ekphrasis, which, as usual in Ovid,
bears metapoetic and meta-artistic resonances. In the context of
metaphorical sexual vocabulary, *vallis* is itself grammatically feminine and
serves to allude to the female body. The *phantasia* of the scene that the
reader forms in her mind's eye comes as a framed picture, in which the
goddess will be enclosed. To read this scene one has to break the 'pictorial' limits. The very essence of ekphrasis here incites in the reader a desire
to intrude, to see "what is inside." The idea of enclosure is further
advanced by the *antrum nemorale*, which itself marks an internal frame in
the scene and draws the reader to an even more interior space.[68] *Antrum
nemorale* also bears connotations of female sexuality because the female
interior is frequently associated with enclosed spaces. Obscurity also plays
a part and the grove likewise points in this direction.[69]

But the scene also presents a sacred space violated by Man, which is
comparable to Cadmus's *silva* (*Met.* 3.28), the untouched forest in which
Cadmus makes his intrusion earlier in Book 3. Likewise, Actaeon's gaze
on the goddess can be paralleled with Cadmus's and Tiresias' outrage of
the sacred serpents.[70] Even more, this closed space is fitting to Diana, the
virgin, who has never been opened by a man; there is a clear analogy
between the space and the goddess's body. The description of the pool as
margine gramineo patulos succinctus hiatus/ "widened into a pool framed by
grassy banks" (*Met.* 3.162) is significant in the construction of space as a
great female opening. The epithet *succincta* (156) entices the reader to
look and desire to see her naked body. *Virgineos artus*/ "virginal limbs"
(164) also enhances this sense.

Ovid's plays on art and nature are extensive. Curiously, this scene, he
tells, is not painted by art, but seems to be because it is beautiful. This
statement implies that art is superior to natural beauty. In any case, with

this reference to *ars* the narrator warns the reader about the metapoetic overtones of the story. With Actaeon, the reader is desirous to look, and, if the ekphrastic scene stands as a synecdoche for the whole *Metamorphoses*, he will be an intrusive eye, which needs to break the physical and narratological boundaries of the book to read. Thus, the external reader, whether male or female in trans-sex identification, shares Actaeon's voyeuristic desire to break the frames of the ekphrasis, thus exerting symbolic violence on the female enclosure. Talking about Actaeon's "desire" may seem to contradict the text's reasoning that he only saw the goddess "by chance" (*Met.* 3.141–43). However, while the youth may have looked at the goddess unintentionally at the beginning, this does not prevent desire, and the imagery and metaphoric language of the text imply such.[71] First, we have the impression that from the moment he sees, Actaeon maintains his gaze fixed on the goddess for quite some time, as there are fifteen lines between the discovery and his actual transformation. Furthermore, in some versions of the myth, such as the one found in Euripides' *Bacchae* (339–41), Actaeon actually boasts of being a better hunter than Artemis. The desire to surpass the goddess in hunting proposes a metaphor for sexual domination given that hunting is a common erotic metaphor and a figure for desire.[72] Moreover, other sources like Hyginus (180) recount that Actaeon was desirous of the goddess. Furthermore, the setting of the scene takes place at midday (*Met.* 3.145), which is a particularly erotic time in *Metamorphoses* and recalls the eroticism of *Amores* 1.5.[73] The imagery of the mountains stained with the blood of prey also points to the links between sex, hunting, and blood. Most interesting is that Actaeon himself mentions the blood of the animals and and the fact that it is midday in his command to his companions (*Met.* 3.148 and 151–52), which could be taken as a veiled expression of sexual desire.

In this first part of the episode, the reader cannot really identify with the female because the focalizer is Actaeon. But the roles are reversed later in the story. Here, the text makes clear the penetrative power of Actaeon's intrusion in the grotto:

> qui simul intravit rorantia fontibus antra,
> sicut erant, nudae viso sua pectora nymphae
> percussere viro. . . .

> As soon as he entered the grotto besprinkled with fountain spray, the nymphs, naked as they were, beat their breasts at the sight of the man. (*Met.* 3.177–79)

John Heath, however, believes that Actaeon's 'innocence' analogizes him almost to the figure of the huntress-girl who, all *inadvertently*, comes to a *locus amoenus* and is then raped.[74] It is difficult to agree with Heath on this point, for he seems to allow no place for the possibility of Actaeon's desire. But Heath is right in proposing that Diana's reaction is based on her 'reading' of rape stories in Ovid's *Metamorphoses* and that she is right to expect sexual violence according to the story circumstances. Heath's suggestion that characters can read stories of the same poem in which they belong presupposes a releasing reading of the character's mind and a certain independence from the main authorial voice.[75] It also signals a self-consciousness of the characters as fictional entities and part of a body of literature, which can be compared with the characters' knowledge that they are part of a 'play,' so common in Roman comedy. Nonetheless, for Heath, Diana's reading is incomplete, for she cannot see a different role for the male than that of sexual assaulter.[76] But the truth is: were it not a goddess that Acteon's gaze came across but simply a beautiful virgin, how do we know that he wouldn't have raped her?

Although the text presents the man in the passive voice, it is clear that he is actively looking and that what the nymphs try to protect the goddesses's body from is his sight. Ovid here plays with us as viewers and shifts the focus of the narration to the eyes of the nymphs, but the central figure in the picture is still the goddess, and the fact that she is said to be "taller than the others" helps this perception. Diana is the spectacle here because the great crime is actually to have seen her in her bath. She is the object of Actaeon's gaze (*visae sine veste Dianae*/ "of Diana seen without clothes," *Met.* 3.185). But one more (literal) layer of opening and disclosure can be observed. It is not the simple fact of seeing the goddess that carries a crime, but the fact that she is naked. Clothing constitutes an element that helps maintain a woman closed, protected from danger and from Man's intrusive gaze, but Diana with her nakedness is, at some level, already open before being penetrated by Actaeon's eyes.[77]

Diana now turns on her side to avoid being exposed to Actaeon's gaze, but she seems to turn her gaze forward in an *oblique* way to speak to him and attack him (*in latus obliquum tamen adstitit oraque retro/ flexit/* "However she stood on her side and turned her face backwards," *Met.* 3.187–88). She seems to be the viewer now. A redressing of the gender balance takes place. Diana exerts her vengeance on Actaeon, transforming him into a stag with a splash of water:

> ut vellet promptas habuisse sagittas,

quas habuit sic hausit aquas vultumque virilem
perfudit spargensque comas ultricibus undis
addidit haec cladis praenuntia verba futurae:
"nunc tibi me posito visam velamine narres,
si poteris narrare, licet!" . . .

Although she wished she would have had her arrows ready, what she had available, the water, she thus took and poured on his manly face, and sprinkling his hair with the avenging water added these words foretelling his future ruin: "Now you are free to tell that you have seen me without clothing, if you can tell!" (*Met.* 3.188–93)

Without her *sagittae*, Diana is *inermis*, a word that also indicates male impotence. But the paradox is that she is really not *inermis*, and in a very feminine response, Diana soon looks for an alternative to the conventional penetrative arrows, but using an element that is *mollis* instead. The splash of water is here a clear substitute for the goddess's weapons, and with it Diana returns the violence (in her eyes) that Actaeon's gaze has exerted on her. The fact that the splash is directed to Actaeon's *vultus virilis* is significant because it is precisely that virile gaze that she wishes to avenge. Compared with Callimachus's similar version of the bath of the goddess, where Tiresias is punished with blindness for what he has seen, the punishment here seems strange. Diana does not directly blind Actaeon—although blindness is suavely alluded to—but deprives him of his power of speech. It is the transformation of her image into text which disturbs the goddess. The verb *narres* is poignant in a metapoetic sense as well. We are here also reminded of Anchises, who, in the Homeric *Hymn to Aphrodite*, was warned not to boast of having had sex with the goddess. The later tradition that records that Anchises became crippled probably due to his 'telling' that he had an affair with Venus is meaningful for Actaeon. The similarities of these scenes to Ovid's own fate are striking and it is piquant that *Tristia* 2.105 mentions Actaeon as a parallel to Ovid's own crime.[78] In this sense, Actaeon the 'narrator' colludes with the image of the poet in exile. Furthermore, although the causes of Ovid's exile are disputed and unclear, some have interpreted Ovid's words in the exile poetry as a confession that he actually saw something. It was even suggested that he was an eyewitness of Julia's affairs or of some crime committed by Augustus himself. In his exile poetry he says that he has seen it but has not reported it. He may have seen something that Augustus wanted to keep secret; therefore, exile as a form of silencing corresponds vividly to

Actaeon's loss of articulate speech.[79] While this theory is no more than one of the several hypotheses that explain Ovid's exile, it is interesting nonetheless as a fantasy that connects punishment and seeing for the poet and that relates him to the fate of Actaeon.[80]

The episode concludes with a tragic play on the question of essence and appearance, what Actaeon really is and what he seems to be in the eyes of the dogs.[81] Actaeon looks at his image reflected in a pool and recognizes his change, a scene that, compared to Narcissus's self-delusion, is striking.[82] The text reads: *ut vero vultus et cornua vidit in unda,/ "me miserum!" dicturus erat: vox nulla secuta est!/* "When in fact he saw his face and horns in the water, he was about to say 'Ah, wretched me!' But no voice followed" (*Met.* 3.200–1). Issues of gaze and knowledge also affect Io, who goes to her father's river and sees her own image. Despite her new form, Io recognizes her old self underneath (*rictus novaque ut conspexit in unda/ cornua, pertimuit seque exsternata refugit/* "When she saw her expression and new horns in the water, she was afraid and, terrified, she fled from herself," *Met.*1.640–41). In this, Io is like Actaeon in Book 3 who also sees his new horns in the water, but different from Narcissus who cannot distinguish self and other.[83] Humorously, Actaeon sees 'himself' although he does not look himself any more, whereas in contrast, Narcissus cannot see himself but another when his own image is reflected. We sympathize with Actaeon's suffering because we are able to distinguish between what he 'is' and what he 'seems' to be.[84] But is this really so simple? What makes Actaeon Actaeon and not a stag? Actaeon has preserved his gaze, his eyes are still his, he can look in the pool and 'see' who he is, he can also recognize his dogs.[85] This act of looking in the mirror in search of self-identity is remarkable. Barkan suggests that the secret that Actaeon saw while looking at the goddess is the secret of self-consciousness: "Metamorphosis becomes a means of creating self-consciousness because it establishes a tension between identity and form, and through this tension the individual is compelled to look in the mirror."[86] Therefore, "metamorphosis is, at the deepest level, a transfiguration of the self."[87] This mirroring is also present in the episode of Pentheus, who looks at his mother in a sacred space.[88] Barkan understands that what Actaeon has seen is his divine aspect, and this costs Actaeon his life.

Speech and silence are an intricate part of many transformations in the poem, present here also. Diana transformed Actaeon into a stag to silence him.[89] Another common way of seeing his punishment is to envision it as a transformation from hunter to prey.[90] But the metamorphosis can also be understood in terms of viewer and object of the gaze. While a hunter, an epitome of masculinity, particularly in sexuality, Actaeon was the one who controlled his prey with his eyes; his gaze was fixed on the prey. As a stag, he is the object of the gaze of his hounds and the target of their desire. The text explicitly marks it: *videre canes/* "the dogs saw him" (*Met.* 3.206). He also begs his hounds to "know their master" ("*Actaeon ego sum: dominum cognoscite vestrum!*" / "'I am Actaeon, recognize your master!'" *Met.* 3.230), but to no avail. What is more, the play on essence and appearance is extended to his companions, who "look around" and cannot see Actaeon, although they see the stag: *ignari instigant oculisque Actaeona quaerunt/* "Unknowingly they urge on [the fierce pack] and search for Actaeon with their eyes" (*Met.* 3.243). Actaeon's transformation into a spectacle is well established by his companions who lament that he is absent and missing the *oblatae . . . spectacula praedae/* "the spectacle of the quarry brought to bay" (*Met.* 3.246), when he is, paradoxically, the spectacle. Actaeon's final wish, at the moment of his dismemberment, is to be the viewer rather than the viewed:

> . . . velletque videre,
> non etiam sentire canum fera facta suorum.

> Indeed he would want to see, not feel the fierce deeds of his own hounds.
> (*Met.* 3.247–48)

The penetrative reading and viewing model works well for the ekphrasis at the beginning of the episode. However, if one understands that Diana turns around and gazes at Actaeon, one could then question how the Mulveyan model works here. One could suppose a simple gender 'inversion,' where Diana's gaze is male precisely because it is objectifying and controlling. The problem is that in this case one should suppose an inverse trans-sex identification: the male external spectator identifies with the gaze of the internal female viewer (and so does the female external viewer, but it is not necessary to call it trans-sex identification—or maybe it is because she still identifies with a "male gaze"?). On the other hand, even if the male identifies with Diana's "male gaze," how does a male reader feel about being a viewer of an objectified male, or even, what if the male viewer, who had up to now aligned himself with Actaeon's eyes, resists switching bands and remains with Actaeon but is now objectified himself (this is rather difficult because the reader is forced to 'see' with Diana). The viewer Actaeon becomes the object of the gaze and his sight becomes feminized because he cannot 'act on it.' The reader needs to shift identifications to remain powerful. But even if one identifies with Actaeon's dogs, the view is partial, because they can't see beyond appearances. The reader then needs to remain outside the constrictions of identification and see the scene in its totality. With male viewers who can turn into objects of the gaze, female objects that become viewers, and hunters with an incomplete gaze, *Metamorphoses* with its shifting patterns and changing forms seems too fluid for Mulvey's model, and thus the metaphor of penetration for viewing and reading, though useful for the ekphrasis, may not be enough to appreciate the complexities of the whole episode.

At this point one questions the usefulness of the concept of focalization when it imposes constraints.[91] However, thinking about focalization helps in understanding an important effect of *Metamorphoses*, namely, that the poem expects the perspectives of the reader to be constantly shifting and that a one-sided view will restrict the appreciation of its richness. This demand that we switch our focalization makes us more active and participating readers and shows that contrasting views can be productive by their very contrast. Furthermore, the gender (and other) destabilizations that the text presents are transferred to the reader and the act of reading, and we find ourselves questioning our own stability and our own sense of identity. Focalization, then, is a dynamic process that opens up a world of questions about the text and about ourselves as readers.

The end of Book 3 narrates the death of Pentheus at the hands of the Maenades.[92] After listening impatiently to Acoetes' recollection of Dionysus's deeds (the god had caused the ship of Acoetes to stand still and to be covered with ivy. When the ship's men jumped overboard, they were turned into dolphins), Pentheus decides to go himself to Cithaeron and see what is going on. Pentheus's eyes, just as in Euripides' *Bacchae*, are important throughout the whole episode. When the priest comes to him, Pentheus's wrath is manifest in his gaze: *adspicit hunc Pentheus oculis, quos ira tremendos/ fecerat/* "Pentheus looked at him with his eyes, which his wrath had made terrible" (*Met.* 3.577–78). But this tension in his eyes may well have to do with Pentheus's avid desire to see the orgy, whether with his mind's eye or with his physical eyes. When he finally approaches Mount Cithaeron, an ekphrastic description frames the sacred space of the women:

> monte fere medio est, cingentibus ultima silvis,
> purus ab arboribus, spectabilis undique, campus:
> hic oculis illum cernentem sacra profanis

prima videt, prima est insano concita cursu,
prima suum misso violavit Penthea thyrso
mater. . . .

Almost in the middle of the mount, there is a field, clear of trees, visible
from everywhere, with borders framed by woods. Here his mother saw
him first looking at the sacred rites with polluting eyes. She was the first
to rush madly on him, the first to injure her son Pentheus with the
hurled thyrsus. (Met. 3.708–13)

The phrase *monte fere medio est* introduces the space where the women will
perform the Dionysiac rites. It is an enclosed space with borders marked
by woods, which acts as a metaphor for feminine sexuality. The text, however, remarks that it is a *spectabilis* space, a place to be looked at.
Although the developments of the Bacchanalia are secret, the word
spectabilis seduces the reader/viewer by giving him a sense of permission to
look, and thus one eagerly moves on.[93] The following line aligns the reader's eyes with those of Pentheus as he is found actively looking on the
scene. But a hint of the tragedy to come is given by the *oculis profanis*.[94]
So Pentheus's eyes open up and penetrate the enclosed space of sacred
femininity, thus implying a symbolic rape and violation. However, as with
all sexual violence, it pollutes the female. Eyes in this scene are not only
penetrative and opening, but also polluting. The game of the gaze, however, is soon turned upside down. Women will have their revenge on
Pentheus's intrusion, and it is now Agave who does the looking (*prima
videt*). The word *violavit* in the following line is poignant in connection
with Varro's reference to rape and the power of the gaze. But how genuine
is the gaze of these women? Agave is frenzied, out of her mind; she cannot see the 'real,' but attacks an image that she fabricates in her own
mind. She is in a way blinded by Dionysus and one can even say that in
the end it is his eyes that do the looking while the women just phantasize
and do not really control their gaze (it is not really a voluntary act of violence on Pentheus).[95] The details of Pentheus's death are meaningful for
his loss of masculinity. The story, and with it Book 3 of *Metamorphoses*,
ends like this:

"adspice, mater!" ait. visis ululavit Agaue
collaque iactavit movitque per aera crinem
avulsumque caput digitis conplexa cruentis
clamat: 'io comites, opus hoc victoria nostra est!'

non citius frondes autumni frigore tactas
iamque male haerentes alta rapit arbore ventus,
quam sunt membra viri manibus direpta nefandis.
talibus exemplis monitae nova sacra frequentant
turaque dant sanctasque colunt Ismenides aras.

"Look, mother!" he said. Agave howled madly at the sight, threw her
neck backward, and tossed her hair through the air. And embracing his
severed head with her bloody fingers she shouts: "Io, comrades, this work
is our victory!" No more quickly does a wind snatch away leaves touched
by the autumn cold, already lightly clinging to a tall tree, than is Penthus
torn limb from limb by impious hands. Warned by such examples, the
Theban women celebrate the new sacred rites, burn incense, and wor-
ship the sacred altars. (*Met.* 3.725–33)

Like Argus, Pentheus suffers decapitation and with the loss of his head,
he loses—among other things—the power to see. This decapitation, as it
was suggested for Argus, implies castration in the metaphor of deprivation
of his phallic eyes. Likewise, the simile of the wind tearing the leaves off
the tree recalls the tree on which Pentheus hides in Euripides' *Bacchae*
(1061ff.).[96] The chopping down of this tree has been seen by Segal and
others as a symbolic castration, and this can also be applied to the allusion to the tree deprived of its leaves—like a man deprived of his phallus—in Ovid.[97]

Spencer suggests that there are many "contrasts" between Actaeon and
Pentheus and that the men are portrayed as "opposites."[98] The problem
with this kind of thinking is that in its effort to show contrasts, it overlooks the many similarities that the actors of the Theban cycle present. In
the Actaeon episode Ovid stages the conflict between identity and
appearance. In contrast with Actaeon, Pentheus does not undergo a physical transformation. Nevertheless, the transformation takes place in the
minds of the women, who see him as a wild boar. One could suppose that
darkness may not help in the recognition of Agave's son, but probably it is
Dionysus who is placing a false *phantasia* in the women's minds and thus
controlling the kind of access to reality they have. Interestingly, the link
between Actaeon and Pentheus is strengthened by the fact that they are
both, in 'reality' or in the imagination, transformed into hunting prey: a
stag and a boar. The inward agony of both protagonists is alike, however,
in that it resumes the anxiety of not being recognized as who one is; it
brings about a conflict of identity and the self. Likewise, the prophecies of

Tiresias are once again realized. As in Sophocles' *Oedipus Rex*, the protagonist loses his sight, and blindness becomes a trade-off for the acquisition of knowledge. In Ovid, the *vates* had predicted, i.e., seen (*"meque sub his tenebris nimium vidisse quereris"*/ "'You will lament that with my blindness I have seen too much,'" *Met.* 3.525) Pentheus's end with a reflection on seeing and the desire to see (*"quam felix esses, si tu quoque luminis huius/ orbus" ait "fieres, ne Bacchica sacra videres!"*/ "'How fortunate you would be if you were deprived of eyes as well, so that you would not see the sacred rites of Bacchus,'" *Met.* 3.517–18).

Pentheus's gaze fails. His powerful and destructive gaze turns out to destroy the gazer. Part of the reason for this is Pentheus's own troubled and insecure masculinity. He is a youth striving to be a man and a king, but who is tied up oedipally with his mother; who has no meaningful father and an odd relationship with his grandfather and the ambiguously sexed Tiresias. In a way, he is similar to Dionysus but with fear of the sexual ambiguity that Dionysus has and rejoices in. In the failure of his gaze, we can place Pentheus with incomplete males striving for masculinity like Narcissus, Hermaphroditus, and Phaethon, and against the visual penetrative competence of Jupiter or Apollo. The 'male gaze' works fairly well here, for women are really deprived of a gaze through divine possession and Pentheus is reified and feminized.

Several critics have demonstrated that the Narcissus episode in Book 3 is enormously rich in issues of looking, art, and eroticism.[99] The story actually begins with another story of seeing: Tiresias. When Juno and Jupiter desire a judgment about which sex, male or female, experiences more sexual pleasure, they bring their case before the seer, who, because he has lived both as a man and as a woman, can answer this question. Tiresias has a special and unique knowledge, but his perspective does not correspond to Juno's wishes, and so, as punishment, the goddess blinds him. In Tiresias' case, and in general but especially in Thebes, seeing is connected with knowledge. Tiresias knows more than what is allowed to mortals, and thus the punishment may be aimed at preventing knowledge. But Jupiter compensates for this by giving him the power to predict the future. In a way, Tiresias' doom has to do with knowing, knowing something forbidden or inappropriate.[100] Curiously, the story of Narcissus is linked with Tiresias'. The fame of the old prophet became greater when Liriope, Narcissus's mother, asked if her child would become ripe in age and Tiresias responded: *si se non noverit* / "If he doesn't know himself" (*Met.* 3.348). It is noteworthy that *noscere* and *videre* are made synonymous, as it is really the act of seeing himself that destroys the boy. *Noverit* here clearly expresses Tiresias' personal conception of what *to see* signifies. The prophecy, as has been well established, plays with the famous Delphic maxim. But, contrary to Gregson Davis's opinion that Narcissus finally returns to the knowledge of his own self-identity, the problem here is that Narcissus does not 'know himself' in the mirror of the pool because he sees another reflected there.[101]

The story, which actually precedes the tale of Pentheus, also presents elements relevant to the issues of gaze, ekphrasis, and gender. After his encounter with Echo and the curse of one of the youths scorned by him, the boy Narcissus comes to a clear pool:

> fons erat inlimis, nitidis argenteus undis,
> quem neque pastores neque pastae monte capellae
> contigerant aliudve pecus, quem nulla volucris
> nec fera turbarat nec lapsus ab arbore ramus;
> gramen erat circa, quod proximus umor alebat,
> silvaque sole locum passura tepescere nullo.

> There was a clear pool, silvery with its shining waters, which neither shepherds nor she-goats that graze in the mountain had touched nor any other cattle, which no bird, no beast and no branch falling from a tree had disturbed. There was grass around it, which the near water nourished, and trees that would never suffer the sun to warm the spot. (*Met.* 3.407–12)

The phrase *fons erat inlimis* acts as a visual and narratological border that Narcissus, and the reader, will break to be able to see. There follows a description of a very virginal landscape that will be penetrated by Narcissus and that recalls the virginal land where Cadmus and his companions come to found Thebes earlier in the book. Furthermore, some connections with the Actaeon episode can be drawn. It is said that Narcissus has been hunting (*hic puer et studio venandi lassus et aestu/ procubuit faciemque loci fontemque secutus,/ dumque sitim sedare cupit, sitis altera crevi/* "Here the boy lay down, weary with the effort of the hunt and the heat, and attracted by the beauty of the place and the pool, while desiring to quench his thirst, another thirst grows in him," *Met.* 3.413–15). The hunter stopping in a 'virginal' locus recalls Actaeon the hunter and his erotic implications. In Narcissus's case, the thirst acts as a clear metaphor for erotic desire (*sitim sedare cupit, Met.* 3.415). It is precisely this desire that will doom the boy.

The problem is that Rhamnusia—a name for Nemesis—by whom the curse of Narcissus's suitor was heard (*Met.* 3.406), plays an odd trick on Narcissus. After reading Actaeon's story, the reader expects to find a virgin nymph or goddess in the *locus amoenus*; but all one sees, with Narcissus, is a virginal *puer*, or rather his reflection in the water. Mulvey's terms of the male gaze that objectifies the female image are not enough to understand the intricacies of the story. One could suppose that Narcissus intruding into the place—which itself has much to do with feminine landscapes (pools surrounded with grassy banks as in Diana's episode)—is the active male viewer. This could be justified by Narcissus's desire to penetrate the image in the metaphor of penetrating the pool with his arms: *in mediis quotiens visum captantia collum/ bracchia mersit aquis nec se deprendit in illis!/* "How many times did he plunge his arms in the middle of the waters trying to clasp the neck he sees. But he did not clasp himself in them!" (*Met.* 3.428–29).

As Elsner has shown, what Narcissus objectifies is himself or his own image.[102] This creates problems because while Narcissus looks at the reflection in the pool, the reflection bounces back, looks at him and repeats every one of his actions, thereby also becoming penetrative and intrusive. Narcissus destabilizes Mulvey's model, because it is impossible to take Narcissus strictly as viewer and his reflected image as viewed. Likewise, it is worth wondering what happens to identification in the scene. A man looking with 'active' Narcissus finds himself looking at a (reflection of a) *puer*. Some believe, as was argued for Hermaphroditus, that this would not represent a problem because erotic relations between adult males and boys were common and accepted in Greece and Rome. But it was still not as unproblematic as critics would like. Furthermore, if the external male or female reader truly focalized with Narcissus he would fall into the same narcissistic delusion as the protagonist. If a woman reader identified with Narcissus, she could, as Mulvey suggests, acquire some power, but it is a limited power, for all she can control and reify with the gaze is a *puer*, and not a full-grown man. Both male and female external viewers who focalize with Narcissus will suffer from visual reification, for the image they look at will also return the look and make them objects of their own gaze. Identification is thus a complex concept. The reader must, and in practice does, constantly shift perspectives and is encouraged to read the story from a multiplicity of angles.

Like Actaeon and Pentheus, Narcissus is also an 'incomplete' or problematic male whose youth makes him a *puer* (*namque ter ad quinos unum Cephisius annum/ addiderat/* "For Narcissus had reached his sixteen years," *Met.* 3.351) stranded on the threshold of mature masculinity, in that he has not stopped being a child. He wishes to be a penetrative and active viewer, but he is also stuck in his auto-eroticism and 'self-penetration,' which can only lead him to death or transformation. In the end, Narcissus the viewer becomes a visual object in his metamorphosis into a narcissus, yet something of his gaze is preserved in the very shape of the flower that keeps on 'looking down' in a fantasy of erotic contemplation.

ARACHNE'S ALTERNATIVES

In the analysis of the previous episodes the question 'what happens if the reader/viewer is a woman?' was only partially addressed. This issue is linked to whether penetration is the only metaphor available for reading. The episode of Arachne and Minerva offers some deconstruction of the penetrative reading model offered before.

The tale of Arachne, recounted by Ovid in *Metamorphoses* 6, has been much discussed in recent years. It tells of a young lady from Lydia, whose father was a dyer of purple wool and whose mother, already dead, was also lowborn. Despite her humble origin, Arachne achieved great fame owing to her extraordinary talents at the art of weaving (*clara, sed arte fuit/* "She was famous for her art," *Met.* 6.8). Even though it was clear that Minerva, master and creator of the art, must have taught her, Arachne in her stubborn arrogance challenged the goddess to a weaving contest. Pallas, dressed as an old woman, tried to warn her against the crime of defying a deity and was ready to grant divine pardon if the girl apologized. But Arachne stuck to her own pride even when the goddess revealed herself. Arachne and Minerva each wove a tapestry. The girl's tapestry was a wonderful work of art, prompting Minerva, in a fit of anger, to destroy the woven cloth and hit the girl three times on the forehead. Unable to bear this offense to her artistic talent, Arachne tried to hang herself with her own threads, so the goddess, "in an act of pity," turned her into a spider.

Both woman and goddess weave a cloth—presumably rectangular—and divide its space in dissimilar ways. Minerva's is symmetrical and hierarchically organized, while Arachne's flows and is a combination of images impossible to represent in actual painting. There is, however, something disconcerting in the experience of reading this scene. When the two weavers set to work the reader can envision a symbolic frame for the woven images to come in: *constituunt diversis partibus ambae/ et gracili geminas intendunt stamine telas* / "They both settle on different sides and stretch the slender warp upon separate looms" (*Met.* 6.53–54). What follows is a description of the process of weaving that transmits the fluidity and transitions of the work (*Met.* 6.55–69), which concludes with the narration of an ancient tale (*et vetus in tela deducitur argumentum*/ "and an old story is traced on the loom," *Met.* 6.69). But while at the beginning the action is in process, now the reader sees a description of the completed tapestries. Nancy Miller notes that Ovid, who is in the rest of the passage very accurate in the description of the weaving process, does not seem to respect here the technicalities of the art of weaving at the loom whereby the tapestry moves up from the bottom and thus the border is integrated from the beginning.[103] If Ovid were describing this process realistically, we would see only fragments of images developing until the whole tapestry is completed. Instead, he jumps to the concluded works. Next we are immersed in the description of the 'stories,' and the text embraces us.

As in the previous episodes there were narratological borders that acted figuratively as borders of pictures, here there is a concrete border for the tapestries. At the end of each ekphrasis, the narrator tells us that the artists take good care in drawing a border. Minerva marks it with a wreath of olive (*circuit extremas oleis pacalibus oras*/ (*is modus est*) *operisque sua facit arbore finem*/ "Around the borders she wove a peaceful olive-wreath (this was the end) and thus she concluded her work with her tree," *Met.* 6.101–2) and Arachne with little flowers (*ultima pars telae, tenui circumdata limbo,*/ *nexilibus flores hederis habet intertextos*/ "The edges of the tapestry, surrounded by a slender border, have woven flowers intertwined with ivy," *Met.* 6.127–28). This is not what they weave 'last,' but the reader is deceived by the narrator's manipulation of description. Miller reads this edge as a female signature, a mark of subjectivity and identity. It is the text of a woman signed by the closing *intertextos* of line 128. Miller ventures that this detail may respond to Ovid's specific intention to lay weight on Arachne's 'signature,' but it can also be an imitation of the Homeric ekphrasis, where the river Oceanus comes at the end as a 'rim' (*Il.* 18.607–8).[104] It is interesting here that two di-spondaic words act as narrative and pictorial borders of the tapestries. *Argumentum* in line 69 opens the description of the tapestries and *intertextos* closes it.

Both the initial symbolic and narrative 'frame' and the emphasis on the borders affect the act of looking at the tapestries: to see, the reader also needs to intrude into their works. But this intrusion is milder than with Actaeon or Pentheus who physically enter feminine spaces. Unlike other ekphrases, as readers and viewers we undergo an awkward process. First we know that some description will come, but what comes is rather the description of weaving. Then there is another narrative frame denoted by *vetus argumentum* (*Met.* 6.69), which in a way we need to break to see and read. Next we are immersed in the images before noticing that there will be a border circling them and our gaze. So we begin by exerting some sort of penetrative power, though a mild one, but then get lost in the images and only know that we have been truly penetrating the text(ile)—or that the text has engulfed us—once we are inside it and we realize that the strong frame of a border surrounds us.

Two reading movements are observed in this highly stimulating episode. The first can be described with the metaphor of penetration; the second—which deconstructs the first—sees the text as swallowing us. In any case the text is viewed as feminine, but there are two very different types of feminine figures involved, which imply two different metaphors for reading. The first and penetrative one, developed in the previous episodes, sees the text as a female in sexual terms. The second is more complex. Here the reader sinks into the text and is surrounded by it.[105] This type of reader-text relationship, in its turn, is twofold. On the one hand, the text can be seen as a big feminine web that entraps the reader. It could even represent the threat of the castrating female. On the other hand, a more comforting relationship with the tapestries envisions the text as a *magna mater* who embraces us and in whom we can plunge and enjoy.

Something similar occurs with the borders. Arachne's border is composed of flowers, common symbols of virginity, as can be appreciated in Proserpina's rape, which occurred while she was picking violets and lilies (*Met.* 5.392). In the metaphor of reading as penetration, by looking at Arachne's work we open it up and we destroy the flowers. It is relevant here that Minerva, who has been identified with masculinity and the godhead, triumphs over the girl, and a symbolic violation is suggested by her rending of Arachne's cloth at the end of the episode (*et rupit pictas, caelestia crimina, vestes* / "And she rent the embroidered tapestry showing heavenly crimes," *Met.* 6.131). But if one accepts the more comforting metaphor for reading instead of the violent one, one can think of the tapestry as a pleasurable pool surrounded by flowers. In this case, Arachne's 'signature,' as Miller calls it, would be a mark of femininity and would signal the possibility of looking at her tapestry in a nonviolent way.

The model of the monolithic male gaze, while useful for some ekphrases, falls short of making sense of larger gender struggles present in *Metamorphoses*. Likewise, while penetration and violence work to some extent as valid metaphors for reading and viewing ekphrases, the episode of Arachne opens our eyes to a different viewing and reading of framed description.

Desire and Paraclausithyron

The paraclausithyron can be described as "the song sung by the lover at his mistress's door, after he has been refused admission to her house."[106] Ovid and the elegiac poets have widely exploited this popular topos in their poetry; notable examples are Tibullus 1.2 and 1.5; Propertius 1.16; and Ovid, *Amores* 1.6. *Metamorphoses*, however, possesses only one true paraclausithyron, the story of Iphis and Anaxarete in Book 14. Iphis' desire for the girl commences with the eyes (*viderat . . . Iphis Anaxareten* / "Iphis had seen Anaxarete," *Met.* 14.698–99; *viderat et totis perceperat ossibus aestum*/ "He had seen her and had caught the fire of love in all his bones," *Met.* 14.700). This description invites us to anticipate a powerful male rapist like Jupiter, Mercury, or Apollo. But the tale diverges from this theme: Iphis goes as a suppliant to Anaxarete's locked doors (*supplex ad limina venit*, *Met.* 14.702).[107] The sexual overtones of the paraclausithyron are solidly acknowledged: a man who wishes to penetrate the doors of a mistress and enter her house, both doors and house being metaphors for female sexuality.[108] Further komastic motifs are present in the story: the garlands at the door, the tears of the lover, and the hard threshold (*interdum madidas lacrimarum rore coronas/ postibus intendit posuitque in limine duro/ molle latus*/ "At times he hung garlands wet with his tears on her doorposts and on the hard threshold he laid his soft body," *Met.* 14.708–9). But Anaxarete's heart is of iron, immovable and impenetrable as a rock. Because of the girl's rejection, Iphis decides on death and hangs himself by the door, and thus the lover himself becomes the garland and his death substitutes for the lover's vigil.[109] The banging of the lifeless body "begs for admittance" (*icta pedum motu trepidantum aperire iubentem/visa dedisse sonum est adapertaque ianua factum prodidit*/ "Struck by the motion of the trembling feet, the door seemed to have given a sound bidding to open and when it was opened, it revealed what had happened," *Met.* 14.739–41). The role that eyes play in the tale is remarkable. Iphis had fallen in love through his eyes but could not achieve penetration. At the time of his death he wishes that the girl take pleasure in his dead body: *"ipse ego, ne dubites, adero praesensque videbor,/ corpore ut exanimi crudelia lumina pascas"*/ "'I myself, you should not doubt it, will be there and will be seen present before you, so that you may feast your cruel eyes on my lifeless body,'" *Met.*14.727–28), and he envisions himself as passive in his being seen (*videbor*). But it is Anaxarete's gaze that brings her doom. When the funeral pomp passes by, Anaxarete is curious to see: *"Videamus" ait "miserabile funus"*/ "'Let us see,' she said, 'this mournful funeral'"* (*Met.*14.751). The images of openness become apparent, which provoke the irony of love and desire at the wrong time:

et patulis iniit tectum sublime fenestris
vixque bene impositum lecto prospexerat Iphin.

And she entered the highest part of the house with its wide-open win-
dows. Scarcely had she taken a good look at the body of Iphis placed on
the bier. (*Met.* 14.752–53)

Her eyes are locked in a frozen stare at the sight (*deriguere oculi,*
*Met.*14.754). Anaxarete's desire to see dooms her and transforms her into
stone, a natural outcome of the *dura puella* she was before.[110] With her
transformation, Anaxarete becomes, apparently, truly impenetrable. Her
case may be seen as the reverse of the Propoetides, who in various readings harden because of 'sexual excess.' But if one considers Liveley's view
that the Propoetides' first denial of Venus actually implied abstinence and
not prostitution, then their transformation into stone can also be seen as
a preservation of their initial frigid condition.[111] Even more interesting is
the end of the story, where Anaxarete's stone statue is placed in the temple of Venus Prospiciens (*Met.*14.761). A statue of a woman leaning forward in a watching position, thus symbolizing the fate of women who
scorn love and thus anger Venus, stood in a temple dedicated to
Aphrodite in Salamis.[112] This statue combines the figures of Anaxarete
transformed and the goddess Aphrodite herself.[113] The moment of looking
forward in the window is frozen in a symbolically charged literalizing
metaphor with Anaxarete's transformation into a statue and may even be
more complex and multifaceted than it appears. The figure of the "woman
in the window" is extensive in mid-oriental and Mediterranean Asia and
is particularly popular in Phoenicia and Mesopotamia. It is found, in the
figure of a goddess, a priestess, or just an ordinary woman, looking out of
a window in the high part of a temple (cf. *et patulis iniit tectum sublime fen-*
*estris, Met.*14.752) and it conveys the meaning that love is on offer there.
The image is apparently connected with sacred prostitution.[114] Thus
Anaxarete, though impenetrable as stone, may actually convey the idea
of sexual penetrability in her eternal fixation in an open window; in this
sense, her link to the sexually available Propoetides turned to stone is
strengthened. The punishment for Anaxarete's hybris is thus brought to
full closure, for what could be worse for a *dura puella* who does not wish
to open her doors (and body) than to be eternally fixed in a gesture of sexual availability.

To conclude, this is the story of a failed male who cannot achieve a
true masculine gaze and whose eyes are nonpenetrative and nonperformative. Iphis' impotence was already pre-announced in his very name,

which serves both for men and women and acts as an intratextual nexus with the story of the sexually ambiguous other Iphis in the poem (*Met.* 9. 688–797). Paradoxically, when Iphis' eyes close forever some power over the woman is exerted. On the other hand, the girl does not let herself be seen, as proper femininity requires, but by the end of the episode, she desires herself to see, to go beyond the limits of the household and know visually what is going on. Anaxarete's behavior literally seals her doom: Venus punishes her with petrifaction for resisting love. The right place for a woman's gaze, then, is narrowly defined between absence and excess. She should not control her gaze by looking too much and at will, but no looking is problematic as well. She should be able to look back and to return the gaze, but not to act upon it, not to initiate it either, and not to reject it.

This is an embedded story told by the disguised Vertumnus to Pomona as an admonition that she should not be a *dura puella* and that she should accept him as lover.[115] As Gentilcore has shown, Pomona is associated with the landscape of her magnificent garden and is at risk of and suffers the intrusion of Vertumnus, who woos her. In a way she wishes to be as closed as Anaxarete's doors, but finally opens up. Because the narrator focalizes with Iphis, the reader is led to identify with his gaze. But his gaze, according to the gist of the story, is an excluded one and lacks the objectifying power of the male gaze. Unlike with Daphne or Atalanta, for example, Ovid does not provide a physical description of Anaxarete; instead the text focuses on the pathos of love suffered by the man. He (and the 'male reader') tries to see her, but he is precluded from such reifying vision. Instead, the lover is transformed into the center of attention, and he becomes a clear object of the gaze in his death. The male gaze of the reader, used to experiencing visual fulfillment in other episodes, is here frustrated. Therefore, if 'he' does not want to be blinded, he will have to opt for a different reading position. With his death, the text turns the reader's gaze over to Iphis, yet the reader cannot really form an accurate *phantasia* of him, as no detailed description is offered. Both male and female readers are encouraged to move to a space where they can either look at the scene as a whole or adopt shifting focalizations. Finally, if women readers identify with Pomona, we can "be convinced' that we should "do as man says" and that if we try to exercise our own will and reject man's power and own our own gaze, we will end up petrified. But the story is likewise a disturbing warning to men that masculinity is fallible and that if men let themselves be conquered by passion, they may end up in madness and death.

A few other episodes play with the idea of paraclausithyron in more veiled and displaced ways. Pyramus and Thisbe re-enact the topos of the paraclausithyron.[116] It is not a door in this case, but a wall (*paries communis*, *Met.* 4.66) that separates the lovers: the episode exploits the poetics of absence. Perhaps the fact that what separates the lovers is a wall adds further drama to the story, for doors can be opened, but walls need to be broken down. It is, as with Narcissus, an impenetrable barrier, but while Narcissus's tragedy focuses on seeing, Pyramus and Thisbe cannot see each other at all.[117] Their relationship is based on the secret exchange of words through a hole in the wall (*Met.* 4.65–77). It is a relation where desire increases by prohibition and by the impossibility of seeing and touching. The analogies of the situation with a paraclausithyron are first perceived in the symbolism of the wall. It is the barrier that the lovers need to trespass, and to it—as in the paraclausithyron—they direct their prayers:

> "invide," dicebant, "paries, quid amantibus obstas?
> quantum erat, ut sineres toto nos corpore iungi
> aut, hoc si nimium est, vel ad oscula danda pateres?
> nec sumus ingrati: tibi nos debere fatemur,
> quod datus est verbis ad amicas transitus auris."

> "Envious wall," they said, "why do you stand between the lovers? How big a thing would it be for you to let us join our bodies in embrace, or if this is too much, to open for our kisses? We are not ungrateful: we confess that we owe it to you that a passage is given for our words to reach each other's loving ears." (*Met.* 4.73–77)

In view of the power of envy as a force that has implications for the gaze, the epithet of the wall is itself meaningful, as the wall may be understood as a metaphor for social constraints and what the lovers fear is the gaze of the family that will prevent them from being together. The interesting adaptation here is that both lovers play the role traditionally assigned to the *exclusus amator*. Furthermore, the wall stands as an obvious erotic icon, with its hole through which they exchange their passion; the desire that it would open (*pateres*) for erotic exchange adds to the sexual symbolism. Like the door in the elegiac paraclausithyron, the wall receives kisses (*partique dedere/ oscula quisque suae non pervenientia contra/* "They each gave kisses to their side of the wall, which did not get through," *Met.*

4.79–80). Further, mention of the deception of the *custodes* recalls the elegiac *puella* who needs to deceive her guardians to be with the lover. It is interesting that the girl herself opens the door of the house, unlike what happens in the traditional paraclausithyron where it remains stubbornly closed (*Callida per tenebras versato cardine Thisbel egreditur/* "Opening the door, clever Thisbe goes out through the darkness," *Met.* 4.93–94). But for all the openness and desire to be visible for Pyramus, Thisbe tries to become invisible to the gaze of parents and society by veiling her face (*fallitque suos adopertaque vultum/ pervenit/* "Deceiving her family and with her head veiled, she arrives," *Met.* 4.94).

The lovers undergo a series of adventures where looking plays a central role. Unfortunately, the eyes of Pyramus and Thisbe only meet when it is all too late. Thisbe, who throughout the episode has desired to see and be seen, suffers this irony of fate: that she can only see her lover in death, and the same twist applies to the function of the mulberry tree, which was meant to cover and protect them from society's gaze and which now simply covers them in death (*at tu quae ramis arbor miserabile corpus/ nunc tegis unius, mox es tectura duorum/* "But you, tree which now covers the wretched body of one, soon you will cover two," *Met.* 4.159). The poetics of the paraclausithyron are felt throughout. The episode presents the complaint against the object of separation, kisses delivered to it (*Met.* 4.80), and the futility of the efforts to break down the barrier. First, Pyramus and Thisbe both desire to penetrate the wall with their eyes, words, and embraces. In the woods, they wish to see each other, but they cannot achieve it. Their eyes only meet at death. The story has its points of contact with the tale of Iphis and Anaxarete, who can open the doors of the beloved and make the girl take heed of him only when it is too late. Pyramus and Thisbe thus embody a failed attempt at mutuality.

CHAPTER THREE

❦

The Fixing Gaze

"Set-piece description is regularly seen by narratologists as the paradigm example of narrative pause." This is how Don Fowler begins his discussion of narration and description as problems raised by ekphrasis. This detention of the story, where "the plot does not advance, but something is described"[1]—this in itself being a questionable statement—has been discussed principally by Mieke Bal.[2] However, the meanings of narrative detention for gender have been less explored. Mulvey observes that "the presence of woman is an indispensable element of spectacle in normal narrative film, yet her visual presence tends to work against the development of a story line, to freeze the flow of action in moments of erotic contemplation."[3] If one thinks in terms of the traditional gender paradigm of activity equaling the male and passivity equating with the female, one could imagine a certain identification of narrative with the active and advancing masculine, or at least with masculine aspects, and description with the passive and static female. When Leonard Shlain relates the female to image and the masculine to literacy, he suggests that the female is metaphorically connected with space while the male is envisioned as time.[4] The poet William Blake seems to have seen the male and the female in a similar way when he says that "Time and Space are Real Beings, a Male & a Female. Time is a Man and Space is a Woman."[5] This can be applied to narratological issues, for descriptions are commonly of spaces and narrations tell about actions in time; thus in a broad way, descriptions in a text may be seen as more feminine moments, and narrations as more masculine ones, though there is much room for discussion on this question.

These plays and interactions between narrative and description affect the gaze and the way in which characters and readers construct their *phantasiae* from the images they see. The present chapter focuses on the relation between gaze and movement, both in characters physically stopping their actions and in the detention of the narrative pace and the gaze by and for internal and external readers. The eyes of males often have the power to fix visual objects, namely, women and boys, while at the same time they delay the narrative. Nevertheless, the image itself has some power to paralyze the viewer and a two-way movement is recognized.

Looking at Statues

CONTEMPLATING THE IVORY MAIDEN

It is common in *Metamorphoses* that, when a woman is described, the flow of the narration is suddenly detained and everything stops in the contemplation of an immobile figure, paralyzed by the gaze of the viewer/narrator, internal and external. In consequence, the 'mind's eye' of the reader also experiences a pause. It is true that not all descriptions of women are construed in these terms, but the stoppage of the narration with a fixed description is almost a commonplace; even in pictures of the female body in action (e.g., Daphne and Atalanta) there is an illusion of detention. Two episodes are particularly rich in interplays between gaze, desire, mobility, and immobility: Pygmalion's ivory maiden and Andromeda.

The story of Pygmalion is well known and is one of the episodes that has received more attention in relation to the gaze. Some points, however, have been overlooked by the critics. In particular, this discussion will argue with Elsner's view of Pygmalion as viewer and will say a few things about the interactions between gaze, movement, and paralysis in the story. Disgusted with the sexual misconduct of the Propoetides, the women of Amathus who had denied the divinity of Venus and were thus forced to become prostitutes and were later turned to stone, Pygmalion constructs for himself a perfect ivory maiden.[6] As mentioned before, critics have seen Pygmalion as the paragon of the visual artist, as the alter-ego of the elegiac poet and as a viewer/reader.[7] But while some like Sharrock see the statue as lacking in self-agency and not having "a mind of her own," yet still being able to fulfill Pygmalion's "erotic fantasies, of being 'a whore in bed,'"[8] some like Liveley try to recover some female agency in the sculpted maiden.[9]

The focus here will be on Elsner's understanding of the story as a myth of the viewer and reader.[10] Elsner thinks that "the ivory statue (which we may see as a figure for the poem) may have been created by Pygmalion the sculptor but it generates him as a viewer-lover."[11] As Lively says, the viewer that Elsner imagines is not genderless but clearly male, and just as Wheeler does not explicitly acknowledge the gender differences in his "all-encompassing" audience, Elsner also falls into the very universalization of the male experience that Fetterly's resisting reader condemns.[12] Proof of this is his affirmation that "the second person of *credas* directly addresses the reader as viewer of the statue and equates the reader with Pygmalion as one who might also believe" and that "as Pygmalion loves and desires, so the reader loves and desires."[13] The problem here is, who is the "reader"? What if the reader is actually a woman? Does she also "love and desire"? We are again in the problematic Mulveyan crux. In a trans-sex identification she is allowed to have the same experiences as the male reader, otherwise she remains outside the pleasure of the scene. Although it is fairly 'acceptable' to talk about power and objectification in trans-sex identification, don't "love and desire" bring a whole lot of more complex issues? Do women "love and desire" images of women? Neither Elsner's nor Mulvey's assumptions work here, Elsner's, because of his male-centered universalization, and Mulvey's because of the 'reductiveness' of her model. Any 'solution' would in itself be self-defeating, yet one may suggest that unilateral 'identification' is not the only model for productive gender-aware readings of the episode, for it imposes too many limits on viewing. To get a full view of the richness of the episode, the reader needs to be prepared to assume various focalizing points and contrasting views simultaneously.

Beyond these criticisms, however, Elsner's contention that Pygmalion is really a myth of the viewer is undoubtedly fruitful and has "opened our eyes" to a different way of looking at the story. It has certainly informed the present reading. Nonetheless, one does not need to think in terms of 'either/or': whether to see Pygmalion as a reader or as a creator, for both aspects can, and need to, be reconciled. Elsner is aware of this, but he feels the need to stress the differences for the sake of his own argument. First, Elsner seems to imply that Pygmalion is a viewer only after the creation of his statue. But the *phantasia* that he must have forged in his mind before setting to work had already generated him as viewer and given him a gaze. The important point about regarding Pygmalion as a viewer before he creates his statue is that it permits us to inquire about what previous viewings and readings inform his work and constitute him as a creator. This is one aspect where Elsner's thesis can be expanded.

The motor of the story is something that Pygmalion has seen (*quas quia Pygmalion aevum per crimen agentis/ viderat/* "Pygmalion had seen these women lead their lives in shame," *Met.*10.243–44), the promiscuity of the Propoetides.[14] So Pygmalion sets out to create his own image of a perfect (and immobile) maiden. Part of Elsner's argument is based on the fact that Ovid dedicates a mere two and a half lines to the creation of the statue and close to fifty to the viewing of the image.[15] But length is not all that counts here and sometimes two lines can tell more than a hundred. Indeed, these few lines are very meaningful for issues of gender, readership, and creativity:

> interea niveum mira feliciter arte
> sculpsit ebur formamque[16] dedit, qua femina nasci
> nulla potest, operisque sui concepit amorem.

> In the meantime he successfully sculpted a statue of dazzling ivory with amazing art and gave it a beauty that no woman can be born with. He fell in love with his own work. (*Met.* 10.247–49)

These lines describe Pygmalion as an active artist whose actions and agency lead to the creation of the ivory maiden. It is noteworthy that in this narration Ovid uses verbs in the preterite to show a succession of actions that suggest narrative progression and performance and place the male as central, active, and mobile character. Taking into account the previous idea that narrative involves a more masculine movement and description a more feminine one, Pygmalion here, through the 'diachronicity' expressed by the perfect, embodies the masculine action and the 'performativity' of the creator.[17] Then again, if Pygmalion identifies with Ovid the creator at the very moment of commencement of creative action, it is a male artist/viewer/reader that lurks behind the image.

Pygmalion's previous readings and viewings inform his creation; he—and any artist—is a viewer before creating a work of art.[18] In the three meaningful lines quoted above, Pygmalion shows that he has both 'read' Roman literature and 'seen' ancient statues. In considering Pygmalion's previous viewings the concept of *phantasia* can clearly be seen at work as a critical tool. One of the central issues in the episode is that Pygmalion wants a chaste woman whom he can marry. The epitome of the candid, immobile, and chaste woman is Lucretia and the passage shows her hiding behind the ivory statue. Thus, in the creation of a wife who is beautifully pale and chaste, Pygmalion is reading Ovid, for an allusion to the image of Lucretia in the *Fasti* is construed in very similar terms as the ivory girl.

This is a difficult point, because the final writing and revision of both *Metamorphoses* and *Fasti* may have taken place simultaneously when the poet was already in exile.[19] Nonetheless, the image of Lucretia, whether already inscribed in the *Fasti* or still as mental *phantasia* of the poet, acts as intertext for Pygmalion's girl.[20] Lucretia is also "snowy"; when Sextus Tarquin conceives a desire for her, the text reads:

> forma placet niveusque color flavique capilli,
>> quique aderat nulla factus ab arte decor;
> verba placent et vox, et quod corrumpere non est.

> Her beauty, her snow white color, and her blond hair please him and her grace made by no art. Her words and her voice please him, and her incorruptibility. (*Fasti* 2.763–65)

Lucretia is almost a statue, except for the fact that she can speak. First one notes the allusion to the skin of both women as *niveus* and the word *forma*, involving its double meaning of beauty and shape. A few lines later in the *Fasti* passage, the description of Lucretia tells us: *hic color, haec facies, hic decor oris erat*/ "This was her hue, this her beauty, this was the grace of her face" (*Fasti* 2.774). Any reference to Lucretia's color is absent from Livy's version, but it accords with Ovid's preoccupation about color and women elsewhere.[21] In Livy, the decisive factors in arousing Tarquin's desire are both beauty and chastity: *forma tum spectata castitas incitat*/ "Her beauty and exemplary purity incite him" (Livy 1.57.10).[22] *Spectata* here clearly emphasizes the condition of Woman as spectacle. The lover is again a viewer and in both Livy and Ovid the narration is focalized through the male, with whom the (male) reader also identifies. Ovid picks up on the two fundamental features of Lucretia's character as construed by Livy (*forma* and *castitas*), but translates them into color imagery (*niveus color*—white having connotations of purity). It is interesting that *castitas* is actually an *invisible* quality, which the plastic artist makes visible. Important also is the comment *sine arte*, as it denotes that her pale beauty/purity is natural and not achieved through cosmetics. Lucretia's *sine arte color* should be compared with *feliciter arte* in Pygmalion's construction. The statue is the work of an artist, and he chooses deliberately to carve it out of ivory, but Lucretia is naturally pale and thus fulfils 'naturally' the male fantasy of the white woman. The reference to *ars* is teasing; for while the ivory statue is pure *ars*, the virtue of Lucretia is that she is not 'artificial.' Paradoxically, what Pygmalion wants is a non-artificial female. This may be seen to undermine the 'artificiality' of Pygmalion's girl, a reading that would agree with Liveley's de-mystifying view of the statue.[23] So Pygmalion has read/seen Lucretia and, with her *phantasia* in his mind, he constructs his ivory wife.

Critics have recognized that there is another statue that informs Pygmalion's creation: Aphrodite of Knidos described in Lucian, *Amores* 13–16.[24] Lucian's statue can be connected with those three meaningful lines that construct Pygmalion as viewer before (or at the same time) he becomes a creator. The artist Praxiteles created a beautiful statue of the naked goddess Aphrodite about to enter her bath.[25] There was a man who was so profoundly in love with the statue that he managed to lock himself inside the temple where the sculpture was and had sex with the 'goddess.' After this a mark appeared in the thigh of Knidian Aphrodite. In Lucian's story the reader focalizes with the male narrator who, in a voyeuristic stance, comes to the temple with his friend to look at the statue, although the apparent intention is aesthetic and not erotic contemplation (it is questionable whether these two forms of viewing can be separated, however). This story functions as an evident intertext for Pygmalion who sexually desires his statue. Like Pygmalion's maiden (and like Lucretia), Lucian describes the statue as of pure brilliance and splendor (τῆς λίθου λαμπρότης, *Amores* 15). Although the original Knidian statue is lost, through copies, art historians have deduced that, although there was some polychromy in Praxiteles' work—as usual in Greek sculpture—the body of Aphrodite seems to have been white or at least covered in a light tint, and over this surface the mark of sexuality would be even more visible.[26] But the statue also recalls for us the issue of the goddess in the bath, a distinctly female pleasure and thus a particularly tempting sight for male desire. Ovid's Pygmalion, then, who in other versions actually fell in love with a statue of Aphrodite, models his own statue on that of the goddess; therefore, one could envision him as viewer and reader of this traditional account.[27] We are here, as with Diana's readings of rape in *Metamorphoses*, envisioning, in a releasing critical maneuver, a literary character with self-agency and life beyond his specific episode who can become a reader. One may suppose, then, that Pygmalion has read and seen this statue of Aphrodite and was already in love with its *phantasia* before creating his statue; therefore, he tries to recreate for his own enjoyment an image of her. In this sense, Pygmalion aligns with other male viewers/lovers of goddesses.

Praxiteles' art is so realistic as to be capable of deceiving the human eye and heart. Indeed, the inability to distinguish between statue and goddess is itself telling. This uncanny ability links Praxiteles to Pygmalion.[28] But in Ovid's tale Pygmalion takes the roles of both the artist and the viewer and thus embodies the figures of Praxiteles and the intruder. Most poignant also is that the text compares the statue's lover with Anchises (ὁ καινὸς Ἀγχίσης καθεῖρκτο, *Amores* 16). This is interesting in light of our observations regarding Actaeon and its relation to the Homeric *Hymn to Aphrodite*.[29] If Pygmalion is associated with the viewer/intruder (like Actaeon) who comes to love a statue of the goddess in her bath, Pygmalion is in some way associated with Anchises as lover of Aphrodite and with Actaeon who sees a bathing goddess. Given that in *Metamorphoses* Pygmalion comes after Actaeon, one may also suppose that Pygmalion informs his construction and his love with his own 'reading' of Actaeon. But Pygmalion is smart enough to make a statue of a woman and not a goddess to fall in love with, and so he avoids the typical punishment of males who view and love goddesses.

On the basis of previous readings and *phantastic* viewings of the figure of Lucretia, the statue of Knidian Aphrodite and perhaps the image of Diana in her bath, Pygmalion forges a perfect maiden with whom he soon falls in love and through whom he becomes artist and viewer, reader and writer. Further, while Elsner is surely right in stressing Ovid's construction of Pygamlion as a viewer, he does not stress sufficiently the importance of his being a viewer and reader *before* creating his statue, for reader and artist are inseparable categories in the story. Literature and art are constructed on the basis of previous readings and viewings.

After the three introductory lines where Pygmalion makes his ivory maiden, the reader's gaze is directed to the finished work and there he experiences a detention of the action in the contemplation of the statue:

> virginis est verae facies, quam vivere credas,
> et, si non obstet reverentia, velle moveri:
> ars adeo latet arte sua. miratur et haurit
> pectore Pygmalion simulati corporis ignes.

> Her face is that of a real maiden, which you would think was alive, and, if shame did not prevent it, you would think she would want to be moved: to such an extent does his art conceal his art. Pygmalion admires her and burns in his heart with the fires inspired by the crafted body. (*Met.*10.250–53)

The verbs now are mostly in the present, which gives an idea of detention and synchronic action, often associated with visuality, while diachronicity is linked to narrative. Thus, the image of the woman detains the action and with its visual charge produces a stoppage in the narrative. The phrase *velle moveri* has often puzzled critics.[30] The statue is so real that, "you would believe that she is alive and desirous to be moved"—although *moveri* could have a middle-reflexive sense here. Yet it is curious that the text does not read *velle (se) movere*, which would imply an active desire of the statue to move, to gain life, but one may think that her 'imagined' desire is the desire of a passive object to be activated by her creator. Note how Pygmalion is most mobile when he "tries her" (note *admovet*) with his hands (*saepe manus operi temptantes admovet, an sit/ corpus an illud ebur* / "He often tried his work with his hands, to check whether she is flesh or ivory," *Met.*10.254) and mouth (*admovet os iterum* / "Again he moves his mouth near her," 282).

There is also the question of why the ivory statue would experience *pudor* at the thought of self-generated movement. Pygmalion wants a woman whom he can marry, and movement is not appropriate in a respectful *matrona*.[31] The paradox is that men do not always want an immobile woman, Pygmalion desires a wife who is a fixed image that does not move, yet he wishes that she would actually stop being just a statue. Here Sharrock's inference that Pygmalion wants a wife/ goddess/ whore is appropriate.

After the description of the ivory maiden, the story turns to Pygmalion's actions as lover. He applies kisses, arranges the statue, and offers gifts, all typical actions of the elegiac lover. But notably, Pygmalion seems to be affected by the immobility of the statue by becoming himself less active. This process, paradoxically, takes place when the statue begins to be mobile or at least 'movable.' Most of the verbs that describe Pygmalion's actions toward the statue are in the present (*admovet, dat, putat, loquitur, tenet, credit,* etc). According to Elsner, this is the section that best shows Pygmalion as a viewer, but also as (elegiac) lover. Again, the sequence of actions in the present gives an idea of synchronicity rather than narrative diachronicity, which has interesting implications for his transformation from artist to lover. It is well known that the elegiac lover is always somewhat feminized and static in his adoration of the *puella*, especially in comparison to the 'man of action.' The image here provokes in turn some fixity in the viewer—such is the case with Perseus, who, like Pygmalion, also *stupet* at a magnificent image (10.287). In this sense, there are further connections between the story and Lucian's tale of Knidian Aphrodite because in the Greek text the curious visitors/viewers are also affected with paralysis at the sight of the statue, especially Charicles, who stood almost petrified before the image of the goddess (ὁ Χαρικλῆς ὑπὸ τοῦ σφόδρα θάμβους ὀλίγου δεῖν ἐπεπήγει τακερόν τι καὶ ῥέον ἐν τοῖς ὄμμασι πάθος ἀνυγραίνων / "Charicles in the excess of his admiration stood almost petrified, though his emotions showed in the melting tears trickling down from his eyes," Lucian, *Amores* 14, trans. Harmon [1993]).

It is significant that when Ovid narrates the scene at the festival of Venus, when Pygmalion is actively seeking a 'result,' he soon returns to the use of the perfect (*constitit, dixit, sensit*, Met.10.274–77) to refer to Pygmalion. But when he returns home, Pygmalion appears to be newly detained in the contemplation of the ivory maiden, when the present is now used: *admovet, temptat, mollescit, subsidit, cedit, remollescit, flectitur, fit, stupet, retractat, gaudet, veretur* (Met.10.282–88). In the end, Pygmalion has suffered several transformations, first from viewer to creator—and from creator to viewer. Finally, from artist to lover, who, after manufacturing an immobile statue, is immobilized himself by the image he has fashioned. However, as usual, there is some continuity in transformation: the creator is still a viewer, and the lover is still an artist at some level. The narrative and descriptive sequencings in the episode are marked by the use of the perfect and the present, respectively. The former shows an advance of the action and implicates a more masculine movement of performativity and action. Description slows down the action and delays the gaze in contemplation, making the readers, internal and external, more 'feminine' and immobile.

FLEXIT AMANS OCULOS: ORPHEUS'S VISUAL FAILURE

When talking about Pygmalion, one cannot forget that this is the story of not one artist but three, and therefore the story of three (or more) viewers. Pygmalion creates his ivory maiden, but Orpheus sings their story and Ovid that of Orpheus. [32] The episode of Pygmalion and his girl mirrors Orpheus's desire to see. The bard lost his own dear Eurydice precisely because he could not resist casting a controlling and longing eye on his wife. The gaze is central to his fate (*metuens avidusque videndi/ flexit amans oculos* / "In fear and desirous to see, the lover turns back his gaze," Met.10.56–57) and will exert a profound impact on the whole of Book 10. Issues of paralysis and mobility are also central in Orpheus's descent to the Underworld. With his music, he is able to paralyze the creatures of Hades and freeze their normal routines:

. . . nec Tantalus undam
captavit refugam, stupuitque Ixionis orbis,

nec carpsere iecur volucres, urnisque vacarunt
Belides, inque tuo sedisti, Sisyphe, saxo.

Tantalus did not try to catch the fleeting water, and Ixion's wheel
stopped in amazement. Nor did the birds pluck the liver, the Belides rest-
ed from their pots, and you, Sisyphus, sat on your rock. (Met.10.41–44)

The verb *stupuit* for Ixion is particularly telling here, for it indicates
Orpheus's power to control and immobilize through music. Let us remember that Orpheus has the capacity to make static objects move and to
freeze moving objects with his art.[33] Here Ovid is drawing on Virgil's
description of how the realm of the Underworld and the inmost Tartarian
halls are astounded at the bard's song (Virg., *Georg.* 4.481–82). Notwith-
standing, while he is a successful musician and poet, Orpheus is an unsuccessful viewer. When he turns to gaze at Eurydice, he is himself stupefied
by her disappearance:

non aliter stupuit gemina nece coniugis Orpheus,
quam tria qui timidus, medio portante catenas,
colla canis vidit. . . .

Orpheus was stupefied by the second death of his wife not unlike the
man who, in terror, saw the three necks of the dog Cerberus, the one in
the middle bearing chains. (Met.10.64–66)

John Heath suggests that Orpheus represents the unheroic failure in comparison with Hercules' success in the Underworld. Instead of paralyzing
Cerberus, through the force of the simile, the guardian of the realm of Dis
immobilizes Orpheus. This sense is also conveyed by the comparison with
Olenos, the husband of Lethaea, in lines 68–69, which brings forth the
fact that Orpheus is not willing to die to achieve his goal.[34] Heath's conception of Orpheus's failure is appropriate and his suggestion that the poet
projects his own desires through the stories he tells in Book 10 is suitable.[35]
But although he justly shows that Eurydice can be assimilated to a "hell-
ish denizen who turns onlookers into stone," Heath does not expose the
gender implications of this.[36] All this leads to a comparison with Perseus.
Like Perseus, Orpheus *stupet*, but not just temporarily as the hero. His stu-
pefaction has profound implications for his life and marks the loss of his
beloved's image, the failure of his gaze, and the collapse of his masculinity. Like Perseus, he faces a 'Gorgon' with the power to petrify, yet unlike
him, Orpheus cannot overcome her power.

What Orpheus then does with the story of Pygmalion is to create a *phantasia* of his own success. The ivory statue can be understood as Orpheus's desiring fantasy to fix his eyes forever, to have an immobile girl who would never move or fade away.[37] Further, in Orpheus's story of loss, when the couple is headed upward to the realm of the living, Eurydice, who follows her husband, is probably the one who looks at him from behind, while Orpheus must not turn around (*ne flectat retro sua lumina/* "That he should not turn his eyes back," *Met*.10.51). In appearance, hers is a mute gaze with no power to control or influence her husband. It is perhaps this prohibition on looking and the knowledge that he is being seen by a woman, which are felt as a weakening of masculinity for the bard, and Orpheus cannot resist it.[38] In contrast, Pygmalion's ivory statue can always be looked at, but, ideally, she cannot look back. However, Orpheus's dream is dismantled by the power of Venus, who turns the statue to life and finally gives her a gaze, thus frustrating Orpheus's desire to fix the beloved forever as a spectacle. But the statue's 'coming to life' could also realize the dream of Orpheus in a different way. Through his art, the bard can move rocks and stones, thus animating them, and he also almost succeeds in bringing Eurydice to life. Pygmalion, Orpheus's *alter ego*, succeeds with his attentions and prayers, and accomplishes the dream of the Thracian bard. So the awakening of the statue is complex from Orpheus's perspective, for on the one hand, it realizes his dream of giving life to his beloved, but on the other, it shows Orpheus's failure to petrify and impose eternal visual control over her image, for Pygmalion's statue comes to life, opens her eyes and—in a releasing reading—could even escape the gaze of her lover.

PERSEUS'S STUPEFACTION

Instead of a concrete statue, the episode of Andromeda and Perseus presents a quasi-statue and has many points of contact with the tale of Pygmalion and his ivory maiden. The hero Perseus visits the land of the Ethiopians and finds Andromeda chained to a rock, Ammon's punishment for her mother's crime. As with Pygmalion, the affair begins with the male gaze:

> vidit Abantiades, nisi quod levis aura capillos
> moverat et tepido manabant lumina fletu,
> marmoreum ratus esset opus; trahit inscius ignes

et stupet et visae correptus imagine formae
paene suas quatere est oblitus in aere pennas.

(As soon as) Perseus saw her chained by her arms to a rough rock, save for
the fact that a light breeze would stir her hair and that warm tears were
trickling from her eyes, he would have thought she was a marble statue.
Unknowingly, he burns with the fire of love. He is stupefied and seized by
the sight of beauty he has seen; he almost forgot to flap his wings in the
air. (Met. 4.674–47)

Perseus sees Andromeda immobile and believes her a marble statue,
except for her wind-blown hair, which can be understood as a sign of her
being still alive.[39] This scene accords well with the observation that
women looked at are normally depicted as inactive. Beauty is equated
with immobility and the male gaze fixes the figure of the girl and slows
down the narrative. The reader, also focalizing with Perseus, stops 'his' gaze
in the contemplation of statue-like Andromeda. Perseus falls in love with
the frozen image. Movement of the hair gives reality to the picture and
anticipates the possibility of movement and pleasure.

It is worth remembering that Perseus constitutes an odd case, since,
although a mortal, he can still fly like the gods, and this endows him with
the possession of a vertical gaze characteristic of deities (despectat, con-
spicit, 624 and 669). Perseus's mobility, which is also seen here in the fact
that he is a traveling hero, emblematizes masculine movement against
feminine fixation, not only with reference to Andromeda but in relation
to all the other female spots/landscapes that Perseus traverses: the
dwelling of the Graeae (773–75), the house of Gorgons (778–79), Libya
(618–20), and the garden of the Hesperides (628).[40] Perseus views
Andromeda, but the passage insists on her 'not seeing.' First, her eyes are
full of tears (manabant lumina fletu / "Tears were tricking from her eyes,"
674) and then it is said that, if she were not tied up, she would modestly
cover her face with her hands.[41] Instead, her tears do the job: manibusque
modestos/ celasset vultus, si non religata fuisset;/ lumina, quod potuit, lacrimis
inplevit obortis / "If she had not been in chains, she would have covered her
modest face with her hands; she did what she could and filled her eyes with
rising tears" (Met. 4.682–84). Andromeda's eyes acquire an alternative
function, which is not to see. Although she does not look, it cannot be said
that her eyes are completely inactive, for they "do what they can" to cover
her face. It is a somewhat frustrating and frustrated attempt, but an
attempt still at some kind of activity. It is peculiar, however, that Ovid
never says that she would cover her nudity if she could. While not looking

at a man's eyes before having been formally introduced to him is what a virgin should do; her embarrassment may also be due to the fact that she is naked. A point to be borne in mind here is, as with Pygmalion, the issue of modesty and marriageability. Andromeda cannot 'look back' because modest women should not do so. Andromeda, then, is the fixed, immobile statue-like beauty that the male gaze freezes for his pleasure and delights in at the prospect of making her mobile. And it is the unbinding of Andromeda which Perseus sees as a passport to marriage (*"praeferrer cunctis certe gener"*/ "'Surely, I should be preferred as son-in-law over all the suitors,'" 701). One may suppose that it is not only the statue-like condition of Andromeda that seduces Perseus, but the fact that she embodies the fantasy of the blind woman. Seeing that silence was a condition praised in women in the ancient world, we may infer that men desire a woman who cannot/does not want to see. Andromeda covering her face in shame conveys the idea that she does not possess powerful, threatening, and castrating eyes, which is precisely what Perseus has been fighting to eradicate in Medusa and the daughters of Phorcys by robbing them of their gaze.

The obvious fact that Perseus actively looks, while Andromeda is clearly the passive object, led to a straightforward application of the monolithic male gaze to the episode. Segal shows the link between the stories of Pygmalion and Andromeda by affirming that "Andromeda is the inverse of Pygmalion's beloved, a living body made into a statue-like spectacle for a male viewer" and insists that Andromeda is only an erotic object and that her "statuesque role is Andromeda's only function in the episode." For Segal Andromeda's body as a statue somehow legitimizes "male erotic viewing under the rubric of art."[42] While this seems true for the most part, it is not appropriate to assign absolutely no agency to Andromeda (she is at least capable of talking and expressing herself, while Pygmalion's girl is not) and even less so to assign Perseus absolute control, for he suffers some destabilization by the very act of looking and almost loses control.

Perseus is as mobile as one can be: he flies around in every direction and needs constant flapping of his wings in mid-air, which is curiously endangered by the paralyzing effects of love (note in particular *stupet* in line 676).[43] Love makes Man weaker, it paralyzes him, and, like a woman, he becomes immobile and passive. The reference to the chains of love in line 679 is interesting in this respect:

> ut stetit, "o" dixit "non istis digna catenis,
> sed quibus inter se cupidi iunguntur amantes."

As he stood he said: "Oh, you do not deserve these chains, but those that
bind fond lovers to each other." (*Met.* 4.678–79)

While some see this expression as one more element of male domination
and power, since entrapment and enclosure are common features of rape,
the "chains of love" also provide a different dimension to the power relations in the story.[44] The reference unavoidably recalls the *servitium amor-*
is of Latin elegy, where it is normally the male lover who finds himself a
slave to love and to a cruel mistress. Perseus's allusion to erotic chains precisely at the moment when he *stetit* and *stupet*, losing control—though
briefly—of himself, evokes feelings of domination experienced by the elegiac lover and hints at the fact that he is feeling entrapped and powerless
like a slave. Perseus could be using the elegiac jargon to express his own
feelings, for here the female object of the gaze and desire, by its very
immobility, controls, even disturbs and overmasters the viewer—which is
definitely more than Segal's assumption that Andromeda is "just a statue." In a more releasing reading, the very fixed image of Andromeda as
statue affects both the male gaze and the narration, which stops and centers on her image. A double-edged play is at work. Not only does Man's
gaze freeze Woman's image, detaining the story; but also Woman's image
paralyzes Man and with him the eyes of the external viewer/reader (again,
for the moment this reading assumes a trans-sex identification for female
viewers). The reader is not immune or detached but becomes affected by
what he sees and reads.

So one way of reading the episode is by identifying with Perseus's gaze,
whether we are male readers or female. Another way is to resist Perseus's
and Ovid's gaze by questioning their reliability and exposing the mecha-
nisms whereby Andromeda is constructed by narrator and focalizer as a
fantasy for and by the male gaze. First, one can disagree with Segal that
Andromeda is the reverse of Pygmalion's maiden, for the story displays
the same metamorphic sequencing observed in Pygmalion. From ivory
statue, the woman is released by love and comes to life. Andromeda is
also constructed as a *marmoreum opus*. The word *opus* cannot but have
metacritical overtones. In this, Ovid plays a trick on his readers (perhaps
his preconceptions play a trick on him) and shows himself as an unreliable
and subjective viewer whose gaze we can resist. When in the *Ars Amato-*
ria Ovid admonishes the male lover to avoid reproaching a woman with
her "faults" (*vitia*), he adduces the example of Andromeda: *nec suus*
Andromedae color est abiectus ab illo/ "And her color was not made a
reproach to Andromeda by him [i.e., Perseus]" (*AA. 2.643*). Andromeda's

color is here, by implication, considered a *vitium*. Her example is again blended with Sappho's tradition in *Heroides* 15, where Sappho writes:

> candida si non sum, placuit Cepheia Perseo
>   Andromede, patriae fusca colore suae.
> et variis albae iunguntur saepe columbae,
>   et niger a viridi turtur amatur ave.

> If I am not dazzling white, Cepheus's Andromeda, dark with the color of
> her country, did please Perseus. White doves are often joined with those
> of varied hue, and the black turtledove is loved by the green bird [the
> parrot]. (35–38)

The color of Andromeda's skin varies according to different versions of the story, giving rise to much discussion about this issue.[45] In the Asian account she is white, and in the African account she is black.[46] Ovid appropriates the African version in the *Heroides* and three times in the *Ars Amatoria*; in Latin elegy Andromeda becomes a paradigm of the black woman who was loved despite her color. In the version adopted by the *Metamorphoses*, the home of Andromeda, daughter of Cepheus, was Ethiopia. Therefore, her picture as a marble statue becomes curious. Since the story takes place in Ethiopia, the reader is led at first to believe that Andromeda is black, but the image of a marble statue is normally associated with pure whiteness of the body.[47] It is quite surprising that critics like Anderson who have a very deep knowledge of Ovid do not seem to be aware of this problem. Anderson comments on the line: "Andromeda had a beautiful body, white like marble, nude like most statues."[48] Apparently Anderson does not register the incongruity of the myth and Andromeda's description simply because he falls in the trap of aligning himself with the gaze of the desiring male subject in the tale. This seems to be a usual maneuver whereby "throughout the history of western art figures of female beauty, whether virginal or provocative, sacred or secular, are regularly assimilated to an ideal of European whiteness, even where ethnic origin might suggest they should be represented otherwise."[49] The version of the story that Ovid had in mind, on the evidence of Sappho's letter and the setting of the tale in *Metamorphoses*, was the African, which makes Andromeda black. But Ovid still describes her beauty with images of whiteness. Like Apollo wishing that Daphne would comb her hair and thus alter her appearance in conformance with his desire, the viewer is here changing the nature of the image. Andromeda is not considered beautiful in her blackness. Thus Ovid's male gaze annihilates what Andromeda *is* and constructs her as a perfect fabrication of man's mind that suits his taste and desire, just as Pygmalion will do in Book 10. But why does Ovid change his presentation of Andromeda in the various places he mentions her? Perhaps it is because in the other Ovidian passages where the heroine appears she is not looked upon directly as the erotic object of the gaze; instead, her color is referred to in a somewhat oblique way. In fact, in *Heroides* 15 it is the character Sappho, a woman, who does the speaking. In *Metamorphoses* 4, on the other hand, Andromeda is a clear object of the gaze that entraps the onlooker, an effect that would perhaps be lost if her blackness were emphasized. Perseus/Ovid silences and distorts Andromeda's image. In agreement with recent views on race in antiquity,[50] and despite all earlier assumptions that color prejudice was almost nonexistent in the ancient world,[51] this appears to be a judgment on race. When something negative is said, Ovid's texts mention "black Andromeda": when something positive is meant, she metamorphoses into a "white statue."

Perhaps, if Andromeda had clearly looked back, Perseus would have been completely petrified, but it is indeed Medusa, his fierce female enemy, who has the actual power of turning brave men into stone. Perseus has defeated her with her own lethal gaze. As Barkan suggests, Perseus is a master of mirror and reflection, which is why he can manipulate the girl's image and even give a reflection of Andromeda that is sieved through his own subjectivity. Interestingly, while most mirrors in *Metamorphoses* only serve the purpose of feminine toilette or self-contemplation, as in the Narcissus episode, Perseus here puts the forces of the mirror to a very masculine and epic task: killing the monster. Like Ulysses and the song of the Sirens, Perseus gets to see the monster and thus acquires the knowledge of the unknown and the 'other' in order to defeat it. While it is the vision of the horrific Medusa which petrifies, the text also suggests that she has a powerful gaze (cf. *Met.* 5.240–41: *sed nec ope armorum nec, quam male ceperat, arce/ torva colubriferi superavit lumina monstri/* "But neither by the power of arms nor by the stronghold he had wrongly taken did he overcome the fierce eyes of the serpent-bearing monster"). Perseus uses his shield as mirror, looks at Medusa reflected in it, and decapitates her when she is asleep. This episode bears resemblances with Argus, who is also doomed when he falls asleep and whose eyes are also meaningful. Loss of sight is here developed through decapitation of a female monster, who thereby loses her sight and her phallic gaze. It is worth remembering that

Perseus was already a robber of female eyes as he had stolen the only eye that the two daughters of Phorcys shared.

At his wedding Perseus tells the story of how he defeated the Gorgon and why she had snakes: once she had been a beautiful girl whose best feature was her hair. Neptune raped her in a temple of Minerva and the goddess punished her by turning her hair into snakes. This is in itself remarkable, for the victim is punished instead of the rapist. Again, as with Juno, goddesses are powerless before gods and thus, they need to perpetrate their vengeance on the victim. The text stresses that Medusa the girl was an object of amazement and visual enchantment (*Met.* 4.795–96). From beautiful spectacle she is transformed into horrifying sight, which it is however forbidden to gaze upon. In an inversion of the sequences of transformations observed in the Theban cycle, here is a female object of the gaze that is turned into a most powerful viewer. This is precisely what makes Medusa intolerable and deeply threatening: that a female may possess a gaze and turn men (literally) into objects (of the gaze).[52] The petrifying power of Medusa's eyes is then a hyperbolic metaphor for any woman who wishes to see and to affect the world with her eyes.[53]

Perseus uses the head of Medusa to destroy his enemies and to vanquish his opponent in the conquest of his bride. Andromeda and Medusa are thus opposites: the bad, monstrous, and powerful woman, who can fix, control, and petrify with her eyes; the one that "cannot be looked at," but who can look at whatever she pleases and who thus needs to be beheaded. Andromeda is powerless, bound, a woman destined for marriage, fixed (turned into stone) by the male gaze, but who cannot, in her modesty, look back at the gaze of Man, thus embodying the fantasy of the blind woman. Very well, but are these two women really so different? Like a ball, Andromeda's image bounces back and almost petrifies her viewer, although Perseus resists. There is something of Medusa in Andromeda; a domesticated Gorgon who can still be controlled and loved, although she can nonetheless surprise you.

The episode clearly displays the male gaze, yet it still invites an exploration of "the risks entailed by the male in his control of the gaze."[54] At first glance, the monolithic male gaze works fairly well, but soon the reader realizes that Perseus's control actually hangs from a thin thread and that his gaze and masculine supremacy are often in danger of destabilization. Likewise, while the male reader (and female in trans-sex identification) can focalize with Perseus and enjoy the pleasure of looking, the resisting reader can disarticulate the viewer's fantasy and expose the strategies whereby Andromeda is constructed as a work of art and deprived of her own identity. We can be fooled by Perseus's gaze and

Ovid's narrative, or we can decompose the layers of reflections that the master of the mirror imposes on us. The first road paralyzes us and leaves us stupefied before Andromeda's image. The second will surely give us more critical mobility.

Fixing the Bride

SLOWING DOWN ATALANTA

Running is a common feature of virgins in *Metamorphoses*. Various characters run away from their suitors until they become fixed in one way or another: Daphne, Syrinx, and Lotis. That fixation is a common aspect of marriage imagery is well known, but here the focus will be on the connection between this aspect and the function of the gaze. The episode of Atalanta and Hippomenes is most emblematic. Venus narrates the tale in Book 10, under the wishful sight of the Thracian bard. This girl of fleeting feet (*laude pedum*, Met. 10.563) has been told by an oracle that marriage will be her bane ("*coniuge . . . / nil opus est, Atalanta, tibi: fuge coniugis usum / nec tamen effugies teque ipsa viva carebis*"/ "'There's no benefit for you in a husband, Atalanta; flee the contact of a husband, and yet you will not flee, and though alive, you will lose yourself,'" Met. 10.567–68). So Atalanta turns herself into a stereotype of the 'running virgin' who lives in the woods (*Met*.10.566–67) just like Daphne, Callisto, and Diana. The insistence of the oracle on the idea of fleeing (*fuge, effugiens*, and later *fugat*, 569) recalls Daphne's flight in Book 1. Again, as in the Daphne episode the emphasis on the feet (563, 570, 653) can be taken as metapoetic, and may assimilate Atalanta to the fleeing *puella* who is at the same time envisioned as an erotic poem.[55]

Atalanta's identification with the *dura puella* of erotic elegy is also observed in the affirmation that she was indeed harsh (*illa quidem inmitis*, 573). In Ovid's presentation of the girl there are obvious intertextualities with Propertius, who mentions that Milanion conquered harsh Atalanta (*Milanion nullos fugiendo, Tulle, labores/ saevitiam durae contudit Iasidos/* "Milanion conquered the cruelty of harsh Atalanta, Tullus, by fleeing from no toil," Prop.1.1.9–10) and refers to her speed (*ergo velocem potuit domuisse puellam/* "Thus he could subdue the fast-footed girl," Prop.1.1.15). But what is rather unelegiac is the episode's insistence on the idea of marriage (564, 567, 571, 576, 613, 618, 620, 621, 634, 635), which is a central issue in the heroine's life. Her virginity is signaled by mobility and running, but at the same time, her speed is described with images of flying, especially in *passu volat alite virgo* (587) and in the simile of the Scythian arrow in 588. Yet the most obvious image of flying is the reference to the *talaria* flowing with the wind as she runs, which has given much trouble to translators and commentators (*aura refert ablata citis talaria plantis/* "The breeze bears back the streaming wings she wears on her swift ankles," Met.10.591).[56] The word *talaria* links Atalanta to three main characters who have winged ankles or sandals, namely, Minerva, Mercury, and Perseus. From a gender viewpoint Atalanta aligns herself with two mobile males who fly around, survey the world, and spot immobile women on land in *Metamorphoses*. The connections with Minerva, although the poem does not show her with wings, may also point to the mobile characteristic of deities, male and female, and to the particular 'masculinity' of Minerva herself.

Atalanta engages in running contests with the promise of wedlock for the suitor who can outdo her in the race. Many young men, however, pay the penalty for losing with their own lives. One day, Hippomenes, wondering who would be so foolish as to look for a bride at such a high price, sits as a spectator at the race deemed so unfair: *sederat Hippomenes cursus spectator iniqui* (Met.10.575). This line is quite remarkable for issues of gazing and mobility. In contrast with Atalanta's running, the text shows a man who is immobile. He is, however, an almost detached spectator who looks down on the whole event as ridiculous, yet at the same time he comes partly in search of scopophilic pleasure to observe the race. But Hippomenes' gaze soon changes when Venus describes what happens to him on first seeing the girl:

> ut faciem et posito corpus velamine vidit,
> quale meum, vel quale tuum, si femina fias,
> obstipuit. . . .

> When he saw her face and her body without clothing, like mine, or like yours—if you were a woman—he was stupefied. (Met.10.578–80)

Posito velamine recalls Diana *sine veste* in Book 3, and thus turns Hippomenes into a sort of voyeuristic Actaeon. Likewise, his paralysis, denoted by the verb *obstipuit*, aligns the boy with Perseus who almost loses control at the sight of Andromeda. Here again, it is not only the viewer who fixes the image, but the image can also affect the viewer. Venus's comparison with her own naked body obviously points to Atalanta's beauty, but the comparison with Adonis—if he were a woman—is problematic, for it

conveys gender ambivalences in Atalanta. She is a girl, but a girl who cannot be fixed in marriage, a mobile girl who possesses, at some level, more
power than her male suitors. The situation is complex, because
Hippomenes, the *puer*, is here viewed as a sort of Adonis, a boy under the
influence of a powerful female.

Soon, however, the narrative shifts to present the figure of Atalanta;
the readers focalize with Hippomenes, and with his gaze. The narration is
somewhat detained:

> quae quamquam Scythica non setius ire sagitta
> Aonio visa est iuveni, tamen ille decorem
> miratur magis: et cursus facit ipse decorem.
> aura refert ablata citis talaria plantis,
> tergaque iactantur crines per eburnea, quaeque
> poplitibus suberant picto genualia limbo;
> inque puellari corpus candore ruborem
> traxerat, haud aliter, quam cum super atria velum
> candida purpureum simulatas inficit umbras.

> Though she seemed to the Aonian youth to go no less swiftly than a
> Scythian arrow, he admired her beauty more: and the race itself gave her
> beauty. The breeze bore back the streaming wings she wore on her swift
> ankles, her hair was thrown back over her ivory back, and the ribbons
> with decorated borders were placed at her knees. Her body had acquired
> a blush of girlish radiance, as when a purple awning drawn over a gleam-
> ing white atrium stains it with borrowed shades. (Met.10.588–96)

While reading this episode the reader wonders for a long time when the
metamorphosis will come. While physical transformation happens only at
the end when the lovers are turned to lions by Cybele, the section presents a gradual transformation of Atalanta into a wife, by first transforming her into object of the gaze and then by gradually slowing her down
and fixing her image. The *visa est* of line 589 places Atalanta for the first
time as the art object to be looked at (the previous description focuses
more on the effects of the image on Hippomenes). As mentioned before,
such phrases are narratological and visual markers that focus our eyes and
frame the description to come. They act as the cinematographic camera
when framing the image for the gaze of the viewer. *Miratur* again points
to the youth's amazement and erotic paralysis. Likewise, the visual infatuation is expressed later in the fixation of Hippomenes' eyes on Atalanta

(*constitit in medio vultuque in virgine fixo* / "He stood in the middle and with his eyes fixed on the girl," *Met.*10.601). But a two-way play is conveyed here, too, where the gazer is also fixed by the image he sees, for the passive *fixo* referring to his *vultus* also implies that while Hippomenes fixes the image with his eyes he is also fixed by it.

The connections with art are relevant here. The reference to *terga eburnea* in line 592, placed in a book where we have just read about Pygmalion's *eburnea virgo*, cannot be taken but as a reference to a statue. The erotic and—hopefully marriageable—girl is conceived with references to an immobile image. It is almost as if Hippomenes cannot conceive a wife because she is fast of feet, but needs to turn her image into something that is static. Right from his first glance, Hippomenes, with whom the reader focalizes, is trying to fix Atalanta and detain her running. The story will become then an effort of the lover to stop her movement and convert her into a 'proper,' immobile, erotic object.

The next indicator of Atalanta's transformation is seen in the way she returns his gaze:

> talia dicentem molli Schoeneia vultu
> aspicit et dubitat, superari an vincere malit.

> With soft expression the daughter of Schoeneus looks at him while he says this and doubts whether she prefers to win or to be overcome. (*Met.*10.609–10)

This is the first time that Atalanta looks at Hippomenes, yet her gaze does not objectify the male, and although later the text insists on his being young and beautiful, there is no detailed description of the body of Hippomenes to match the way we see the body of Atalanta. Differing from the former characterization of Atalanta as hard (*inmitis*), her face (and eyes) is now *mollis*. Next, there is a monologue where, as often in female characters, the girl expresses her doubts and battles with her soul. Notably, she begins to think of herself in the passive regarding viewing. Atalanta recognizes that what has ensnared Hippomenes is her image: "*a! miser Hippomene, nollem tibi visa fuissem!*" / "'Ah, miserable Hippomenes, I wish I hadn't been seen by you!'" (*Met.*10.632). Soon Hippomenes competes with her in running and finally vanquishes her with the help of Venus's golden apples.[57] But the race constitutes a constant effort of the male to stop and delay the female. In this sense, the repetition of the word *mora* is relevant. Venus is the first to use the concept when she recognizes that there was little time to give Hippomenes help (*nec opis mora longa dabatur*,643).[58] Further, the crowd cheers to Hippomenes and tells him not to tarry because he will win: *pelle moram: vinces!* (659). In part it is his image that delays Atalanta in her running: *o quotiens, cum iam posset transire, morata est/ spectatosque diu vultus invita reliquit!/* "Oh, how often, when she could pass him, did she tarry and unwillingly left behind the face that she had contemplated for a long time" (Met.10.661–62). In this case Atalanta assumes the position of viewer, who, like Perseus, is stopped by the image. But she is still mobile like a man. Soon, however, Hippomenes throws one of the golden apples on the side of the path and avid Atalanta stops to pick it up: *obstipuit virgo nitidique cupidine pomi/ declinat cursus/* "The maiden was stupefied and the desire for the brilliant apple made her turn away from her course" (666–67). The yearning for a fruit, as in the episode of Proserpina, is a common symbol of sexual desire and even presages the loss of virginity. But Atalanta, with a new burst of speed, makes up for her *mora* (669) and leaves the youth behind. The same trick is played again: *et rursus pomi iactu remorata secundi/ consequitur transitque virum/* "And after being newly delayed at the tossing of a second apple, she followed on and passed the man," Met.10.671–72). The conclusions of the race and the story are piquant:

> an peteret, virgo visa est dubitare: coegi
> tollere et adieci sublato pondera malo
> inpediique oneris pariter gravitate moraque,
> neve meus sermo cursu sit tardior ipso,
> praeterita est virgo: duxit sua praemia victor.

> The maiden seemed to hesitate whether she should go after the apple or not: I forced her to pick it up and added weight to the apple she held. Equally with the weight of the burden and with the delay I impeded her, and lest my speech be slower than the race itself, the maiden was overtaken, and the winner took his prize. (Met.10.676–80)

Note that Atalanta is now referred to in the passive: she "seems/ is seen" (*visa*) and "she was outstripped" (*praeterita est*). Further, *duxit* is interesting in light of the implications of the verb as an expression of a male "taking a wife" (*uxorem ducere*). The verb *impedio* makes for a loaded pun, for it is precisely Atalanta's *feet* that the weight of the apples hinders. And so Atalanta is newly detained (*moraque*), but this time her transformation is complete. With the loss of the race she has become a 'delayed' girl and thus she is marriageable. She has now left behind the trace that most

marked her individuality, her excellence in running. Anderson rightly
observes that by desiring Hippomenes' victory early, she is in a way
accepting a form of death: "We might be tempted to read this dilemma as
Ovid's poetic representation of the universal dilemma of woman (or man)
in love: she must 'die' as an independent *puella* in order to become a
wife."[59] To conclude the story, Venus draws attention to herself as narrator and to Adonis as audience. The same *mora* with which Atalanta was
affected is what Venus fears might affect her narrative. This coincidence
is also interesting from a reader-response viewpoint, for Venus is aware
that when we see Atalanta delayed, the gaze of the reader/viewer is
delayed with her. In this sense it is noteworthy that, as Anderson shows,
there is a largely dactylic rhythm in lines 669–70 when Atalanta speeds
up, but then the spondees prevail in 671 as she slows down.[60]

Jupiter bids Peleus to take his place as lover and seek a union with Thetis,
the virgin goddess of the sea (*Met.*11.227–28). As seen in chapter 2, the
whole setting of the scene where Peleus encounters the goddess is an
ekphrasis that turns her into a visual artifact. Ovid creates a double framework whose boundaries are doubly marked in a Chinese box structure. In
the internal frame delineated by *est* in line 235 there is a little
"*Metamorphoses*":

> illic te Peleus, ut somno vincta iacebas,
> occupat, et quoniam precibus temptata repugnas,
> vim parat, innectens ambobus colla lacertis;
> quod nisi venisses variatis saepe figuris
> ad solitas artes, auso foret ille potitus;
> sed modo tu volucris: volucrem tamen ille tenebat;
> nunc gravis arbor eras: haerebat in arbore Peleus;
> tertia forma fuit maculosae tigridis: illa
> territus Aeacides a corpore bracchia solvit.

There Peleus takes hold of you when you are lying conquered by sleep,
and because, though entreated by his prayers, you reject him, he prepares
to offer violence, entwining both arms around your neck. He would have
accomplished his attempt if you had not changed often into varied forms
resorting to your usual arts of transformation. Now you were a bird; he,
however, held you as a bird. Now you were a sturdy tree, but Peleus held

tight to the tree. The third shape was that of a spotted tigress. The son of
Aeacus was terrified by it and let loose his arms from your body.
(*Met*.11.238–46)

Thetis' protean character, stressed also by *ambiguum* in line 236 (*ambiguum, magis arte tamen*), vividly recalls Proteus's mutability in the *Odyssey*, narrated by Menelaus in Book 4, who also needs to be held tight to be overmastered.[61] The scene presents all the ingredients of *Metamorphoses*: love, rape, sexual violence, and a succession of physical transformations. Here is a goddess who changes forms, not to rape but to avoid being raped, and a mortal man who succeeds in raping a goddess, though with the help of some god, as Thetis recognizes. If one takes one step backward, one sees that it was Jupiter who in fact desired Thetis, but was discouraged by the prophecy that she would engender a child who would surpass his father (*Met*.11.222–26). Instead, Jupiter bids his grandson Peleus to pursue Thetis in love. From these lines the reader understands Peleus as a surrogate of Jupiter's desire. Thetis, for her part, tries to avoid rape through metamorphosis, like Daphne or Syrinx, but is unsuccessful. Daphne and Syrinx could change form thanks to the help of their divine relatives; but Thetis, though a deity herself, is powerless against the desires of males.

It could even be said, with standard feminist critique, that this description of Thetis makes a spectacle of a woman whose rape gives pleasure to the male viewer. Most noteworthy is this framed detention of the reader's gaze, which also fixes Woman in sexuality. Thetis, to remain a virgin, needs to keep on moving and changing, but the formula to obtain the girl is given to Peleus: "keep a firm hold of her no matter how many times she changes." Proteus actually advises: "*ignaram laqueis vincloque innecte tenaci*"/ "'Bind her unaware with snares and tight bonds'" (*Met*.11.252). Bonds and chains pertain to the common imagery of love and marriage and symbolize the power and control that Peleus will hold over the goddess. And this is exactly how Thetis is gained. The firm arms of Peleus holding her lead to her surrender, her rape, and their union, which is understood as marriage in the text:

> exhibita estque Thetis: confessam amplectitur heros
> et potitur votis ingentique inplet Achille.
> Felix et nato, felix et coniuge Peleus.

> Thetis was revealed as herself: the hero embraced the exposed goddess, attained his desires and filled her with the mighty Achilles. Peleus was blessed in his child, blessed also in his wife. (*Met*.11.264–66)

This episode leads to the question of sex as an event that fixes women; modern English slang expressions for lovemaking (from the controlling perspective of the male) like "to nail/screw" respond to this conception. But Thetis is also fixed as a visual image, and *exhibita Thetis* makes us think of a picture in an 'exhibition.'

One can recall a related story where the wandering island of Delos only becomes fixed and stops its wanderings when Latona finally gives birth to Apollo, immortalized in the Homeric *Hymn to Delian Apollo* and in Callimachus's *Fourth Hymn to Delos*.[62] The story is also briefly mentioned in Ovid's *Metamorphoses* 6.184ff.[63] Latona, impregnated by Zeus, is denied a place on earth to give birth. She then wanders until Delos (mobile at the time and not attached to the bottom of the sea) offers itself as the place of birth for the divine twins. Solomon draws an interesting connection between Delos' wanderings and female hysteria.[64] Hysteria was considered a female disease whereby the *hyster* (womb) was dislodged and floated loose in the body, causing various complications. "The cure for 'hysteria,' 'wombness,' was sexual intercourse, the purpose of which was to impregnate the woman, thereby anchoring the womb down with a fetus."[65] With these ideas in mind, one may reconsider the sexual act of marriage as an act of fixation; the virgin would be like the loose, wandering womb, who can move, change, and run until a man comes to fix her. In this same light, the virgin island of Delos, untouched before, and movable, becomes lodged, anchored, and fixed by an act of giving birth, which becomes symbolically its own pregnancy and procreation. This is exactly Thetis' fate for, while a virgin, she is free to move and change constantly. Her fixation implies matrimony and readiness for procreation and motherhood. The emphasis on Thetis' future child is also relevant, as she needs fixation and immobility to conceive, in accordance with ancient sexual beliefs.[66]

QUASI-BRIDES

The previous examples merge marriage, sexuality, and immobility; but there are some other episodes in which, although the relation is not so clear-cut, something of this imagery can be appreciated. The previous reflections about Delos are useful when studying other stories of *Metamorphoses*. Since his birth, Apollo is someone who 'fixes' as, with his new presence he contributes to fix the wandering island. This capacity to fix (especially his lovers) will be prominent in his characterization in *Metamorphoses*. Let us look at Daphne, for example. It is true that, unlike Atalanta, Daphne rejects marriage and sex. It has been established, however, that her transformation brings forth a form of symbolic (and displaced) marriage with the god and thus, not surprisingly, she loses the mobility of the virgin and becomes rooted, though not through actual intercourse.[67] Many plays on fixation and the gaze run through the episode, as was discussed earlier, and Daphne becomes a spectacle to the eyes of the god who experiences love as a visual fixation. Apollo grasps a frozen image of the virgin but, in her running, she tries to evade him. The long chase begins, and for about twenty-five lines, there are no specific references to the gaze because the passage concentrates on the fleeing, the movement, and Apollo's wooing (*Met.*1.502–25). Then the text presents a new description of the running virgin that freezes her movement through the focalized gaze of the god:

> fugit cumque ipso verba inperfecta reliquit,
> tum quoque visa decens: nudabant corpora venti
> obviaque adversas vibrabant flamina vestes,
> et levis inpulsos retro dabat aura capillos,
> auctaque forma fuga est. . . .

> She fled and with him she left behind his unfinished words, and even then she seemed fair. The winds disrobed her body and the opposing breezes caused her garments to flutter, and a gentle wind bore back her streaming hair. And the flight enhanced her beauty. (*Met.*1.526–30)

Before the chase continues, a poignant simile is introduced, where a Gallic hound sees (*vidit*, 534) a hare and runs after her. The previous detention of Daphne's image through Apollo's eyes prefigures her final 'arborization' and gives way to the god's desire to fix her and possess her. This fixation is finally achieved, though in a twisted way, as a change that prevents a straightforward possession by Apollo, but which realizes his desire to control and immobilize her (note how he still surrounds her as a tree with his arms and kisses the bark). The ending is paradoxical. Daphne obtains what she wants, the preservation of virginity, but Apollo also manages to fix her in a symbolic marriage.

The story of Syrinx parallels that of Daphne. Pan is attracted to her through the eyes (*Pan videt hanc*/ "Pan sees her," *Met.*1.699). This causes the nymph to run from the fixing eye of the pursuer, but she ends up being fixed as a reed and finally objectified as a reed-pipe in a symbolic (and displaced) union. The desire of fixation is newly achieved, though in an awkward way. Little is known about Lotis. Ovid tells us that she became a lotus tree after running away from Priapus (*Met.* 9.347–48). Supposedly, something similar occurs in this story. Finally, fixation can also be understood in another form. Philip Hardie suggests that these characters also become 'inscribed' with the mark of their lovers and are a perpetual memorial for the god's love.[68] The laurel will always be a mark of Apollo, and the reed an emblematic instrument of Pan. The fixation is not only visual, but also verbal as these women become in a way 'written.' Inscription and fixation go together; this is particularly the case with Apollo's inscription of his beloved Hyacinthus.

Fixed Boys

In sexual relations boys occupy a position similar, yet not equal, to that of women because they are also often envisioned as the passive partners, and therefore there are similar issues of mobility and fixation in the affairs of gods and boys.[69] Likewise, in some sense it is felt that women are like children, but they just never grow up, while male youths do.

NARCISSUS

We begin our discussion of the erotic role of *pueri* with Narcissus. This boy, consumed by his own love, pines away and turns into a flower. It has been widely recognized that Narcissus's self-fixation is achieved through his eyes, and that even in the Underworld he remains fixed to his own image in the Stygian pool. Narcissus's psychological fixation is literalized in the physical fixation of his gaze. When he first reclines by the pool and tries to drink water, he is 'stupefied' by the image he sees. The scene is intriguing, leaving the reader to wonder if this is the first time that Narcissus ever tries to drink from a pool. Being a hunter one would think that Narcissus is no stranger to pools and streams and that he must have quenched his thirst in them before. Or was he so lucky before not to look into the water while drinking? Yet this seems to be a particularly 'mirroring' pool (cf. *Met.* 3.407). Perhaps this new 'knowledge' of himself to which Tiresias refers is the gaze of the male on the verge of maturity. Although as a child he may have physically seen his image, the image he now sees is a different one, that of the adolescent growing up. One can also think that Tiresias' prophecy only takes effect after the curse by one of Narcissus's rejected suitors: *sic amet ipse licet, sic non potiatur amato!/* "May he himself thus love, thus may he not conquer his beloved!" (*Met.* 3.405). But then again, it is doubtful that Narcissus would not recognize his own image when reflected, unless he is 'blinded' by a higher force, and what he sees is not really the image of himself that he recalls but a 'fictional' *phantasia* of something else.[70] Narcissus is paralyzed by the beauty of the image he sees (*Met.* 3.416), just as Perseus will be in the following book. Relevant as well are the connections of immobility and statue-like beauty in the episode:

> adstupet ipse sibi, vultuque inmotus eodem
> haeret, ut e Pario formatum marmore signum.

> He himself is stupefied at himself, and immobile, he is fixed with the same expression as a statue carved out of Parian marble. (*Met.* 3.418–19)

The passage also states that the reflected image has *eburnea colla/* "ivory neck" (422) and a snow-white face slightly tinted by a blush (*et in niveo mixtum candore ruborem*, 423), just like Atalanta. Narcissus thus captures in himself the immobility of the lover paralyzed by the image of the beloved; but this immobility, when reflected in the pool, is transformed into a more reified immobility like that of statue-like Andromeda and Pygmalion's ivory maiden.[71] He is, at the same time, viewer and statue. The passage is focalized through Narcissus's eyes. If we follow the suggestion that Narcissus had known his image before and is now seeing something different from his 'real' image, he is in a sense a creator of a particular *phantasia* that envisions the beloved as a statue, undergoing the same process as Pygmalion and Perseus. The connections with art and statues are shown further when he begins to lament and beat his breast:

> dumque dolet, summa vestem deduxit ab ora
> nudaque marmoreis percussit pectora palmis
> pectora traxerunt roseum percussa ruborem,
> non aliter quam poma solent, quae candida parte,
> parte rubent, aut ut variis solet uva racemis
> ducere purpureum nondum matura colorem.

> While he grieves, he removes his tunic from the upper fold and beat his naked breast with his marble-white hands. The beaten breast took on a pink hue, no different from apples, which are often partly red and partly white, or as grapes in clusters of varied hue acquire a purple tint when they are not yet ripe. (*Met.* 3.480–85)

The 'statue-likeness' of the reflection is now transferred to Narcissus himself. His hands are now of marble and beat on the snow-white body. The chest, as locus of love and passion, turns red accordingly and now recalls the blush of the young virgin erotically aroused (Pygmalion's statue awoken). Narcissus pines away. Richard Spencer suggests that the episode of Narcissus contrasts with Pygmalion's in that "the sculptor desires a partner to love, who will fulfill his life; Narcissus loves only himself. Pygmalion gives bodily form to the object of his love; Narcissus loses his bodily existence by fascination with the object of his love."[72] This kind of reasoning is another good example of why Spencer's approach is flawed, for, again, the insistence on contrast precludes him from seeing similarities and intermediate options. In this case, there is not only contrast between Pygmalion and Narcissus but also 'likeness.' In a very 'narcissistic' way, Pygmalion falls in love with a part of himself, a product of his own imagination, an emanation of his artistic mind. The symbolism of the reddening apple is used once more to indicate the proximity of sexual maturity. Like Narcissus himself, the *poma* is partly red, partly white. The fruit simile, however, denotes a progression: the second example of the grapes deepens the reddish tonality (*purpura*) and marks the change with the highly significant *matura*, yet *nondum* certainly undermines this sense.

After "melting down like wax" (a metaliterary element in itself), Narcissus is turned into a flower and this is all that remains of his body (*Met.* 3.509–10). This final metamorphosis has been unjustly discredited by some critics who claim that "the metamorphosis is at best very marginal to the story."[73] But the final transformation actually involves and preserves the fixation typical of erotic viewing. The new flower not only implies the fixation to earth of Narcissus's own body, but also, as a complex metaphor, preserves the fixed gaze of the viewer with the inclination of the flower toward the ground. This is more than simply "tangential," as some would like to see. He becomes now something to be looked at, a spectacle himself, for whom looking and being looked at were the causes of his tragedy. Interestingly, if the narcissus were placed by a pool it would also preserve the circular instability of Narcissus's gaze, eternally looking at a reflection that eternally looks at him. Yet this would be an empty gesture, for the flower is blind and lacks understanding of what it is reflected in the pool.

HYACINTHUS AND ADONIS

Other youths in *Metamorphoses* are transformed into flowers and thus become fixed to the ground and prevented from self-motivated movement, namely, Hyacinthus and Adonis. The connections with the gaze in these characters are not as clearly displayed as in the episode of Narcissus.

Yet they become in one way or another fixed as visual mementos. In Book 10 Apollo falls in love with Hyacinthus, who dies after being struck by the god's discus. The language used in the description of this accident recalls rape, with its emphasis on *vulnus* (Met.10.187–93). The boy is then transformed into a hyacinth. With this transformation the *puer* is fixed to the ground but also fixed as writing and inscription by the god of poetry (Met.10.205–6).[74] One can think here of an analogy between the erotics of poetic composition and sexual fixation (Met.10.207–16).

Adonis dies in a fight with beasts and is eternally preserved as a flower by Venus. The flower springs from the blood of the boy and acquires its deep red tonality. The youth, thus fixed in the earth as a flower, is always available to the controlling eye of the goddess. However, the flowing character of the anemone (Met.10.737–39) and Adonis' immobility are problematic. He is a flower rooted to the ground, but it can easily be swept by the winds. This instability may point at a failure of Venus, who, being a female, cannot completely fix her beloved.

To this short list one could add Cyparissus, who is transformed into a tree (Met. 10.106–42), fixed to the ground, and turned into a memorial. Although it is not clear whether Apollo is the direct author of his transformation, the god is surely the author of its meaning and symbolism as an eternally mourning tree. The transformation of the boy into a cypress recalls Daphne's metamorphosis in Book 1.

Nailing Her Down to Earth: Travel and the Poetics of Absence

Barthes, in *A Lover's Discourse. Fragments*, tells us:

> Historically, the discourse of absence is carried on by the Woman: Woman is sedentary, Man hunts, journeys; Woman is faithful (she waits), man is fickle (he sails away, he cruises). It is Woman who gives shape to absence, elaborates its fiction, for she has time to do so; she weaves and she sings; the Spinning Songs express both immobility (by the hum of the Wheel) and absence (far away, rhythms of travel, sea surges, cavalcades). It follows that in any man who utters the other's absence *something feminine* is declared: this man who waits and who suffers from his waiting is miraculously feminized. A man is not feminized because he is inverted but because he is in love.[75] (original emphasis)

In the Homeric poems the majority of women are fixed in one place while their men move in a myriad of adventures by sea and land. The exemplary case is the figure of Penelope, always waiting in the palace of Ithaca while Odysseus travels homeward from the coasts of Troy. In the *Iliad* as well, women remain within the walls of the city viewing the war fought by men. Representations of the female in the *Iliad* and *Odyssey* are notably different. While the first appears as an essentially masculine poem with scarce and scattered emersions of female characters, in the *Odyssey* women people the story and are fundamental agents of the hero's fate.[76] The most prominent female characters that relate to Odysseus are Athena, Calypso, Nausicaa, Circe, and, finally, Penelope. A piquant coincidence in the relationship between the last four characters and Odysseus is especially relevant to the conceptions of man and woman that this chapter delineates. In all four cases the hero arrives on an island where a woman is waiting: Calypso in Ogygia, Nausicaa in Scheria, Circe in Aeaea, and Penelope in Ithaca.[77] Man is the traveler, the one who cleaves through the waves, constantly passing from place to place. Women remain on land, fixed in a safe and unmovable space on solid earth. This overall picture of women in the *Odyssey* conforms to Barthes's quotation.[78]

In Latin literature this division can be seen in the *Aeneid*, where Dido stays on land and Aeneas travels to and from Carthage.[79] It is also prominent in Latin elegy.[80] Unlike the *Heroides* and other classical texts, *Metamorphoses* does not present many examples of women cursing the sea for carrying their men away while they stay behind abandoned on land. Still, the poetics of absence can be traced in many episodes where a male void, abandonment, or rejection is experienced as a dolorous event in the life of women, as for example in the letter that Byblis writes to her brother giving expression to her unattainable love. Dido and Ariadne are briefly mentioned and the abandonment by men through the sea is felt, though not explicitly exploited. One episode in Ovid's epic does raise explicitly this dichotomy between sea as masculine and land as feminine: Ceyx and Alcyone in Book 11. These other episodes are not so rich in gaze issues, but the poetics of absence in *Metamorphoses* is displayed in a different way of traveling in the poem: air. Sometimes this tradition where men travel and move whereas women become fixed to land is driven to an absurd extreme through 'literalness,' in which women who suffer their men's absence are literally immobilized.

LEUCOTHOE AND CLYTIE

In Book 4 Ovid tells the story of Clytie, one of the daughters of Oceanus, who was desperately in love with the Sun god. It is truly surprising how little attention this episode has received, especially when it offers an enormously rich source for discussions of viewing and gender. The Sun loved Leucothoe, so one night when she was spinning with her hand-maids, the god, disguised as her mother, wooed her and possessed her. But Clytie in her jealousy (*invidit Clytie*, *Met.* 4.234) divulged the story and informed her rival's father. The punishment Leucothoe received is strange: she was buried alive:

> ille ferox inmansuetusque precantem
> tendentemque manus ad lumina Solis et "ille
> vim tulit invitae" dicentem defodit alta
> crudus humo tumulumque super gravis addit harenae.

> Although she prayed and stretched her arms to the rays of the Sun saying, "He raped me against my will," the cruel and merciless father savagely buried her in the deep earth and heaped a mound of heavy sand over her body. (*Met.* 4.237–40)

The Sun tried to revive Leucothoe, but she was literally stuck to the ground (*dissipat hunc radiis Hyperione natus iterque/ dat tibi qua possis defos-sos promere vultus;/ nec tu iam poteras enectum pondere terrae/ tollere . . . caput/* "The son of Hyperion rends this with his rays and opens a path though which you could lift up your buried face, but now you could not lift your head crushed by the weight of the earth," *Met.* 4.241–44). He actually tries to penetrate to her with her rays but is unsuccessful. The rays of the Sun are often described in Greek poetry as "striking things"; during the Augustan period the Sun is, more than ever before, identified with Apollo and his rays are assimilated to arrows.[81] Here, however, the Sun's rays are paradoxically used to 'unfix' her. He cannot save Leucothoe, but instead, he transforms her into a shrub of frankincense so that she can "reach the sky" in some way (251). In this transformation one can see a fixation of the beloved by the Sun god. The interesting play on gender and movement is seen in the fact that the Sun is a mobile god, who travels across the sky constantly, without ever stopping. In opposition, his beloved is fixed, rooted to the ground (*virgaque per glaebas sensim radicibus actis/ turea surrexit tumulumque cacumine rupit/* "And a shrub of frankin-cense with deep-driven roots rose slowly through the clods and broke through the top of the mound," *Met.* 4.254–55). The same fixation is reflected in Clytie, who pines away with love for the Sun and becomes, as a flower, stuck to the ground. The only movement she can achieve is a circular one following the journey of the god throughout the sky:

> illa suum, quamvis radice tenetur,
> vertitur ad Solem mutataque servat amorem.

> Although roots hold her, she turns toward her beloved Sun and, though changed herself, she preserves her love for him. (*Met.* 4.269–70)

Book 4 begins with a festival of Bacchus, which all the Thebans, including the matrons, celebrate. These women leave their houses and their wool-work to participate in the frantic revels of Dionysus's dances. But not the daughters of Minyas, who stay inside, weave, and tell stories to the rhythm of the spindle (*Met.* 4.32–35). The scene where the Sun finds Leucothoe clearly recalls the Minyeides and is an obvious remake of Livy's portrayal of Lucretia:

> . . . et inter
> bis sex Leucothoen famulas ad lumina cernit
> levia versato ducentem stamina fuso.

> And among twelve servants he sees Leucothoe by the lamplight, spinning fine threads with whirling spindle. (*Met.* 4.219–21)

In this sense, Leuconoe, one of the daughters of Minyas, rewrites herself (and her sisters) in the figure of Leucothoe, who acts as a fantasy about what they believe a good and desirable woman would be like in the eyes of the male viewer. This image of Woman, as with Lucretia, is conceived as a static picture fixed in the eyes of the male viewer, who detains the narration and delays our reading with his. Like Pygmalion and Perseus, the Sun falls in love with his eyes, and the Sun's very declaration of love to her is an image that embraces the act of seeing: *"ille ego sum" dixit, "qui longum metior annum,/ omnia qui video, per quem videt omnia tellus,/ mundi oculus: mihi, crede, places"/* "'I am the one who measures the long year,' he said, 'the one who sees all things, through whom the earth sees all things, I am the eye of the world. Believe me, you really please me'" (*Met.* 4.226–28). The Sun god is the great eye of the world. He sees everything, and, thanks to him, things can be seen. Woman becomes an object of his mighty eye, his desire, and his lust. The revenge exerted on him by Venus is therefore effectual:

> . . . quique omnia cernere debes,
> Leucothoen spectas et virgine figis in una,
> quos mundo debes, oculos. . . .

> And you, who must see all things, now look only at Leucothoe and fix your eyes on only one maiden, eyes which you owe to the world. (*Met.* 4.195–97)

The Sun's eyes become fixed in the girl, but they fix her at the same time. The lover, in his weakening and near feminization, loses his power to move, which is why the Sun faces problems as he travels across his usual celestial path: *modo surgis Eoo/ temperius caelo, modo serius incidis undis,/ spectandique mora brumalis porrigis horas/* "Now you rise too early into the dawn sky, now you set too late on the waves and prolong the wintry hours by lingering to look at her" (*Met.* 4.197–99). This slowing down of the Sun's journey implies a slowing down of time in the day and affects the narration, decelerating it as well. The Sun, the great seer, now has his eyes fixed on only one thing and this fixation is transmitted to the object of love in her metamorphosis. The slowing down of the Sun can also be compared to the *mora* that affects Atalanta. The great paradox of the story, as Anderson notes, is the fallibility of the Sun's eye, which in fact does not "see it all," as he misses precisely the cruel punishment suffered by Leucothoe, or when he finally sees what has happened to her it's all too late.[82] Notably, the Sun's 'eye' is even blind (he is also deaf) to Leuconthoe's needs. In her suffering she appeals to her lover (*tendentemque manus ad lumina Solis/* "stretching her arms to the rays of the Sun," *Met.* 4.238), but he cannot see. This is a somewhat humorous and debasing picture of the mighty Sun god, who has little power against the cruel behavior of a human father. When he finally sees the cruel spectacle of Leucothoe's 'death,' the text draws a comparison with the Phaethon episode: *nil illo fertur volucrum moderator equorum/ post Phaethonteos vidisse dolentius ignes/* "They say that the charioteer of the winged horses had seen nothing more painful than that after Phaeton's conflagration" (*Met.* 4.245–46). As in the case of Phaethon, the Sun cannot control the fate of a loved one and his gaze is weakened. Although the big eye of the world can 'see,' his gaze is impotent. As Barthes says, "*something feminine is declared*" (original emphasis) because he loves.

As with some metamorphoses in the text, the agent of change (normally a god) is not explicit in Clytie's transformation, but one is led to think that the Sun may have something to do with it. Her metamorpho-

sis is the perfect inversion of the Sun's suffering. Clytie's eternal visual fixation may well be a punishment for her crime and the god's suffering, but
it is also a continuation of her previous state of erotic fixation. Segal
believes that Clytie's transformation into a flower connotes innocence
and gentleness, but this does not seem right.[83] First, we do not know if
Clytie is actually a virgin, as he supposes. Second, for a woman to actively love and look are deviant actions; therefore, it is difficult to see the
flower as a sign of Clytie's innocence. Perhaps, we ought to rethink the
connotations of flowers as they present more complications than is apparent. Just as the Sun had his sight stuck on Leucothoe and could "barely
move," now Clytie loses her individual mobility precisely through the
eyes. In this continuation of her state of dependence on love for the Sun,
there is a geometrical inversion of the previous scene:

> nec se movit humo; tantum spectabat euntis
> ora dei vultusque suos flectebat ad illum.
> membra ferunt haesisse solo. . . .

> She did not move from the ground. She only gazed on the face of the
> traveling god and turned her face toward him. Her limbs, they say, were
> fixed to the ground. (*Met.* 4.264–66)

Haessisse here recalls *haerent telae* of line 35, where the daughters of
Minyas are fixed to their task of weaving. Clytie is now immobile, capable of only one movement that follows the Sun with her eyes. Likewise,
she is stuck to the ground, just as Leucothoe buried by her father, who cannot lift her head. Clytie's punishment mirrors Leucothoe's fate.

PHAETHON AND THE HELIADES

At the end of the first book of *Metamorphoses*, the Sun god has an affair
with a woman called Clymene and from this union a son is born:
Phaethon. From the beginning of the story, the Sun is both something to
see and the great seer of the world. Clymene swears to her son Phaethon:

> bracchia porrexit spectansque ad lumina solis
> "per iubar hoc" inquit "radiis insigne coruscis,
> nate, tibi iuro, quod nos auditque videtque,

hoc te, quem spectas, hoc te, qui temperat orbem,
Sole satum; si ficta loquor, neget ipse videndum
se mihi, sitque oculis lux ista novissima nostris!"

She stretched her arms to the sky and turning her eyes to the rays of the
Sun said: "By this light, my son, glorious in its gleaming rays, who sees
and hears me, I swear this: that you are the son of this Sun, whom you
see and who rules the world. If am not telling the truth, let he himself
forbid me to see his light, and let this light be the last for my eyes."
(*Met*.1.767–72)

In the couple of Clymene and the Sun, there is a contrast between a
woman established on earth and a god who moves across the skies. In
search of his own identity, the boy wishes to drive the chariot of his
father. The achievement of masculinity for Phaethon is understood in
terms of adventure and movement. If he can advance across the sky, he
will be like his father and prove his ancestry. But Phaethon is only a child,
and not a divine one, and so he fails in his intent. Yet the apparently simple desire to drive his father's chariot has further implications for seeing
and the gaze. As Phaethon calls his father at the beginning of Book 2 ("*o
lux inmensi publica mundi*" / "'O common light of the vast world'" *Met*.
2.35), the god is the great eye of the world, which can see it all (*Sol oculis
iuvenem, quibus adspicit omnia, vidit*/ "The Sun saw the boy with the same
eyes with which he sees all things," *Met*. 2.32). The first image that con-
fronts Phaethon upon arriving at his father's palace is the magnificent
work on the doors. These doors show the whole living world, the skies,
the lands, and the waters with their creatures. Much has been said about
the meanings of this ekphrasis, but it can be suggested that the images on
the doors are a representation of the things that the Sun can see in his
flight, which is confirmed by the god's own explanation of the perils of
the journey (*medio est altissima caelo,/ unde mare et terras ipsi mihi saepe
videre/ fit timor/* "In the middle of the sky the path is very high, from where
it often scares even myself to see the sea and the lands," *Met*. 2.64–66).
These marvels exposed to Phaethon early awake in him a desire to see and
to be a great seer like his father. Later when Phaethon finally sees the chariot of the Sun—*Vulcani munera*/ "the gift of Vulcan"—he is mesmerized
and his avid eyes experience a deep visual pleasure (*dumque ea magnan-
imus Phaethon miratur opusque perspicit* / "And while daring Phaethon
looks and marvels at the work of art," *Met*. 2.111–12). It is clear from this
verse that Phaethon's ambition is a desire not only for masculine action,
but also for sight and knowledge. Like his father, he wishes to drive the

chariot of the Sun and to be the great eye of the universe. But Phaethon is only a child and thus incapable of his father's mighty sight. Indeed, his eyes are incapable of holding the dazzling images that the Sun god deals with daily. Phaethon is often blinded:

> protinus ad patrios sua fert vestigia vultus
> consistitque procul; neque enim propiora ferebat
> lumina. . . .

> Right on he directed his steps toward the face of his father and stop-
> ped at a distance, for he could not bear the radiance any closer.
> (Met.2.21–23)

Later on in his celestial journey, Phaethon is blinded again by the light of the fires that ignite the Earth and cannot tolerate it: *sunt oculis tenebrae per tantum lumen obortae/* "He was blinded by such bright light," Met. 2.181). This physical blindness also embodies the metaphoric blindness of the ignorant, the one who does not know or understand the perils ahead and stubbornly plunges into his own death. For not only is masculinity experienced as strength, as the desire to move across the skies and hold the reins, but being as masculine as the father also implicates the power to see and to hold the gaze, which the doomed *puer* does not achieve.

Curiously, the lengthy tale of Phaethon does not present a physical metamorphosis (unless one sees the conflagration of the universe as a form of change); however, it is succeeded by a clear transformation of his sisters, the Heliades, into trees:

> plangorem dederant: e quis Phaethusa, sororum
> maxima, cum vellet terra procumbere, questa est
> deriguisse pedes; ad quam conata venire
> candida Lampetie subita radice retenta est.

> They beat their breasts in mourning. Phaethusa, the oldest of the sisters,
> when she wanted to lie on the ground, complained that her feet had
> hardened. When fair Lampetie tried to come toward her, she suddenly
> grew roots and was held back. (Met. 2.346–49)

There follows a detailed description of the transformation of the hair into foliage, the arms into branches, and the bark creeping along their bodies. Its opening in particular marks the essential feature of the Heliades' new being: fixation. The reference to *terra* in line 347 is poignant if one keeps in mind Leucothoe's body buried in the ground and Clytie's fixation as a flower. Then, Phaethusa's feet become immobile, preventing her displacement and self-mobility, and finally, the mention of Lampetie's 'root-ification' crowns the image of fixation to the ground. This is a type of immobility that has sprung from their tears and excessive mourning. The tears also solidify and become amber drops; after Phaethon's unsuccessful travels, his sisters become fixed and rooted forever. In part, the story of Phaethon and his sisters repeats the contrast between the Sun and Clymene. Both males travel across the sky, though the boy is tragically doomed, and both mother and daughters are bound to earth, though the latter to a literal extreme.

Mulvey's theory of the monolithic male gaze is based on the infallibility of men looking; it does not allocate a place for males who fail in their gaze. Both in Phaethon and in the Sun there is a failure of the masculine gaze. Thus, if the external male viewer identifies with the Sun or Phaethon he will, with them, experience a failure of his own and a subsequent weakening of his masculinity. These two figures, among others, reveal that Mulvey's model is too limited for the gender complexities of *Metamorphoses*.

Deviant Exiles

TREASON AGAINST THE FATHERLAND

The previous section explored the issue of travel as a marker of masculinity in contrast with women's immobility and fixity to land. Conversely, there are cases in *Metamorphoses* where women do travel and where connections between traveling, displacement, and the gaze can be observed. Exile will here be used in a broad sense, following the original meaning from *ex* plus the Latin stem *sal-* (*salio*) for any individual who is displaced from his/her land either by force or by personal decision, and not in the more restricted sense of someone who has been forced to leave her land by some kind of persecution.

Medea

Let us begin with Medea, a paradigm of the exile. When her story begins in Book 7, she is no more than a girl, but a girl who promptly falls in love and would give it all to gain her beloved. Her desire springs from an image of Jason. The text first describes how she became passionate for the hero (*concipit interea validos Aeetias ignes*/ "In the meantime, the daughter of King Aeetes was ignited by the overpowering fire of love," Met.7.9); shortly thereafter we realize that she has just seen him: "*cur, quem modo denique vidi,/ ne pereat timeo?*"/ "'Why am I afraid that he whom I have only just seen may die?'" Met. 7.15–16). The visual impression proceeds in a double edged-way. Medea, struggling with her own emotions between duty and desire, states:

> sed trahit invitam nova vis, aliudque cupido,
> mens aliud suadet: video meliora proboque,
> deteriora sequor. . . .
>
> But a new force drives me against my will. Desire persuades me one way, my mind another. I see the better course and I approve of it, but I follow the worse. (*Met.* 7.19–21)

These formulaic utterances have profound intertextual echoes, serve as a defining trace of Medea's character, and hint at woman's libido and inability to do the right thing.[84] At a surface level, *video meliora* seems to refer to Medea's knowledge of the right path to follow.[85] Her previous comment that she has just *seen* Jason bears the hidden sense that what is '*meliora*' may well be Jason, in her eyes. In addition, the monologue presents a key problem in the story: why does Medea burn for a foreigner? (*Met.*7.21–22). Medea's 'barbarism' and the problems of treason against one's land have been widely explored and they remain central in the issues of movement and immobility that are here discussed. Medea knows that her proper role is to stay on land and safeguard her family, but love is more powerful. As Carole Newlands points out—though perhaps stretching Medea's transformation too far—the heroine undergoes a change from dutiful daughter and innocent girl to rebellious woman, and finally monster.[86] This first instance of hesitation stages the commencement of Medea's transformation; in this change her decision to travel is central. To love Jason is to accept the foreign and, with it, the prospects of her leaving the land, of venturing to sea and following a new husband at her own will. But traveling like the epic hero will turn woman into a monster.

Medea's doubts about going or staying show the beginning of a gender destabilization, because not only has she decided to travel but she even wishes to have the honors of a man and a hero: *non magna relinquam,/*

magna sequar: titulum servatae pubis Achivae/ "I will not leave great things behind, I will follow great things: the title of savior of the Achaean youth" (*Met.* 7.55–56). It is worth recalling that at the beginning of the story it is Jason who, as a typical epic hero, is actually an exile because he had left his own country for a foreign land, but this will rapidly be reversed when Medea is the one who leaves. Soon Medea encounters Jason again and the text newly focuses on the act of looking:

> et iam fortis erat, pulsusque recesserat ardor,
> cum videt Aesoniden exstinctaque flamma reluxit.
> erubuere genae, totoque recanduit ore,
> utque solet ventis alimenta adsumere, quaeque
> parva sub inducta latuit scintilla favilla
> crescere et in veteres agitata resurgere vires,
> sic iam lenis amor, iam quem languere putares,
> ut vidit iuvenem, specie praesentis inarsit.
> et casu solito formosior Aesone natus
> illa luce fuit: posses ignoscere amanti.
> spectat et in vultu veluti tum denique viso
> lumina fixa tenet nec se mortalia demens
> ora videre putat nec se declinat ab illo.

> And now she was strong and her conquered passion had receded, when she saw the son of Aeson and the dying flame was rekindled. Her cheeks turned red and all her face became pale again; and as a tiny spark, which was hidden under the ashes, is often fed by the winds, grows and, newly awakened, regains its old strength; so now, when she saw the youth, the gentle love which you would now think was losing strength, blazed up again at the sight of the youth standing before her. And it happened that the son of Aeson was more beautiful than usual that day: you would pardon her for loving him. She looked at him and fixed her eyes in his face as if she had just seen him for the first time and in her madness she thought she was not looking at a mortal face, nor did she turn herself away from him. (*Met.*7.76–88) [87]

The passage is most illuminating. First, the relation between the light perceived through the eyes (*lumina*) is transformed into the flame of fire, the well-known luminous metaphor for love. As in many other episodes where the image is frozen by the gaze of the lover, in this passage the description stops and Ovid pauses the narration to 'paint' a static picture of the object of desire. Contrariwise, here the scene does not emphasize

Jason's image; in fact, he is barely mentioned despite a playful intrusion of the narrator, who is focalizing with Medea (85). While in other scenes the one who looks is somewhat fixed by the image he himself fixes, Medea's fixation is much more emphasized. Her eyes do not seem to entrap Jason or control his image; on the contrary, after being intensely looked at by Medea, he is still able to perform a confident free speech.[88] However, soon enough, Jason will become a spectacle. His fight against the serpent and the army sprung from its teeth will be watched by all as a show, and among the public is, of course, Medea.[89] It is worthwhile repeating that when women are spectacles in a positive sense, they are commonly (but not always) pictured statically. Men who are watched, as they are here, are in action. Interesting as well is the fact that when the Greeks finally triumph, Medea, who had been watching, is prevented from embracing Jason by her modesty, which stands in the way (*Met.* 7.144–45). Having looked and loved, Medea becomes mobile. She will now travel with her new husband. Her gaze, however, does not control or possess Jason and objectify him in the same way a male's gaze is capable of doing.

Following Medea in her adventures, her first voyage is from Colchis to Iolchos, a trip that determines her destiny and her devious transformation. She has now made the unwomanly move, from land to sea. But a new trip will take place. After they arrive in Iolchos, Jason begs Medea to rejuvenate his father, Aeson, for which a series of movements out of the house are necessary. First, she comes out of the palace into the deep woods (*egreditur tectis*, *Met.*7.182) in order to invoke the help of Hecate and the powers of magic. This exit from the house is an obvious intertextual wink to the beginning of Euripides' *Medea*, where she leaves the palace. But this exit is not enough and she will now travel across the sky in a dragon-drawn chariot (220ff.). Medea's eyes become meaningful from the sky, from where she sees and selects the herbs she will collect. A parallel may be drawn between her and the Sun, her grandfather, who looks at the world from above and is the great eye of the universe. This is what Medea does: she travels through the skies and looks down at the world, which recalls the ending of Euripides' *Medea*. Moreover, her gaze is controlling; it knows nature and recognizes the plants that will bring her power. Seeing them is the first step to actual collection and possession of the herbs. The connection with the Sun becomes more apparent from Medea's comments at the beginning of the magical invocations: she will be more powerful than the Sun ("*currus quoque carmine nostro/ pallet avi*"/ "'Even the chariot of the Sun, my grandfather, pales at my song,'" *Met.* 7.208–9). Medea also indicates that it is her song that will control the Sun's chariot—a piquant reference in view of her future trip across the sky. The woman with powerful vision is now on her way to being a 'monster.'

From onlooker, Medea soon becomes a spectacle herself, but a spectacle that she nevertheless controls. While she performs the rite of rejuvenating Aeson, many curious eyes are poised on her. Still, she can deny them the power to intervene, to control: *hinc procul Aesoniden, procul hinc iubet ire ministros/ et monet arcanis oculos removere profanos/* "She orders Jason to go far way, she orders the attendants to go far way from there, and warns them to take their profane eyes off her secret rites" (*Met.* 7.255–56). Medea is the spectacle; she is also able to control what can be seen and what cannot, showing a power uncommon in a woman. After rejuvenating Jason's father, she plays a deceitful trick on the daughters of Pelias and newly escapes death in her flying dragon, from where she can see the whole world. What she sees actually includes various metamorphoses, thus turning Medea into a figurative reader of the whole epic (350ff.).

In addition, at the beginning of the episode a struggle between proper femininity and deviancy is staged in Medea's soul, a struggle that is centered on loving Jason and escaping with him or staying in her fatherland. The previously discussed opposition between male as traveler and woman as bound to land is here problematized. However, in her act of seeing, Medea does not seem to control or fix Jason entirely. But because this woman looks—which in the story equals "loves"—and because she is 'deviant,' she becomes mobile, as she will travel by sea with her man. By looking and loving, she also loses control of herself and her sense of duty, which represents a great danger in a woman. Of course, men also lose some control through their loving gazes; yet it does not seem to be a problem for men, for in most cases they can overcome their paralysis. If one compares, for example, Apollo losing control of himself at the sight of the beautiful Daphne with Medea's case, one sees that although Apollo can only think of his love, the story—at least for Apollo—does not end in tragedy or horror and, in the end, he still exercises some power over the laurel. Medea, who dared to gaze upon Jason, gradually becomes a monster. By looking, Medea becomes mobile and ends up flying across the skies, the place most remote from land, where proper women remain bound.

Scylla

In the following book, with Medea's story still fresh in readers' minds, the narrator presents a new tale of gazing, desire, and displacement. The young girl Scylla, daughter of king Nisus, watches the war between her father and King Minos from the city towers. Teichoscopia in general is a curious situation in which women are allowed to look and men who fight become a spectacle for their eyes. It is also a rich place for gender issues because it allows the reader to see the scene through the woman's eyes, in the same way that soliloquies by female characters give us reflections of women's minds. The main point of the warrior's existence is not to be looked at, as it is the case with women commonly, but to accomplish glorious deeds that place them beyond the personal in transcendent aspirations, to achieve *kleos* through action. Still, Scylla looks on, which is the beginning of a transgressive move on her part: *bello quoque saepe solebat/ spectare ex illa rigidi certamina Martis/* "Also during the war she often watched the combats of brutal Mars from there" (*Met.* 8.19–20). It has been noted that Ovid's Scylla is modeled on Propertius's Tarpeia in elegy 4.4.[90] Not only the general theme of treason to the fatherland is taken over in *Metamorphoses*, but also the dangerous image of women who look:

> vidit harenosis Tatium proludere campis
>   pictaque per flavas arma levare iubas:
> obstipuit regis facie et regalibus armis,
>   interque oblitas excidit urna manus.

> She saw Tatius exercising in the sandy fields and lifting his adorned arms over his horse's golden mane. She was stupefied by the looks of the king and his royal arms; and the urn fell from between her distracted hands. (Prop. 4.4.19–22)

But in *Metamorphoses*, Scylla's greater transgression is that her desire to look is blatantly linked to the desire to know. Scopophilia in general goes hand in hand with epistemephilia, but in this passage, the breakage of boundaries is even more complex. The girl, who up to now had been bound to the enclosed space of the palace, breaks the limits of her knowledge, her quotidian world, and her desire through her sight:

> iamque mora belli procerum quoque nomina norat
> armaque equosque habitusque Cydoneasque pharetras;
> noverat ante alios faciem ducis Europaei,
> plus etiam, quam nosse sat est. . . .

> And now with the delay of the battle she had also learned the names of the heroes, the weapons, the horses, the attire, and the Cydonean quivers.

> Before all others she had learned the face of the leader, the son of
> Europa, even better than she should have. (*Met.* 8.21–24)

But knowledge in women is dangerous and not free from madness (*vix
sanae virgo Niseia compos/ mentis erat/* "The Nisean maiden was barely in
her right mind," 35–36). What can women do with knowledge but love?
Thus Scylla conceives a passion for her enemy. Her desire leads her to wish
to break limits and transgress her world, even to switch bands and to
move and displace. She wishes to leap down from the tower into the
Cretan camp and to open the doors of the city (*est impetus illi/ turribus e
summis in Cnosia mittere corpus/ castra vel aeratas hosti recludere portas,/ vel
siquid Minos aliud velit/* "An impulse drives her to throw her body from the
highest towers into the Cretan camp, to open up the brazen doors to the
enemy, or to do whatever else Minos may want," *Met.* 8.39–42). The
transgression originated in looking is not only moral but also spatial; it is
a desire to leave her space and pass onto Minos' territory. But the opening of the gates has sexual overtones and may reflect Scylla's own fantasies
about Minos, with whom she has fallen in love. One could envision here
an analogy between the female body and the house or city, which is not
uncommon and is present in other stories of *Metamorphoses*. Scylla's
desire is driven to an extreme. After a long hesitation in a monologue on
the choice of treason to the fatherland or helping the beloved that recalls
Medea's, she decides to cut her father's purple lock, seat of his power,
which is an obvious symbolic castration. The power of the father is
intended to be 'given' to the beloved. In contrast with Jason, who does
not seem to have high 'moral standards,' Minos rejects such a devious
love. Although Minos does not refrain from taking advantage of Scylla's
treason, he rejects such a devious love in words referring to land and sea:

> . . . tellusque tibi pontusque negetur!
> certe ego non patiar Iovis incunabula, Creten,
> qui meus est orbis, tantum contingere monstrum.

> May both land and sea be denied to you! For sure I will not permit such
> a monster to touch Crete, cradle of Jove, my own land. (*Met.* 8.98–100)

From this moment onward, Scylla, who wanted a voluntary exile to follow her love, is set in a liminal space, neither on land nor at sea. She cannot return to the fatherland because it is destroyed and because it would
reject her (114–16), but a new land does not await her. Thus, there is no

way of being a woman available to her any longer. It is the loss of the sight of Minos which drives her to follow him by sea: "*me miseram! properare iubet! divulsaque remis/ unda sonat, mecumque simul mea terra recedit*"/ "'Wretched me, he orders his men to hasten! And the waves resound as the oars part them, while my own land and myself are receding from him'" (*Met.* 8.138–39). We are here again in the presence of the poetics of absence, where a woman complains at the abandonment of her beloved. But unlike other women who stay on land, Scylla ventures to sea by clinging to the Cretan boat and begins to surf on the waves in this awkward way. Her attempts are soon dismantled by her father, now transformed into an osprey, who frightens her. She loosens her grip from the boat and ends up transformed into a Ciris, a bird which still bears the mark of her crime (Ciris from κείρω, "I cut").

Scylla's transformation into a bird stages the transformation from her enclosed and contained femininity to the boundary transgressions initiated with her gaze and her desire. It is the sight of Minos that leads her to movement and the desire of exile. Seeing for this woman becomes dangerously tragic. It leads to the opening of the floodgates of sexuality, embodied in the doors, and to the wish to leave land for the sea, to transgress the proper space for a woman. The final transformation into a bird that can fly and conquer the sky takes her one step further in her distancing from land. This is an unsuccessful story: Scylla's desiring eyes end up turning her into a *monstrum*, as Minos observes, but she does not succeed in gaining the object of her lust, while Medea does. Unlike Medea, who is a magician with supernatural powers, Scylla must be a warning to girls that not everyone can be a Medea. Even Medea, however, does not get away with it in the end as she loses both her husband and her children.

Ariadne

When Minos leaves the land of king Nisus, the narrative moves to Crete. Very briefly Ovid tells the story of Ariadne who, in love with the foreigner Theseus, helped him to kill the Minotaur and return safe and sound from the labyrinth (*Met.* 8.169–82). This story echoes Scylla, as if Minos' rejection of her would have earned its vengeance in his own daughter. The elements of treason to the father, love for a stranger, and desire to follow him through the sea to a distant land are all present in the *Metamorphoses* version of the myth, although the stress is duly laid on Ariadne's rescue by Bacchus and her transformation into a star. The gaze is, however, not mentioned directly in the passage. Ariadne is a character most appealing to Ovid, as she appears frequently in *Ars Amatoria* (especially *AA* 1.525ff.) and in *Heroides* 10, which she 'writes.' But it is probable that Ovid is drawing on the reader's knowledge of Catullus 64, where the gaze of Ariadne is highlighted. As soon as Theseus arrives in Crete, the girl fixes her eyes on him:

> hunc simul ac cupido conspexit lumine virgo
> regia, quam suavis expirans castus odores
> lectulus in molli complexu matris alebat,
> quales Eurotae progignunt flumina myrtos
> aurave distinctos educit verna colores,
> non prius ex illo flagrantia declinavit
> lumina, quam cuncto concepit corpore flammam
> funditus atque imis exarsit tota medullis.

> As soon as she saw him with desiring eyes, the royal maiden, whom a chaste and soft little bed—breathing odors like myrtles that spring by the streams of the Eurotas or like the flowers of varied color that the spring-time breeze draws forth—still nourished in the soft embrace of her mother, did not take her burning eyes away from him before she caught the flame of love deep in her whole body and burned completely in her inmost marrow. (Cat. 64.86–93)

The parallelisms with Medea and Scylla are now complete. She sees, she loves, she commits treason to her father and she leaves. Like Medea and Scylla, Ariadne has lost any possibility of being a woman. She has lost her fatherland but has no other alternative country (*Her.*10.64) or male authority to respond to. She is left in a liminal space, on the shores that separate land and sea, symbolic of the transitional moment between life and death, humanity and divinity that she is undergoing. Her fate can only end with an alternative. Bacchus rescues her, makes her his wife, and turns her wedding coronet into a star (*AA*.556–57; Prop.3.20.18). The stories of Medea, Scylla, and Ariadne are all versions of the same female type. One who sees, who betrays the fatherland and the father, who loves a foreigner and wishes to travel with him far away. In all three stories the outcome is unsettling. They neither succeed in keeping their men, nor can they return to their families and countries. They are left in a liminal space where they cannot be proper women. Their ultimate transformations are clear metaphors for their marginality.

INCEST AND DISPLACEMENT

Movement, displacement, and exile are also present in the stories of Myrrha and Byblis who commit incest and upset intrafamilial relationships. As in other cases, the physical displacement symbolizes the deviation of these characters from standard moral and societal norms. Both stories have points in common with Medea and Scylla. Myrrha and Byblis suffer from a forbidden passion. Unlike the heroines of Books 7 and 8, they do not love an 'enemy' but someone close to them. Here also, a love driven to excess ends up converting Cinyras and Caunus into enemies, while both Myrrha and Byblis suffer exile.

Byblis

The story of Byblis in Book 9 is a milder version of the more horrifying tale to come in Book 10 and prepares the reader for it. Byblis falls in love with her twin brother, Caunus.[91] Much has been said about the narcissistic overtones of the tales of Pygmalion and Myrrha, where the creator first falls in love with his creation and then it is the creation that desires her creator. But Byblis in love with her twin brother is not far from this. It is, presumably, his image that enthralls her, an image that, one can confidently assume, bears a close resemblance to her. We may compare another version of the myth of Narcissus where he is in love with his twin sister. After the girl died, Narcissus would go to a spring to find some relief in his own image that so closely resembled that of his beloved.[92] Further, of course, by loving her brother, Byblis loves her own blood, and thus Byblis cannot break the limits of the self necessary for societal interchange and dutiful marriage.

Although there is a physical acquaintance and interchange between brother and sister (458–59), it is Caunus's image that feeds Byblis' passion. It is relevant that Ovid follows this statement by drawing attention to the gaze:

paulatim declinat amor, visuraque fratrem
culta venit, nimiumque cupit formosa videri
et siqua est illic formosior, invidet illi.

Gradually her love degenerates, and when she comes to see her brother she is all adorned. She is too keen to look beautiful, and if any other woman seems more beautiful to him, she envies her. (*Met.* 9.461–63)

Unlike Medea and Scylla, the accent here is not on a woman seeing the
beloved but on being herself the object of the male gaze, as a 'normal'
woman is. However, Byblis' vigil prevents the awareness of deviant desire;
it is only in her dreams that her *cupido* spreads full sails. Then she can actually do the looking: *saepe videt quod amat: visa est quoque iungere fratri/ cor-
pus/* "She often sees what she loves: she sees herself joining her body to
her brother" (*Met.* 9.470–71). Soon, with the realization of desire, from
subject of the gaze Caunus becomes object of the gaze: *ille quidem est oculis
quamvis formosus iniquis/ et placet /* "He is indeed beautiful, even to hostile
eyes, and he is attractive" (*Met.* 9.476–77). This development indicates
Byblis' own transformation into a deviant woman. Afterward, she writes
a letter to Caunus in which she confesses her passion, but she is violently rejected. Once again, Byblis expresses her amatory enterprise with nautical metaphors, a common vocabulary for matters of love, which is
meaningful in view of the imagery of Medea and Scylla that Byblis may
be 'reading' and using to construct her own image:

> . . . ne non sequeretur euntem,
> parte aliqua veli, qualis foret aura, notare
> debueram, tutoque mari decurrere, quae nunc
> non exploratis inplevi lintea ventis.
> auferor in scopulos igitur, subversaque toto
> obruor oceano, neque habent mea vela recursus.

> To make sure the wind blew fair, with some part of the sail I should have
> checked what the wind was like, and I should have sailed safely, now I
> have spread full sails to unexplored winds. Thus I am cast against the
> rocks, I am shipwrecked and overwhelmed by the whole ocean, and my
> sails cannot bring me back. (*Met.* 9.589–94)

Byblis envisions love as sailing, which, despite being a common
metaphor, may hint at the breach of the limits of 'landed' femininity.[93] She
does not end up at sea but becomes an exile. The devious woman who has
'given free sail' to her desire and who has dared to look 'actively' in an
erotic manner, cannot stay in her accustomed space. Her brother leaves
the city, disgusted with her wooing, and goes off to found a city, a very masculine enterprise. His purpose is therefore determined and magnificent,
transcending the personal. But Byblis, whose very desire was a sort of
return to herself (she confesses: "*non hoc inimica precatur, sed quae, cum tibi
sit iunctissima, iunctior esse/ expetit et vinclo tecum propiore ligari*" / "'It is not
an enemy who prays this, but one who, though most closely joined to you,
wishes to be even more closely joined and to be bound to you by a tighter

bond,'" *Met.* 9.548–50), follows him but ends up wandering with no clear purpose: *siquidem patriam invisosque penates/ deserit, et profugi sequitur vestigia fratris/* "Since indeed she abandons her fatherland and her hated home, and follows the footsteps of her exile brother" (*Met.* 9.639–40). The outcome of sexual deviancy and visual desire is physical displacement. Byblis wanders in the open, first following her love, but then, possessed by madness, she loses any sense of direction and disintegrates into a pool.

Myrrha

Myrrha falls in love with her father, Cinyras. This love is experienced not only with heart and soul, but sight plays a most important role in the story. At the beginning, Myrrha is the object of desire of many suitors (*Met.*10.316–17), in a traditional standing for women. But soon she becomes the subject of desire and, with it, the subject of the gaze:

> ire libet procul hinc patriaeque relinquere fines,
> dum scelus effugiam; retinet malus ardor euntem,
> ut praesens spectem Cinyran tangamque loquarque
> osculaque admoveam, si nil conceditur ultra.

> It is well to go far away from here and to abandon the boundaries of my fatherland, as long as I can avoid crime. An evil passion holds me back even as I try to go, so that present, I may see Cinyras and touch him, talk to him and kiss him, if nothing else is allowed. (*Met.* 10.341–44)

The phrase *oscula admoveam* recalls the character of Pygmalion when he applies kisses to his ivory statue. It is poignant that Myrrha mentions exile as an alternative to crime and to seeing, when later in the story she will be condemned to a long wandering due to her fault. Regarding the gaze, it is interesting that when Cinyras asks her what type of husband she would prefer, Myrrha's deceiving answer is *"similem tibi"* / "'like you'" (*Met.*10.364). This constitutes a playful intratextual gesture toward the story of her great-grandfather Pygmalion. In his case, *"sit coniunx . . . similis mea . . . eburnae"/* "'May my wife be similar to the ivory maiden'" (*Met.*10.275–76) is directly related to physical appearance and the visual. This weight is felt in the Myrrha episode. But a witty inversion is displayed. While Pygmalion was in love with his creation, in Myrrha's tale the creation (the daughter) loves the creator. Still, the plays on desire are more complex, as in fact, Cinyras unwittingly enjoys sexual intercourse with the girl.[94]

The conclusion of the story leads us back to exile. After being discovered by Cinyras, already pregnant by him, Myrrha flees sure death at the hands of her father and wonders around with no direction:

> Myrrha fugit: tenebrisque et caecae munere noctis
> intercepta neci est latosque vagata per agros
> palmiferos Arabas Panchaeaque rura relinquit
> perque novem erravit redeuntis cornua lunae,
> cum tandem terra requievit fessa Sabaea;
> vixque uteri portabat onus. . . .

> Myrrha fled, and was saved from death by the shades and the grace of the
> dark night. She wandered through wide fields and left behind palm-bear-
> ing Arabia and the Panchaean country. She wandered around for nine
> months and when finally, exhausted, she rested in the Sabaean land, she
> was barely able to carry the weight of her womb. (*Met.* 10.476–81)

Myrrha wanders and finally becomes fixed as a new tree to give birth,
which recalls the wanderings of Latona to give birth in Delos. But what
is of interest here is the fact that as someone who has committed a crime,
she must leave, be displaced. Curiously, it is not her father, who has also
performed a condemnable union, who leaves the city. Both Myrrha and
Byblis are characters that have their eyes fixed in a narcissistic and forbidden love; in a way, they can have eyes only for something that is kin
to them, and are not able to unite with the different. It is the sexual crime
that makes them errant, exiled women who do not have a home. The only
way out of this impossible situation seems to be transformation: Byblis
into a pool and Myrrha into a tree.

Gaze and movement affect the flow of the narrative. Men usually look
at women and "freeze their image." With this visual detention, a stoppage
in the narrative is produced and the eyes of the external viewer/reader
also experience the power to control the mobility of the female images.
Nevertheless, the play is double, for the female can also paralyze the viewer and deprive him of his masculine activity. Further, the erotic object is
often construed as an immobile statue for the viewer to enjoy. Making a
statue of the beloved serves the purpose of visual control and marriage
and procreation need the fixation of women. Yet some women are lost to
deviancy through their gazes. They begin by looking and end up committing crimes, abandoning the fatherland, and wandering through the world
as exiles like Scylla and Medea. A woman who allows herself to gaze in an
erotic way becomes deviant and mobile and is forced to live in a liminal
space for which usually the only possible outcome is transformation.

CHAPTER FOUR

❦

Phantastic Text(iles)

Recovering the Visual, Recovering the Gaze

We don't know what women's vision is. What do women's eyes see? How
do they carve, invent, decipher the world? I don't know. I know my own
vision, the vision of one woman, but the world seen through the eyes of
others? I only know what men's eyes see.[1]

The preoccupations of this chapter are similar to those of Viviane
Forrester in the passage cited above. In the previous chapters discussion focused on the power of the male gaze and how women could also
adopt it or identify with it as external and internal viewers. But is there
any truly 'female gaze'? Is there a way of knowing what 'women's vision is'
in *Metamorphoses*? What do women's eyes 'see' in the Ovidian poem? As
Forrester says, "I know my own vision" of the poem, but can we find a way
of knowing what the view of other women is? Is it worth trying? The
answer is yes, however difficult or problematic it may be and even when,
before starting, one expects to find no 'definite' solutions.

The first objection we face is that there is no true 'feminine' vision to
be found in *Metamorphoses*, for this is a male-authored text. So, which of
Richlin's options should we follow? Stop reading, "take the poem apart,"
or replace it with a female-authored one? The first and the last alternatives are not options that will be pursued here, for we don't want to
deprive ourselves of the pleasure of reading and 'viewing' *Metamorphoses*.
While it is essentially true at some level that it is not possible to recover
a woman's gaze here in the same way as it could be with a female-
authored text—although one should not be too naïve about the level of
immediacy that even a female-authored text would give—there are still

possibilities available. To find a woman's gaze, one needs to prioritize the women in the poem in their own right and bring them into the spotlight. While the voice of the 'author' cannot be completely occluded, let us for the moment leave him in the dark. Some aspects of female gazes have already been touched upon, but here the focus will be on this and on the episodes where there is a clearer emergence of the 'female gaze.' It must be said that together with concrete seeing, other types of metaphoric viewing such as understanding, realizing, and knowing will also form part of the discussion. Two means of expressing female imagination, textiles and speech, will be approached. We will explore the female *phantasiae* that preempt, lurk behind, and are expressed in visual constructions in textiles, which are in the poem the only form of direct 'pictorial' representation and 'plastic art' allowed to women. Therefore, we will concentrate on stories that involve weaving and will analyze the meanings of the textiles and the implications of viewing and reading them, focusing on the stories of Arachne and Minerva and on Philomela's rape. The production of images through weaving is normally placed in a highly visually charged narrative context. This context influences, interacts with, and is meaningful for the production of female visions through textiles. Although weaving is also an important component of the tale of the Minyeides, their main means of expression is verbal; therefore they will be treated in the following chapter. The episodes of Arachne and Philomela, and all matters related to weaving, have always been duly linked to issues of writing, textuality, and narrative. While this is a major part of weaving as a metaphor, it is the intent of our study to stress its visual components and to think about it as a means available to women to create visually and to have a gaze of their own. The purpose of this chapter, then, is to redeem the visual with all its pertinent traces as a feminine expressive feature that bestows a gaze upon women. This will transpire specifically in the reading of Philomela's weaving, but will also be present in other narratives. Chapter 5 will in turn search for female vision by exploring the *phantasiae* and visual constructions that women produce in their own narratives and the reception of their stories by other women.

Recovering the value of visuality in female productions brings us back to the differences between image and text. Up to now, there was an insistence on the power of the male gaze to fix and penetrate images. Yet for all the visual capabilities of males, women have also demonstrated visual powers. Some critics like Shlain have even considered that the reign of the visual is a particularly female domain. Although Shlain seems at times rather reductive, his theory about the implications of the invention of writing and the alphabet for gender, which are meaningful for issues of visual imagery and textuality, is a thought-provoking exercise in reassigning a gaze and a visual power to women.[2]

Shlain, an American neurologist, believes that the change from matriarchal thought to patriarchy[3] was caused by the advent of literacy and the invention of the alphabet, which fostered a development of the left hemisphere of the brain (involving sequential, diachronic, and abstract functions like speech, numeracy, and the idea of doing) and favored a masculine outlook, while the more feminine world of the image, which corresponds to the functions of the right side of the brain (including the perception of feelings, the idea of 'being,' images and music), was soon disdained.[4] In sum, Shlain proposes that "a *holistic, simultaneous, synthetic,* and *concrete* view of the world are the essential characteristics of a feminine outlook; *linear, sequential, reductionist, and abstract* thinking defines the masculine" (original emphasis).[5] This polarization may be accused of being reductive or too determined by biology, but Shlain responds by saying that every human being is endowed with features of both, and that we should understand Man and Woman as a complex combination of masculine and feminine aspects, although in general feminine traits prevail in women and masculine in males.[6]

Shlain's ideas are compelling because, whether one actually believes in them or not, it is striking that a twentieth-century male physician from San Francisco would write a 400-page book about "the history of the world," which strives in every line to assign the world of the image to the female. By doing this, even if inadvertently, Shlain is striving to unearth the gaze that has so often been denied to the female. Much feminist criticism has dealt with issues of feminine writing and how both orality and the written word have empowered women by giving them a voice. Such approaches have been very fruitful and have redeemed women of their passive roles in patriarchal societies. Image as a female means of expression and communication in itself and not as a metaphor for writing has not received its due attention in *Metamorphoses*. By focusing on visuality it will be possible to find traces of a 'female gaze.' Just as by studying female speech we give women a voice, by discussing female visual productions we give them a gaze.

Recapturing Old Threads

WEAVING AND IDEAL FEMININITY

As Miller puts it, "the language of textiles tends to engender . . . a metaphorics of femininity."[7] Throughout classical art and literature—and more modern times as well—weaving has been regarded as a feminine skill and seen as a virtue of the ideal female.[8] Ideal femininity, one must remember, is a Greco-Roman fantasy (or rather fantasies) about the perfect woman, which is present in literature and does not, of course, coincide necessarily with historical reality.[9]

In Homer, most references to actual weaving have to do with women, but a metaphorical use of the verb ὑφαίνειν as a description of a mental process is also present.[10] In Homer there is much metaphorical weaving: "Odysseus and Menelaus 'weave' words and counsels; Odysseus, the suitors, Nestor, and others 'weave' stratagems and wiles." Interesting also is that Athena, with all her gender complexity, is the only female in Homer for whom weaving is not only a literal occupation.[11] However, this tight association between women and weaving is a cultural construct and not a 'natural' relation (although it is of course undeniable that women did weave). Suffice it to recall, for example, that Lucretius tells us that at the beginning it was Man who wove, but then the task was handed over to women because it was too *mollis* for masculinity (Lucretius, *DRN* 5.1354–60).[12]

Weaving and its precursor, spinning, were also primary activities of the Roman *matrona*. When Lucretia in Livy 1.57.9 is lauded as the utmost example of *pudicitia*, she is found *deditam lanae/* "dedicated to wool work"; and in many other literary instances weaving and spinning are associated with female virtuosity. Plutarch, for instance, in *Rom. Quaest.* 30, while discussing the matrimonial formula *ubi tu Gaius ego Gaia,* "Where you are Gaius, I am Gaia," recalls a bronze image of Gaia Caecilia with sandals and a distaff signifying, respectively, her industry and her housewifery. Likewise, when the virtue of a woman wants to be highlighted in epitaphs we see similar praises, as in the famous *domum servavit, lanam fecit/* "She kept the house, she made wool" (*CIL.* 1.1007) or in the *Laudatio Turiae* 1.30: *domestica bona pudicitiae obsequi, comitatis, facilitatis, lanificiis tuis adsiduitatis cur memorem?/* "Why should I mention your domestic virtues: modesty, obedience, affability, good nature, industry in wool-work . . . ?" (*CIL.* 6.1527). What is more, during the wedding ritual, the bride would carry a loom and a distaff as a symbol of her new role in her husband's house.[13] The ideal of the woman weaving inside the house (in the *atrium* for the Romans) was deeply rooted in the Greek and Roman worlds. This symbolism was evoked in the Augustan age, where the concept of *pudicitia* was tightly linked to *lanificium,* which Augustus tried to emulate by making his family spin (Suet., *Aug.* 64.2).[14] The Romans idealized the past to such an extent that historical events were scarcely distinguishable from legends, and the legends of the founding of Rome and the early Republic were employed in the late Republic and early Empire for moral instruction and propaganda. As a result, the wealthy aristocratic woman of Augustan times, even one who played high politics, was expected to weave and spin.[15]

COMMUNICATIVE AND UTILITARIAN WEAVING

Not all kinds of weaving are emblems of female *castitas* and *pudicitia* or fit within ideals of 'proper' femininity. As Joplin says, women can use their textiles to elevate themselves from the "safe, feminine, domestic craft—weaving—into art as a new means of resistance."[16] Thus we propose that when women weave recognizable images and not just decorative patterns, they are able to communicate their own gazes and ideas in textiles. By doing this, they adopt a transgressive stance and appropriate prerogatives not normally allowed to them: they acquire a voice and a gaze.[17] One can draw a distinction between 'utilitarian' weaving and artistically commu-nicative weaving. Thus, just as making a clay teapot for the sole purpose of serving tea is not the same as creating a statue of clay, there is a differ-ence between making a textile with the utilitarian purpose of clothing or sheltering from the cold, and weaving a tapestry to be aesthetically con-templated. It is true that both functions could coexist in the same object, as in the quilt that covers the marriage bed of Thetis and Peleus in Catullus 64; but the distinction is still valid and useful for the episodes of *Metamorphoses* to be discussed in this chapter. Let us here look at some examples. In Book 3 of the *Iliad*, Iris finds Helen weaving scenes of the Trojan War in a great cloth:

τὴν δ' εὗρ' ἐν μεγάρῳ ἡ δὲ μέγαν ἱστὸν ὕφαινε,
δίπλακα πορφυρέην, πολέας δ' ἐνέπασσεν ἀέθλους
Τρώων θ' ἱπποδάμων καὶ Ἀχαιῶν χαλκοχιτώνων,
οὓς ἔθεν εἴνεκ' ἔπασχον ὑπ' Ἄρηος παλαμάων ·

She found Helen in the hall, where she was weaving a great purple web of double fold, and thereon was scattering many battles of the horse-tam-ing Trojans and the brazen-coated Achaeans, that for her sake they had endured at the hands of Ares. (Hom., *Il.*3.125–28)

While men wage wars, a woman weaves them; hence Helen's tapestry is a reflection of the male activity, which mirrors the whole poem itself. In the epic, "Helen is both woven and the weaver of speech."[18] The interesting detail about Helen's tapestry is that both the web and the subject she depicts are in process and thus the action is somehow reflective of the poetic development. The tapestry is not only a female narration of the deeds of men in war, but also an act of 'reading' and 'picturing' a reality both external to and inclusive of the weaving character. By weaving the war Helen also fixes the mobile warriors with her gaze, and in this she also deviates from common gender patterns. Helen does not simply weave decorative patterns; she is actually able to express her own view of the war through weaving—although Homer does not give much information of what that view is. Helen, who deviates from her proper tasks of wife and mother, is probably the most controversial woman in the classical imagination. Therefore, it is not surprising that she has this capacity to represent visually and communicate her own gaze through weaving.

Let us contrast this with Andromache's weaving, also in the *Iliad*:

ἀλλ᾽ ἥ γ᾽ ἱστὸν ὕφαινε μυχῷ δόμου ὑψηλοῖο
δίπλακα πορφυρέην, ἐν δὲ θρόνα ποικίλ᾽ ἔπασσε·

But she was weaving a web in the innermost part of the lofty house, a purple web of double fold, and therein was scattering flowers of varied hue. (Hom., *Il.*22.440–41)

Maria Pantelia believes that both Helen and Andromache "express themselves through the images they depict on their webs."[19] But while Helen depicts the Trojan War, Andromache designs flowers of different colors, a subject quite conventional and unchallenging, most appropriate for a good woman. It is uncertain, however, whether Andromache is actually expressing herself, her own voice, or rather reproducing a stereotypical vision of what women can produce. Nevertheless, some attempt at creativity and personal voice is seen in her use of different colors and designs, but the images are not as communicative as those in Helen's tapestry and embody the stereotypical male view of what women can do: just draw flowers.[20] Yet Pantelia does recognize that Helen's tapestry has a higher "historical standing" than Andromache's.[21] One may suggest, therefore, that only women who do not comply with models of femininity, who are 'deviant' in one way or another, can create beautiful and figurative works of weaving that convey significant meanings or rather, that 'weaving communicatively' makes them deviant. Andromache, for her part, is the reverse example: she produces figures, but they are decorative, un-signifying, and 'womanly.'

In the case of the Roman matron, in general, whenever weaving is mentioned in the description of virtuous women, little or nothing is said about any possible artistic quality of the product. The remarks are normally limited to the comment "she wove, she weaves" as an equivalent of "she did/does her duty." Also, weaving is directed to the production of family goods and clothing; it is essentially a female *industria*. Distinctively, in Arachne's story the signifying power of the object is clearly highlighted, and with her 'signature,' she leaves a mark as woman and artist, which contrasts with the 'silence' and erasure typical of ideal females.

WAR, WEAVING, AND SPEECH

In the episode of Helen discussed above there is a particular gender dichotomy at play. While men fight, a woman stays in the house and weaves. This Homeric distinction is also significant for the present readings of *Metamorphoses*. A most paradigmatic correspondence to weaving in the masculine sphere is war; this division of tasks is indicated in Hector's speech to Andromache:

ἀλλ' εἰς οἶκον ἰοῦσα τὰ σ' αὐτῆς ἔργα κόμιζε,
ἱστόν τ' ἠλακάτην τε, καὶ ἀμφιπόλοισι κέλευε
ἔργον ἐποίχεσθαι· πόλεμος δ' ἄνδρεσσι μελήσει
πᾶσι, μάλιστα δ' ἐμοί, τοί Ἰλίῳ ἐγγεγάασιν·

Now, go to the house and busy yourself with your own tasks, the loom and the distaff, and bid thy handmaids ply their work: but war shall be for men, for all, but most of all for me, of them that dwell in Ilions. (Hom., *Il*.6.490–93)

In Latin Literature, the dichotomy war (man) / weaving (woman) is clearly signaled in Ovid's *Heroides* 14, where Hypermnestra writes after having spared the life of her husband, Lyncaeus: "*quid mihi cum ferro? quo bellica tela puellae?/ aptior est digitis lana colusque meis*"/ "'What do I have to do with the sword? What does a girl want the weapons of war for? More fitting to my fingers are the wool and the distaff?'" (65–66). Propertius also provides an interesting example. Elegy 4.3 is a letter from a wife to her husband at war. While Arethusa is waiting for Lycotas, she weaves garments for war:

texitur haec castris quarta lacerna tuis.
. . . .
noctibus hibernis castrensia pensa laboro
et Tyria in chlamydas vellera secta suo.

This is the fourth cloak woven for your warfare.

· ·

On winter nights I work on your camp garb and sew together stripes of
Tyrian wool for a military cloak. (4.3.18; 33–34)

The relationship between war and weaving becomes complementary, as
she actually weaves cloaks to be used in war and thus indirectly contributes to it. Arethusa is a model wife and her weaving has a concrete
practical aim.

Together with war, another male attribution opposes the female act of
weaving. The respectable woman in antiquity was expected, in general
terms, to remain silent, have no voice, and even become imperceptible.[22]
This is a recurring problem for women who speak or weave communicatively in *Metamorphoses*. In this regard we may recall what Telemachus
says in the *Odyssey* when he emulates Hector's speech:

ἀλλ᾽ εἰς οἶκον ἰοῦσα τὰ σ᾽ αὐτῆς ἔργα κόμιζε,
ἱστόν τ᾽ ἠλακάτην τε, καὶ ἀμφιπόλοισι κέλευε
ἔργον ἐποίχεσθαι· μῦθος δ᾽ ἄνδρεσσι μελήσει
πᾶσι, μάλιστα δ᾽ ἐμοί· τοῦ γὰρ κράτος ἔστ᾽ ἐνὶ οἴκῳ·

Now, go to the house, and busy yourself with your own task, the loom
and the distaff, and bid your handmaids ply their tasks; but speech shall
be for men, for all, but most of all for me; since mine is the authority in
the house. (Hom., *Od*.1.356–69)

Telemachus in this scene employs the exact same words found in Hector's
passage in the *Iliad*. The words μῦθος and πόλεμος occupy the same position in the verse and are thus interchangeable and put in parallel. The idea
that the reader expects to find is war, but Telemachus replaces it because
war does not apply to him. Penelope's son appropriates speech as a sign of
masculinity and uses it in particular in an attempt to affirm his own
authority over the household. Hector and Telemachus embody the male
discourse that affirms that war and words are for men. However, it can also
be suggested that Telemachus is trying to achieve masculinity and present
himself as a man, but, of these two core features that define maleness,
speech and war, he can only go halfway; he only manages to be a man in
one aspect.

The contrast between speech and weaving can also be looked at from

the standpoint of poets and poetry. As seen before, an all-pervading association between weaving and singing is recognized, especially in Greek
literature. McIntosh Snyder is particularly astute when she observes "the
mechanical parallels between the weaver's loom and the poet's lyre, that is,
between striking the 'strings' of the loom with the shuttle and striking the
strings of the lyre with the plektron."[23] This parallel could have been
latent in Aristotle's comment in *Politics* 1253b.37 that "if shuttles wove of
their own accord and plectra played lyres all by themselves, craftsmen
would not need assistants and masters would not need slaves." One can
here establish a gender-determining parallel: while women weave at the
loom, poets play the lyre, which, though it strictly speaking alludes to
music, cannot be separated from the art of poetry. Poets are of course
overwhelmingly male in both practice and ideology, but women and men
make use of a very similar instrument, technically and structurally. Yet the
tasks they undertake with them are sharply dissimilar: women weave and
men sing.[24]

DIVINE AND HUMAN TEXTILES

The tale of Arachne and Minerva is particularly rich in issues of visual representation and female creativity. The purpose of this section is to examine how these two very different females look at the world and to explore
what the episode has to say about female gazes.

Various readings for the Ovidian passage in question have been proposed.[25] First, the story was strictly seen as a morality tale. Brooks Otis
locates it among other 'vengeance episodes' in Books 3–6.400.[26] Focus has
also been on the connection of the ekphrases with Ovid's own aesthetic
conceptions. In the center of her tapestry, Minerva places Jupiter presid-
ing over her dispute with Neptune. Twelve gods surround Jupiter, each
with a distinctive emblem. The two contestants each perform a miracle to
assert a claim to Athens. In addition, Minerva draws four smaller panels in
the corners, which show what happened to other mortals who defied the
gods—a message that Arachne 'fails' to decode, as many critics see it. A
more feminocentric reading would perhaps see a deliberate refusal to conform to Minerva's viewpoint. For her part, Arachne weaves a series of
scenes where transformed gods rape human women. Minerva's work is
defined by harmony and balance of composition, while Arachne's is a
panoply of stories, without a defined structure. In fact, it has been recognized that Arachne's tapestry is impossible to imagine as a real picture.
Laird even draws a distinction between obedient and disobedient

ekphrases, i.e., those that can be easily transferred to pictures as opposed
to those impossible to represent as a picture, although they are often sup-
posed to be a description of one. Arachne's, of course, would be disobedient.[27] The fluidity of form in her work can be thus identified with Ovid's
own aesthetics in the *Metamorphoses*, in that it is distant from Minerva's
'order' and thus less aligned with Augustan *gravitas*.[28] A political reading
views Arachne as opposed to established powers and often centers on the
polemics of Ovid's Augustanism or anti-Augustanism. The Arachne
episode may reveal an anti-Augustan poet. Minerva's work has the order,
separation, control, and boundary setting typical of what is often seen as
Augustan. In fact, Augustus's moral politics are frequently viewed as
embodying the denial of change, exactly the opposite of what *Metamorphoses* is about—despite the fact that change is actually what Augustus
achieved.[29] Further, the art of Pallas is official, hierarchic, and political—
thus masculine—while Arachne's design follows the artistic and literary
trends of the Hellenistic period and the Alexandrian poets, and is therefore in tune with what is seen as Ovid's Callimacheanism. Harries identifies Arachne with the poet because she is "a highly gifted artist equipped
with every skill except that of knowing how and when to defer to divine
superiority." The fates of Arachne and Ovid are intertwined; indeed,
Arachne becomes the prototype of the exiled poet.[30] Finally, there is also
a feminist dimension to the opposition of Minerva and Arachne. Modern
feminists have appropriated many mythological figures in order to
empower the voices of contemporary women. While the raped and
tongueless Philomela weaving a message to her sister is a striking example,
Arachne, who weaves images of raped women, is also an emblem of
female rebellion silenced by patriarchal authority. Nancy Miller, for
instance, argues that "against the classically theocentric balance of
Athena's tapestry, Arachne constructs a feminocentric protest" and that
"the goddess destroys the woman's countercultural accounts."[31]

The narrative context of the story is highly charged with gender and
visual implications that shape and influence the textile productions of
Minerva and Arachne. First, the whole scene has a spectacular character.
Arachne's art of weaving was so wonderful that audiences would come
and watch her at work:

> huius ut adspicerent opus admirabile, saepe
> deseruere sui nymphae vineta Timoli,
> deseruere suas nymphae Pactolides undas.

The nymphs often left the vineyards of their Timolus in order to see her wondrous work, the water-nymphs of Pactolus often left their waters. (*Met.*6.14–16)

These lines are meaningful because they establish Arachne's work as a visual object (*opus admirabile*) and because the nymphs come as spectators of her work. But also, as Joplin suggests, "the loom represents the occasion for *communitas,* or peace, a context in which it is possible for pleasure to be nonappropriative and nonviolent. In this, Arachne suggests Sappho, who was also the center of a community of women and who also, in Ovid, meets a deadly end."[32] In Book 5 the nymphs were judges of the singing contest between the Pierides and the Muses, an audience that identified and empathized with the tales narrated by Calliope and other internal narrators. Now, the fact that the nymphs admire and respect Arachne's work humiliates and enrages Minerva, as, in a tacit way, this implies a judgment on the part of the nymphs. Minerva is, already at the beginning, a loser. Furthermore, not only does Arachne's work become a visual object, but also her own person at work is the object of delight for the nymphs' eyes: *nec factas solum vestes, spectare iuvabat/ tum quoque, cum fierent: tantus decor adfuit arti/* "It was not only pleasing to look at the finished cloths, but also to see the process of their making. Such was the grace of her art" (*Met.* 6.17–18). This is a thought-provoking scene. Here is a group of women viewers of a female visual object. The circumstances and implications, however, are very different from the common scenes of men looking oppressively at women. Furthermore, as mentioned before, men as visual objects tend to be represented as "doing something," while women looked at convey the feeling of inactivity. Yet Arachne is active in her work. This is a form of spectacle where both viewers and viewed take pleasure in and gain something from. The verb *iuvo* here clearly shows that the nymphs gain something from the scene, although their eyes do not control, penetrate, or annihilate the image. This, one can postulate, may be an interesting characteristic of women looking at women.

Once Minerva appears in the picture, there is a most interesting play on seeing and the power of the gaze. When Minerva, disguised as an old lady, comes to the girl and counsels her to surrender to the goddess, Arachne looks at her with sullen eyes (*torvis* [*luminibus*], *Met.* 6.34). But for all the visual capabilities of Arachne, she cannot penetrate the meanings of the old woman; she cannot see behind the appearances. Perhaps this would not even make a difference because even when she knows that she is fighting Pallas, this does not deter her from her hubris. Unlike Juno, Arachne does not seem to have the capacity to see what is behind, for she does not 'suspect.' If we believe that Minerva is a goddess connected with envy, apparent especially in Book 2, then Arachne, with her gaze askew, defies the goddess on one more level. Let us remember here that Envy and Minerva are the holders of the *torva lumina*. Arachne not only claims to surpass the goddess in the art of weaving, but she also holds a powerful gaze, a central element in the visual artist.

WEAVING THE GAZE

The aesthetic differences between both tapestries have been well estab-lished by the critics, but to put it in the context of the discussion of female discourses and audiences, one can say that Minerva constructs a self-centered image that lays all the weight on her person, the divine pow-ers and hierarchy.[33] She begins by picturing the dispute over the naming of Athens and continues by placing herself in the divine family, not without showing in the margins how irreverent mortals were punished for disre-specting the gods.[34] On the contrary, Arachne weaves the stories of rape and suffering of women subject to the sexual violence of gods. This is a much more appropriate theme for an audience of nymphs, who, although not explicitly said to be judges of the context, can well be expected to act like judges, given their role in Book 5 and their presence as audience in Book 6. Arachne exposes the crime of rape (note that the text calls these images *caelestia crimina, Met.* 6.131) and in particular displays the fact that male gods transform themselves into animals or other beings in order to deceive and rape women.

    The tapestries of Arachne and Minerva are very different in theme and ideology; yet for all their differences, they both offer alternatives to the male gaze. When Minerva depicts herself and other gods, she combines static pictures with mobility. After the god of the oceans is said to make a *fretum* spring from the earth, Minerva concentrates on her own image:

> at sibi dat clipeum, dat acutae cuspidis hastam,
> dat galeam capiti, defenditur aegide pectus,
> percussamque sua simulat de cuspide terram
> edere cum bacis fetum canentis olivae;
> mirarique deos: operis Victoria finis.

To herself she gives a shield, she gives herself a sharp-pointed spear, and a helmet for her head. The chest is protected by the aegis. She weaves the earth smitten by her spear's point bearing a pale olive tree with its fruits, and shows the gods admiring it. Victory is the end of her work. (*Met.* 6.78–82)

The anaphoric use of *dat* has the effect of focalizing our attention on the different attributes of the goddess, which have to do with warfare. Unlike Arachne, who weaves images of others, Minerva's self-construction points at a self-display typical of narcissism.

It was mentioned in chapter 2 that Ovid presents the ekphrases of the finished tapestries and not of the work in process. His technique is so masterful that it manages to deceive sagacious readers like Anderson, who comments on this section: "We can almost see Minerva weaving into the warp one item after another of her military attire, for she depicts herself as the armored deity that the Athenians revered and Phidias exalted in his magnificent chryselephantine statue."[35] This is an inherent problem of ekphrasis. The description of an image with written words implies a transformation from a synchronic, holistic, *all-at-once* type of perception to a linear, sequential, diachronic, and *one-at-a-time* type of experience. Anderson and other readers are deceived because they prioritize a synchronic/textual reading over the reception of a visual *phantasia*.

Minerva wishes to present an image of herself as warrior goddess and leaves aside other aspects of her character—such as weaving. This has to do with the fact that Minerva envisions power as masculine and thus she decides to stress these aspects in her tapestry. Now, one point is particularly relevant for gaze issues: within her military attributes, Minerva mentions the aegis. This breastplate with the fearful head of Medusa on it formed part of the goddess's regular iconography and had the purpose of freezing enemies into stone with fear. It was such a well-established feature that Ovid did not need to mention this in the ekphrasis. However, it has an enormous significance because one can think that Minerva identifies with Perseus trying to use the gaze of the Gorgon to paralyze the (artistic in this case) powers of her opponent. But she also identifies with Medusa herself as one who looks and wishes to control what she sees—which is actually what Minerva strives to do with Arachne's productions. We see again a complex web of masculine and feminine aspects in her self-presentation.

Minerva's description of herself has close intertextualities with a work of plastic art, the above-mentioned statue by Phidias. Can we suppose, then, that the goddess has 'seen' the statue and models her own image on it? Beyond this type of speculation, what matters is that she presents herself in a static and statue-like stance that suggests obvious echoes of Andromeda and Pygmalion's ivory maiden. But while other female statues in the poem are fairly passive, at least in appearance, Minerva here presents herself as a publicly recognized power. There is an interesting play on gaze, mobility, and immobility. While on the one hand Pallas pictures herself as a statue-like image, the phrase *percussamque terram* implies that there was action before. Likewise, while the gods do the looking and Minerva is the object of their gaze, they do not seem to paralyze and objectify the image. Minerva, however, grants them the active and vital role of judging the work and ultimately declaring it victorious. So, Minerva is a female artist who is looking at gods looking at her in awe. While she at first seems to focalize with the internal viewers and make herself a static visual object, she then deconstructs the illusion by looking at the viewers themselves. It is also relevant that, as Anderson suggests, the admiration of the internal spectators of the transformation (the creation of the olive tree at Minerva's stroke) acts as a "stage-direction" and has metacritical implications for the whole epic on how one should read metamorphosis.[36] We should not fall asleep like Argus, but look in amazement at the spectacles before our eyes.

The fact that Minerva constructs a group of viewers for her own image may well be a product of her *invidia* toward Arachne, who is herself always surrounded by a crowd of admiring spectators. This is in accordance with the goddess's gender complexity. She shows herself with weapons and not with wool-work; she wants to present a masculine picture of her power but she also wants to be looked at—though not eroticized. In this sense, the depiction of Minerva would conform with Mulvey's thesis that the only way for women to be powerful is to identify with the male.

In the four corners of the tapestry Minerva recalls four stories of divine 'justice.' The first is the tale of Haemus and Rhodope who were transformed into mountains for usurping the names of the gods. Thus, these two human beings are paralyzed for their outrage. The following two scenes are notable for gender constructions in *Metamorphoses*. First comes the story of the Pygmaean queen who challenged the majesty of Juno and was transformed into a crane after the goddess conquered her in a *certamen* (*hanc Iuno victam certamine iussit/ esse gruem*, Met. 6.91–92). We know of no *certamen* in other versions of the story (e.g., Antoninus Liberalis 16).[37] One may suppose that Ovid introduces the idea of a contest here to stress the connection with Arachne and Minerva. *Certamen* is a sure hint to Arachne that she should not engage in one. Arachne could be the myth of the 'failure' of the reader, for while she strives to stimulate the female audience to read beneath appearance (to unmask the gods travestied in animals), she is unable to 'suspect.' But Minerva also identifies with Juno, who is such a visually significant deity, especially in the first books of *Metamorphoses*. The third story also involves Juno, who changed Antigone into a stork. In other versions she vied with Juno boasting about her lovely tresses, but Ovid insists on the idea of competition (*pinxit et Antigonen, ausam contendere quondam/ cum magni consorte Iovis /* "And she pictured Antigone, who once dared to vie with the consort of mighty Jupiter," *Met.* 6.93–94). This is noteworthy because after Minerva has presented herself as master of warfare, she keeps on warning Arachne about the hubris in engaging in *certamina* with the gods. The final corner of Minerva's tapestry depicts Cinyras bereft of his daughters. Ovid is the only source of this tale, but with the information he provides one can suppose that the daughters challenged some goddess about their beauty and were changed into the marble steps on her temple.[38] In any case, this is again a story of female petrifaction and a father who embraces the cold steps of the temple.

Minerva draws a border of olive around her tapestry (*circuit extremas oleis pacalibus oras, Met.* 6.101) and thus draws a limit to her story and her tapestry. Ovid's humor is at play here, for this is a very ironic move on Minerva's part. After so much combative imagery and allusions to *certamina*, she circles the conflictive images with an icon of peace. Again, one is reminded of the *Pax Augusta* obtained after so many battles. But the olive is also a symbol of victory, already included in the contest between Minerva and Poseidon over the possession of Athens. In that case, the tree was an emblem of her victory over the god. The border of olive wreath acts as a symbol of Minerva's desire for victory, which, paradoxically, she does not achieve in the story. Probably, the reason why she does not triumph in the contest is that she has a self-centered gaze that cannot empathize with the preoccupations of others and does not engage with the suffering of the nymphs.

What Minerva sees, then, is a world where to be powerful she needs to assume a masculine stance and warn Arachne that she should not engage in *certamina*. Minerva also represents the divine gaze, which must impose control over humans. She is, however, at some level, somewhat blind. Minerva draws, in the corners of her tapestry, examples of men punished by gods. But what she does not realize is that Arachne will not be able to read those images, for not only do both weavers perform their tasks simultaneously and "in different parts of the room"—which would make it difficult to see the opponent's tapestry—but also, if the tapestry moves up from the bottom, not even the reader can see the images in the top corners until they are finished. By now, Arachne would have woven her textile and it would be too late to back off on her hubris. Most critics, however, have tried to see Minerva's scenes of punishment in the tapestry as explicit warnings. This interpretation depends mainly on a sequential reading of the passage, which follows the actual sequential nature of the text (the description of Minerva's tapestry comes before the description of Arachne's tapestry). A more holistic reading would take into account that both weavers weave simultaneously and that weaving, though an action-in-time (like the painting of a picture), is not meant to be 'read' as a diachronic and linear event. The question is, why does Minerva weave all this, then? Perhaps Minerva is blind to this question of the impossibility of reception of her images because she is too self-absorbed in the construction of her own divine image. But one can also suppose that what Minerva wants is not to scare off Arachne, as most critics suppose, but simply to express her gaze and leave her presence in the text of *Metamorphoses*. Perhaps, what Minerva is here doing is constructing her images with the external viewer in mind, for she is warning the reader about what is coming up, because while we can read Minerva's tapestry sequentially, Arachne cannot.

Ovid devotes twenty-six lines to Arachne's tapestry. She depicts the rapes of several women; however, she does not focalize with the male rapists and thus she does not paralyze or turn the images into erotic objects. On the contrary, she can take a distance and find a viewing place from where she can appreciate the whole scene. It is perhaps precisely because of this perspective that Arachne's tapestry is better, because it finds a more original and holistic place from where to look and because its anti-mimetic and anti-realistic features constitute a challenge to the imagination of the viewer.

Ovid's description of Arachne's tapestry begins with an allusion to the rape of Europa. This first scene shows that Arachne has 'read' and understood Ovid's *Metamorphoses*, for Ovid develops the story of Europa in Book 2 of his epic:

> Maeonis elusam designat imagine tauri
> Europam: verum taurum, freta vera putares;
> ipsa videbatur terras spectare relictas
> et comites clamare suas tactumque vereri
> adsilientis aquae timidasque reducere plantas.

> Arachne pictures Europa deceived by the appearance of a bull, a real
> bull, real waves you would think they were. Europa herself seemed to
> watch the land left behind, to call her companions, to fear the contact
> with the leaping waves, and to draw back her fearful feet. (*Met.* 6.103–7)

Arachne is resolved to give us the female gaze and the female perspective,
which Ovid had alluded to in Book 2. The insistence on illusion and
falsehood is striking here (*elusam, imagine*) contrasted with the appearances of reality (*verum taurum . . . putares*) and may actually be understood as a warning to women that they should 'suspect,' that they should
see beyond appearance and make use of the 'oblique' quality of women's
gaze. This warning is extended in twenty more stories of rape by disguised
gods. First come Asterie deceived by Jupiter turned into an eagle and Leda
suffering him as a swan. Next the text mentions how Jupiter disguised as
a satyr raped Antiope (*satyri celatus imagine/* "hidden under the appearance
of a satyr," *Met.* 6.110). We observe again the insistence on appearances
that need to be uncovered and that are being uncovered by Arachne. She
is using the 'oblique' gaze in her textile. The references to Jupiter's imper-
sonation of Amphitryon to rape Alcmene and to his disguise as a golden
shower to rape Danae serve the same purpose. He also cheated Aegina as
a flame (*Aesopida luserit ignis, Met.* 6.113). The verb *luserit* recalling
elusam before points at deception as well. He then cheated Mnemosyne
as a shepherd and Deo's daughter, Proserpina, as a spotted snake. Neptune
changed into a bull rapes Canace (*mutatum torvo, Neptune, iuvenco,*
*Met.*6.115), he deceived (*fallis, Met.* 6.117) Iphimedeia as the river-god
Enipeus (*visus Enipeus*), and Bisaltis as a ram (*visus . . . aries*). Demeter
suffered him as a horse, Medusa as a bird, and Melantho as a dolphin.
Unlike Minerva, who uses Medusa in her monstrous aspect, Arachne
places her among the innocent victims of rape.[39]

Phoebus's passage is also enlightening in the matters of disguise and
deception. Transvestism is even more explicit with him, for Arachne
shows him literally 'dressing up' for the show (*est illic agrestis imagine Phoe-*
bus,/ utque modo accipitris pennas, modo terga leonis/ gesserit, ut pastor
Macareida luserit Issen/ "Phoebus is there in the disguise of a countryman
and she showed how now he wore a hawk's feathers, now the hide of a
lion; how he cheated as a shepherd Macareus's daughter Isse," *Met.*
6.122–24). Bacchus uses a false image (*falsa uva*) to entice Erigone and
Saturn begets the Centaur as a horse.

Arachne depicts gods disguised. But while the text can tell us that
these are indeed gods disguised, the tapestry can only present them in

their borrowed form. This is an important distinction, for while the external reader is instructed on what is really going on, the internal viewers of the tapestry need to decode it. Presumably, they can only see a ram, a bull, a dolphin, and they need to exercise a cooperative act of imagination. Arachne then expects her viewers to 'suspect' the images they see; she invites them to read behind the appearances, to exercise an active act of fantasy and female imagination, and asks them to recall their own previous viewings and readings of the myth. Minerva's tapestry seems to be much more straightforward on what is going on in the scene. If one connects these two modes of envisioning the role of the audience with the more standard reading of the two types of art, non-hierarchic Callimachean and more boundary-setting Augustan, one may suppose that the first, Ovidian, and Arachnean mode implies much more responsive and cooperative readers who can act upon the text and 'complete' it with their imagination. Minerva's art seems instead to impose a certain way of understanding her images, but in this, too, she is unsuccessful.

TAKING ARMS, ASSUMING A VOICE

Minerva's construction of herself brings forth issues of her own complex sexuality as she strives to depict herself with the masculine *vis* of a warrior. But we will suggest that Arachne not only challenges the goddess in the art of weaving, but that she also defies her, in a veiled way, in her aspect of warrior goddess. As seen before, weaving is associated with femininity and having a voice is viewed as an unfeminine prerogative. Arachne, by the very act of weaving, strives to be communicative and to possess a voice and a gaze. Also, in her own desire for competition she emulates the goddess in her combative aspect. In the first encounter between Minerva and Arachne, the issue of the *certamen* is raised and preannounced when the girl challenges the disguised goddess with the insistence on competition (*Met.* 6.25; 6.42). This aligns Arachne with the Pierides, who also quest for a contest with deities: "*Thespiades, certate, deae*"/ "'Strive with us, Thespian goddesses'" (*Met.* 5.310) and *dirimant certamina nymphae*/ "Let the nymphs decide the outcome of the contest" (*Met.* 5.314).

The warrior goddess's love of combat is readily visible in myth and in cult. In the *Iliad* she is often seen standing beside a favorite and the myths recount how she participated in the battle between gods and giants as an outstanding warrior on the side of the gods. In cult, the Greek Athena is identified with Nike, Victory, not only in battle but also in athletic contests.[40] Homer's *Iliad* 5 also emphasizes her profile as a deity of war, by contrasting her and Enyo, the goddess of war, with Aphrodite, who has no place in the battlefield (330–33). But she is also the inventor of weaving. Both domestic and warlike facets are well exemplified in *Iliad* 5.733–37, where Homer describes how Athena took off the finely woven robe that she had made with her own hands and armed herself for battle. But when the goddess's masculine and feminine characteristics are transmitted to humans, clear-cut gender definitions need to become apparent.[41] This is particularly relevant for Arachne because by engaging in the contest with the goddess Minerva, she metaphorically transforms her textiles into weapons.[42] Returning to the dichotomy between weaving and war corresponding to the female and male universes, Arachne becomes some sort of warrior by the very act of weaving, thus producing a new inversion of the established gender patterns and transforming the visual images she creates. Ultimately, the weaving contest is one of gazes that strives to show which gaze will prevail. First, weaving can be read in various cases as female weapons that women wield to defend themselves. Penelope deceives the suitors by this means, Philomela communicates her story, and Arachne defies the goddess.[43] While Minerva tries to avoid a confrontation, Arachne seems eager to engage in a contest. She denies that Pallas had been her teacher and challenges the deity: *"certet" ait "mecum: nihil est, quod victa recusem!"*/ "'Let her strive with me,' she says, 'there is nothing I would not forfeit if I lose'" (*Met.* 6.25). Later, once the goddess in the aspect of an old woman has advised her, the girl stubbornly reaffirms: *"cur non ipsa venit? cur haec certamina vitat?"*/ "'Why doesn't she come herself? Why does she avoid this contest?'" (*Met.* 6.42). It is here worth noting that autodidactism is a common feature of the myth of the artist and it appears in several artists' 'biographies.'[44] Arachne, by this denial of Minerva as teacher, not only affirms her independence as artist but also places herself in a tradition of artists who "taught themselves."[45]

Battle and contest are of course not the same thing, but the semantics of competition are normally envisioned as the territory of men only. Women were, in a Roman context, expected to be peaceful and submissive, unchallenging in all aspects of their lives, except perhaps in their virtue. In Livy 1.57, however, it is her husband who 'enters' Lucretia in the contest of the best wife. Thus, it can even be said that the competition is between men, while the women, as 'properties,' are elements of such dispute. More specifically, women weave for the hearth and the family, but they do not enter contests against each other over this task. It is all the more telling, then, that vocabulary related to contest pervades this episode, with Arachne being presented as the defiant competitor. She does not fear Minerva when she appears in her mighty power (*Met.* 6.45) and she resembles an epic hero in search of the glory of victory. *Certamen*, the word used by Ovid to refer to the weaving contest, is in many other instances in Latin literature used for battle.[46] The scene becomes, therefore, loaded with overtones of antagonism:

> perstat in incepto stolidaeque cupidine palmae
> in sua fata ruit; neque enim Iove nata recusat
> nec monet ulterius nec iam certamina differt.
> haud mora, constituunt diversis partibus ambae
> et gracili geminas intendunt stamine telas:
> tela iugo vincta est, stamen secernit harundo.

> She insists on her challenge and runs to her own fate with foolish desire for victory. The daughter of Jove neither holds her back nor warns her any more, nor does she delay the contest any longer. Without delay they both set their looms in different parts and stretch the fine warp. The web is bound upon the beam, the reed separates the threads. (*Met.* 6.50–55)

The semantics of battle is persistent: *inceptum* and *ruo* are commonly found in war contexts, and the disposition of the contestants (53) recalls the language of single combat, as in Livy 7.10.9, for example, when Titus Manlius fights against the Gaul: *ubi constitere inter duas acies/* "When they took their stand between the two armies." In pursuit of victory and glory, Arachne rushes on to her own death (*in sua fata ruit*); her determination to win recalls the courage of the hero risking his own life against the enemy. By assuming a combative attitude and defying Minerva, Arachne takes up a masculine stance. In this sense she deconstructs and reshapes the polarity of the weaver/fighter as she merges both masculinity and femininity in the single act of entering the weaving contest. By using her textile as a metaphoric weapon, Arachne enters into a 'battle of gazes' where each contestant strives to impose her own vision. Arachne's case thus constitutes a notable paradox, for she uses weaving, an essential female attribute, to reverse ideal femininity.

Why, however, does Arachne punish another woman? It is worth thinking perhaps that not every relationship between women is necessarily sisterly. Miller has suggested that Pallas in this story embodies male power and represents the established gender parameter. She actually advocates a phallic identification of Athena with Olympian authority: "we recall that Athena identifies not only with the gods, but with godhead, the cerebral male identity that bypasses the female."[47] This point had already been raised in Hesiod, who states that the goddess gestated within Zeus's belly (νηδύς, *Theog.* 886–90). In Latin literature Horace, referring to the glory of Jupiter, shows the goddess's proximity to him: *nec viget quicquam simile aut secundum/ proximos illi tamen occupavit/ Pallas honores,/ proeliis audax . . . /* "And nothing has a similar strength or second to him, but Pallas, brave in battle, has secured glory next to his" (*Odes* 1.12.18–21).[48] But more specifically, Athena is tightly identified with Zeus and with the masculine in Aeschylus's *Oresteia*. In her judgment of Orestes' crime in the *Eumenides*, the goddess affirms:

μήτηρ γὰρ οὔτις ἐστὶν ἥ μ᾽ ἐγείνατο,
τὸ δ᾽ ἄρσεν αἰνῶ πάντα, πλὴν γάμου τυχεῖν,
ἅπαντι θυμῷ, κάρτα δ᾽ εἰμὶ τοῦ πατρός·

> No mother gave me birth, and in everything save marriage I approve with all my heart the masculine and am entirely on the father's side. (Aesch., *Eum.* 736–38)

Athena feels closer to the masculine; yet her character is not so simply clear-cut; rather, she is a problematic figure from a gender standpoint. The goddess combines the masculine and the feminine, the warrior and the weaver. Perhaps Arachne's challenge points in this direction. Firstly, one may say, she is also motherless, and a particular attachment to her father can be viewed in her choice of profession—he was a dyer of wool. Arachne's identification with her father, Idmon, i.e., one who has knowledge, has to do with intellectualism in particular. Significantly, Arachne is struck *in the head* by Minerva: *Idmoniae ter quarter Idmoniae frontem percussit Arachnes/* "Three times, four times she struck Idmonian Arachne on the forehead," *Met.* 6.133). Arachne not only bears 'the name of the father' here, but this name is particularly meaningful for its connections with the semantic field of knowledge and ideas. Although she is expected to weave only, as a woman does, the girl wants to possess feminine and masculine endowments, to weave, to have a voice and an intellect, and to compete. In a way, she struggles to be like Minerva, and her sexual intermingling with her brother, recorded in the scholia to Nicander's *Theriaca*, may well symbolize the merging of the masculine and the feminine, of weaving and arms. Arachne is required to be a woman only, but she does not accept the terms of this equation: she threatens to subvert them in her weaving, but the goddess destroys the woman's countercultural attempt. Perhaps, one can even see in Minerva's 'breaking' of Arachne's cloth (which could be metaphorically assimilated to her virginity) an image of rape by a female deity with masculine endowments. In this case, there would be a coincidence and identification between the girl, her woven characters, and her audience. Her tapestry, in a way, would anticipate her fate. But unlike Philomela, Arachne, through 'figurative' rape, loses both her tongue and her ability to communicate through weaving. But even more, her transformation into a spider involves a loss of humanity, as her artistic talent disappears with the metonymy of the shrunken head:

> fitque caput minimum; toto quoque corpore parva est:
> in latere exiles digiti pro cruribus haerent,
> cetera venter habet, de quo tamen illa remittit
> stamen et antiquas exercet aranea telas.

> Her head shrinks, her whole body is also small. Instead of limbs, slender fingers cling to her side, the rest is all belly, from where, however, she spins a thread and, as a spider, she exercises her old art of weaving. (*Met.* 6.142–45)

The adjective *antiquas*, applied to Arachne's *telas*, is misleading. Does this mean that she can still weave (*exercet*) her old cloths in the same way? Of course not, because otherwise, there would be no punishment; and the spider's web is not a work of signifying art in the same sense as Arachne's tapestries. Thus, *antiquas* is ironic, a playful twist. Arachne is now all belly, all instinct and no brains. One can even read Arachne's enormous *venter* as an allusion to women's primary function in ancient societies, pregnancy and reproduction. The 'minimization' of her head can be interpreted as a symbolic 'decapitation' and suppression of female identity.[49] One can understand the struggle between Arachne and Minerva as either an example of anti-sisterhood between women or take it as a standard gender struggle between the male and the female, Minerva arrogating the male for herself in the 'right' to fight, to look, and to speak.

So what does Arachne see? She sees a world of violence against women, but she also sees that women and she herself as artist have the capacity to bear witness. As a viewer and artist, Arachne also asks women to 'suspect' and to exercise their oblique gazes. By weaving, Arachne also assumes a gaze for herself and doubly infringes upon the precepts for proper femininity: she looks, she 'speaks' her mind, and she fights. By her very desire to win the contest, Arachne becomes a sort of warrior and so claims for herself arms, speech, and gaze, contradicting the mandates that Homer puts in the mouths of Hector and Telemachus. Unlike silent women who weave 'silent' and 'blind' textiles with a utilitarian purpose, Arachne, who is verbally defying, expresses her gaze through weaving, makes her gaze a 'weapon,' and engages in a very 'unfeminine' contest in order to forward the causes of women.

GERMANAEQUE SUAE FATUM MISERABILE LEGIT

Wheeler does not incorporate Philomela, Arachne, or Minerva in his chart of narrators, because they do not use a verbal medium for expression and because the reader really hears their stories through the words of the main narrator.[50] However, they do tell stories through weaving, even if these tales are mediated by the voice of the author. This section addresses the tale of Procne and Philomela, concentrating specifically on Philomela's self-construction in visual images through weaving. As in the previous episode, the aim is to recover the visual in the search for the female gaze.

The story is well known and has been discussed amply, especially in feminist critique.[51] Emphasis has normally been laid—and understandably so—on the question of power, silence, and voice.[52] But this concern with voice has overshadowed the importance of the visual in the tale. The motor of the tragedy is a desire to *see*. Procne begs Tereus to bring her sister to her:

> . . . "si gratia" dixit
> "ulla mea est, vel me visendae mitte sorori,
> vel soror huc veniat: redituram tempore parvo
> promittes socero; magni mihi muneris instar
> germanam vidisse dabis." . . .

> "If my love finds any favor," she said, " either send me to visit my sister or let my sister come here. You will promise your father-in-law that she will return shortly. It will be a great gift for me if you let me see my sister."
> (*Met*.6.440–44)

It is common to use 'seeing' for 'being with' in a metonymic way, yet when we 'are' with somebody we normally 'see' her too. One can say that Philomela is, from the beginning, an object of the desire to see; thus the passive nuance of *visendae* becomes most meaningful. Philomela, or rather the *phantasia* of Philomela formed in Procne's mind's eye, is envisioned as an image to be looked at. This is the case if one accepts the reading *visendae*—which is Heinsius's emendation—and not *visendam*, which is the reading of the major manuscripts, in which case Procne would want Philomela to see *her*.[53] Heinsius's suggestion seems more appropriate, because it would suit better the presentation of Philomela as a spectacle that the beginning of the episode conveys. In any case, this desire to see becomes, as is typical in Ovid, displaced and distorted. When Tereus arrives in Athens, he is possessed by Philomela's *forma* and soon becomes the erotic viewer. Ovid plays with this issue of seeing in the very name of the protagonist, for Tereus is etymologically linked with the idea of 'watching' (τηρέω, "to watch over, guard"). The early image of seeing in a more general sense is soon transformed into a more violent desire and the narration, as it does with other "pretty women," stops to describe Philomela and thus fixes her:

> ecce venit magno dives Philomela paratu,
> divitior forma; quales audire solemus
> naidas et dryadas mediis incedere silvis,
> si modo des illis cultus similesque paratus.
> non secus exarsit conspecta virgine Tereus.

> Look! Here comes Philomela, rich in great apparel, but richer in beauty; such as we often hear that the naiads and dryads walk about in the middle of the woods, if only one gave them similar apparel and refinement. As soon as he sees the maiden, Tereus burns with love. (*Met.* 6.451–55)

It is worthwhile wondering whether Ovid's emphasis on Philomela's adornment may respond to a typical macho-oriented maneuver to justify men's violence on women's provocation by making themselves attractive. The comparison with the naiads walking in the woods is also significant. Wheeler is right in signaling that metacritical issues transpire in the simile. *Audire solemus* may well point to stories about nymphs entering woods that we have actually heard in the poem—*audire* would support Wheeler's thesis on its 'oral' quality. Specifically, Wheeler and Anderson refer, correctly, to intertextuality with the Apollo-Daphne story.[54] But what is problematic is that they seem to universalize the experience of the reader. This is what Wheeler says, for example:

> Here the audience participates in the act of imagining the beauty of Philomela. The comparison to nymphs is not drawn from the visual experience of everyday life, but from what the audience is accustomed to hearing ("audire solemus"). "We" are thus encouraged to remember liter-

ary descriptions of beautiful nymphs entering groves. This could, of course, be an appeal to the audience's knowledge of a poetic *topos*. However, given "our" direct experience of such scenes in the *Metamorphoses*, the poet is reminding "us" rather of nymphs such as Daphne and Syrinx.[55]

The problem is: who are "we"? Wheeler does not distinguish between a male and a female audience. So, "the audience participates in the act of imagining the beauty of Philomela." But what if the audience is a woman? Wheeler does not tell us, for example, that the allusion to Daphne or Syrinx "provokes in the reader an anxiety at the forthcoming rape," or that "we are invited to imagine the violent dangers that beauty can bestow upon a woman." These would be, of course, more gynocentric readings of the simile. Not surprisingly, Tereus, like Apollo, like the male reader, burns with Philomela's image. As Segal observes, his desire is expressed in his eyes and the gaze here equals a desire for possession:[56]

perque suam contraque suam petit ipsa salutem.
spectat eam Tereus praecontrectatque videndo
osculaque et collo circumdata bracchia cernens
omnia pro stimulis facibusque ciboque furoris
accipit. . . .

She [Philomela] herself begs that she may see her sister, for (and against) her own welfare. Tereus looks at her and by looking he imagines his future pleasure; and the vision of her kisses and her arms around her father's neck are all like goads, fire and food for his passion. (*Met.* 6.476–82)

It is now Philomela who wants to 'see' her sister, but her desire to see Procne is at the same time watched by the greedy eyes of Tereus. But at the same time, both she and her father are effectively blind, for they cannot 'see' Tereus's devious desire, which, if we trust Ovid, should have by now shown some external signs (*quantum mortalia pectora caecae/ noctis habent!/* "How much dark night rules in mortal hearts," *Met.* 6.472–73). The passage shows quite clearly how desire is constructed from the imaginary picture that the viewer forges in his mind: by seeing Philomela, Tereus fantasizes about her possession. More interestingly, what he sees stimulates his imagination; he is aroused not only by what is visible, but by what remains unseen: *in illa/ aestuat et repetens faciem motusque manusque/ qualia vult, fingit quae nondum vidit et ignes/ ipse suos nutrit cura removente soporem* / "He burns with the thought of her and recalls to his mind her face, her movement, and her hands, which he desires; and he imagines what he has not yet seen. He himself feeds his fire and his anxious love does not let him sleep" (*Met.* 6.490–93). Philomela is a spectacle, an object to be looked at, and thus we do not really hear her voice until after the rape. It is true that we know that she "coaxes her father to let her see her sister" (475–77) and that she cries out for help at the moment of her rape, but these instances are conveyed in indirect speech, which always creates a distance between actual utterance and narration. But after rape, it is as if her power of speech had been directly 'opened' by sexuality: Philomela begins to curse and complain. Tereus then duly silences her by cutting out her tongue. Beyond the well-established explanations of Philomela's silence, it is worth arguing that it is not only what Philomela says that disturbs her raptor, but the fact that, with her voice, she has destroyed the visual illusion. Philomela is an object of visual desire, a spectacle, a delight for the gaze of the one who wishes to possess her; a sort of ivory maiden who, with her voice, has come to life and destroyed the work of art.

The journey is also an important event in Philomela's life. The story has an appearance of morality and order, because it is 'sororal' love that motivates Philomela's journey. A sense of something ominous, however, is felt all the way, as if there were something inherently wrong and uncomfortable in a woman leaving her father and fatherland, which is transmitted in Pandion's excessive sorrow and concern for his girl's departure. Further, there is the transition between Athens as a civilized place and Thrace as a barbaric land, where barbaric crimes will be committed, as Segal shows.[57] Were Philomela a boy, none of this would take place. Although we do find fathers like Evander concerned about the welfare of their sons, the tragedy implied in a woman traveling has a different depth and extent. Philomela's departure stages a fundamental transition in the sexual life of the girl. On land, she is the object of the father's gaze; he is the one who sees her (although the text does not make this explicit, one can well assume that her beautiful image is a spectacle for her father's eyes) and who receives her caresses. The image of Philomela embracing her father is poignant in this respect.[58] But the story centers around the distortion of family bonds, as Philomela complains later (*omnia turbasti,* 537), and her second embrace with her father presents a twist: *et quotiens amplectitur illa parentem,* / *esse parens vellet: neque enim minus inpius esset* / "And whenever she embraces her father, he wishes he were her father— indeed, if he were, he would not be less impious" (*Met.* 6.481–82). Tereus wishes to occupy the place of the father, as is symbolically the case with brides who pass from the control of fathers to their husbands. Her embarkation on the ship breaches the limits of 'landed femininity' and a sense of unease is transmitted in the text, as if the very fact of traveling tainted women with shades of danger and deviancy. Thus, as soon as they jump on the ship Tereus affirms that "he has won" and he does not turn his eyes away from her (*et nusquam lumen detorquet ab illa*, Met. 6.515). The simile that completes the characterization of Tereus's gaze involves an eagle looking down on its prey and controlling it with the sight (516–18), which brings forth issues of the verticality of the powerful gaze and recalls the controlling eyes of the hunter. The passage from land to sea embodies a transition between the world of the father's gaze and domain to the gaze and control of Tereus, her rapist. But it is only when Philomela has become a complete exile, when they arrive at Tereus's shores, that he accomplishes the rape. Being in a foreign land turns women vulnerable, but also, as the story will demonstrate, associates them with the unknown, the uncanny, and the abnormal.

Philomela, raped by her brother-in-law Tereus and silenced by him after he cuts out her tongue, finds resource in weaving to communicate her story to her sister Procne. By this means she also arrogates a gaze for herself, which substitutes for the words that she cannot pronounce. Philomela weaves "purple marks on a white background" (*purpureasque notas filis intexuit albis*, Met. 6.577). These marks are a clear symbol of violent sexual intercourse: Philomela sees herself as a white virgin surface (or page) that has been stained by rape. This accords well with some of the imagery that constructs her character. There is a peculiar simile used to describe the ravished Philomela where Ovid tells us that she is like a dove stained with its own blood: *utque columba suo madefactis sanguine plumis* (*Met.* 6.529).[59] Although it is true that not all *columbae* are necessarily white, the image of the white dove is a pervasive one in literature and we can therefore assume that a white bird is implied to favor the contrast with the drops of red blood. Let us remember here that the combination of red over white is a common one for virgins, as seen particularly in the blush of characters like Atalanta, Diana, Daphne, and Pygmalion's ivory maiden. Later in the narrative, Philomela has to 'recreate' her story to communicate it to her sister. This act of representation implies a previous act of reading and visualization of her own rape, a personal point of view. Marder recalls that "the text does not specify whether the weaving describes the rape through pictures or words. . . . The Latin word *notas*, translated as 'signs,' can mean marks of writing on a page, punctuation, perforation, as well as marks on a body, such as brand or tattoo and, by extension, a distinguishing mark of shame and disgrace."[60] The depiction of her story reproduces graphically the scene of rape. She was a white dove, a white background stained by the mark of man's violence. Philomela for her part stains the white cloth with purple signs. She reads her own rape as a combination of red over white; she reproduces it in the same way, and by narrating it she symbolically re-enacts it.[61] Interestingly, Ovid silences Philomela's version and replaces it with his own, but Procne can still read that silence in silence.

Philomela's story has commonly interested critics for its implications for female writing, voice, and power. Although this aspect is surely important, a different interpretative alternative that focuses on women as plastic artists and communicators through visual images will here be favored. This position is admittedly not entirely new: in Sophocles' lost tragedy *Tereus*, Philomela wove images and not text.[62] Some critics, like Nagle for example,[63] actually do recognize that this is a possibility but, probably because of the modern interest in metacritical issues, most students of Ovid prioritize what the episode has to say about writing and de-emphasize the importance of Philomela as plastic artist. When discussing the episode informally with other readers of the poem, I find it fascinating that they tend to say, "Oh, I always thought she wove pictures. Maybe I need to reread the text." This experience is illuminating because it shows that readers instinctively tend to think of the work of a woman weaver as visual rather than textual, although of course their response may be conditioned by the fact that most decorated cloths have pictures and not words. The text actually reads:

> . . . grande doloris
> ingenium est, miserisque venit sollertia rebus:
> stamina barbarica suspendit callida tela
> purpureasque notas filis intexuit albis,
> indicium sceleris; perfectaque tradidit uni,
> utque ferat dominae, gestu rogat; illa rogata
> pertulit ad Procnen nec scit, quid tradat in illis.
> evolvit vestes saevi matrona tyranni
> germanaeque suae †carmen† miserabile legit.

> Grief has great wit, and cunning comes in painful circumstances. She spread a barbarian web on her clever loom and interwove purple marks on the white background, evidence of the crime she had suffered. When it was finished she handed it to a slave and with a gesture asked her to bring it to her mistress. The servant, as she was asked to, brought it to

> Procne not knowing what she was carrying. The wife of the cruel tyrant
> unrolled the cloth and read her sister's tale. (*Met.* 6.574–82)

The tradition seems to identify Philomela's web with a form of writing.
Wheeler bases all his interpretation on writing and orality on *carmen* with
no mention of other possible readings of the passage.[64] Segal also sees
Philomela's tapestry as text and draws on the textual implications of her
work:

> Behind Philomela's weaving is Ovid's own web of words (*textus*) that
> recreates events which are spectacular for their suppression of speech.
> The *notae* of Philomela's weaving are virtually "letters" of a written mes-
> sage—in fact, a "song" or "poem," *carmen*, like the present one—which
> Procne "reads" (*legit*, 582), as if "unrolling" a scroll (581f.): *evolvit*
> *vestes.*[65]

However, Segal recognizes the visual power of Philomela's *phantasia* and
its reception by Procne: "Procne does not weep, for she has neither words
nor tears, but is totally absorbed in the 'image' that those 'purple marks'
have made her see (583–86)."[66]

While text is surely an important way of reading the tapestry, it limits
the scope of what Philomela's web has to offer and should be accompa-
nied by a reading of the cloth as visual images. This turns Procne into a
viewer who can appreciate the situation and read her sister's tapestry in a
visual way. The first question is raised by *notas*. While it is true that the
word may imply "letters," it may simply indicate "marks," and thus raises
the possibility of having pictorial images rather than letters. The text
quoted corresponds to most standard editions of *Metamorphoses* and reads
carmen miserabile legit. However, this version restricts the meaning of
Philomela's cloth to a written poem. Some editors have, however,
acknowledged the possibility that *carmen* is corrupt and suggested instead
readings like *fatum*, *crimen*, and *textum*.[67] While *textum* points in a similar
critical direction to *carmen*, other possibilities are opened by *crimen* and
fatum.[68] There is, some would argue, the problem of *legit*, but although it is
true that *lego* is most commonly used for reading, it is also used for seeing
or perusing with the sight, as in Virgil, *Aeneid* 6.755 and 6.34.[69]

As mentioned before, in Sophocles' lost tragedy *Tereus*, Philomela
seems to weave in pictures. If this is true, Philomela in *Metamorphoses*
may well be another plastic artist representing images in a cloth and in
this sense she would align with Arachne as both expose the tragedy of

rape. Now if Philomela is the artist, Procne is the reader-viewer whose gaze is placed on the image of her sister as object. Therefore, Philomela becomes not only the object of Tereus's lust and gaze but also the object of her sister's sight. The outcome is, however, very different. Procne as a woman looking at another woman does not objectify, control, and use her; she is instead able to comprehend what lies beyond the picture and empathize with her sister's feelings. Procne's gaze represents an oblique 'feminine' place, where she can look at the whole process of rape but without identifying with the male gaze. As viewer of the rape she can act upon it by rescuing her sister. While men looking at women in *Metamorphoses* seem to present a fairly constant pattern of reification, control, and power over the female image, women looking at women present more variety. The nymphs look at Arachne in admiration but with no desire of possession; Procne looks at (the picture of) Philomela with sympathy and sisterly feelings.

But Philomela is not only an object of the gaze; she acquires a gaze herself, for the tapestry shows her own vision, her own *phantasia* of what has occurred. We can then return to Forrester's question: what do women see? Philomela sees herself as a victim of violence, as a stained body that struggles to become visible despite the erasure of her (images) that the narrator performs. And the experience of the 'stained body' is a particularly feminine one that only women can truly comprehend and that Procne will be able to understand because "a picture is worth a thousand words."

Later on in the story, the centrality of the eyes is also prominent. Once Procne rescues her sister, Philomela, with a proper womanly conduct, does not want to look at her in shame of the 'crime' committed (605–6). But soon vengeance becomes a priority and the sisters plan a crime against the adulterer. It is remarkable that among the possible vengeances, Procne mentions: "*aut linguam atque oculos et quae tibi membra pudorem/ abstulerunt ferro rapiam*" / "'With a sword I will cut off his tongue, and also his eyes, and those parts which stole your honor'" (*Met.* 6.616–17). This sentence is remarkable, as it encompasses the three elements that constituted Tereus's offense and which belong to the traditional male domain. He had first raped her and used his own sexuality, of which Procne wishes to deprive him. Second, he has cut off Philomela's tongue and dispossessed her of speech and a good punishment would imply his own silencing. But Tereus has also committed the crime of seeing and desiring the forbidden and therefore he deserves to have his eyes torn out. He will be visually castrated and thus deprived of his phallic gaze. Furthermore, the women undergo a gradual transformation from objects to be looked at to viewers; thus Procne soon places her eyes on her son Itys, whom she will later control and destroy: *quid possit, ab illo/ admonita est oculisque tuens inmitibus "a! quam es similis patri!"/* "His presence suggested what she could do, and looking at him with harsh eyes she said: 'Alas, how much you look like your father!'" (*Met.* 6.620–22). This identification of Itys with the father is noteworthy if one recalls that the physical resemblance of the son to his father is a vital component in the ideology of the Roman family (cf. Catullus 61.214–15 and Hor. *Odes* 4.5.23 for examples). Itys is visually identified with the father, and Procne in a perverted way can look at him and exercise the power of her eyes on the child as a surrogate for the husband. A gender subversion is here realized, although an incomplete one. It is the woman who can look at the male, but she can do it only perhaps because Itys is a child. Something similar occurs in the myth of Medea, who kills her children to attack her husband. Despite the standard feminist views on the story pointing at women's empowerment, it is worth wondering to what extent this power is attained. In the end, Procne and Philomela cannot attack Tereus directly but need a weaker and more vulnerable target in the person of Itys.

So, what has happened to Philomela? At the end of the story, Ovid presents her as a monster, dripping blood from her criminal hands. From the beautiful maiden at the beginning of the tale, a delight for the male gaze, she has become a sort of Fury: *sicut erat sparsis furiali caede capillis/* "As she was, with her streaming hair drenched with the blood of the mad carnage" (*Met.* 6.657). But she is still a spectacle, which, with its image, terrifies the onlooker and enthralls him at the same time. She is also similar to Perseus when she hangs Itys' head to provoke horror in the father. Instead of a symbolically beheaded woman, with no voice and no eyes, she has now beheaded a man, or rather his surrogate, a potent metaphor for Tereus's castration. Many metamorphoses have already been accomplished at this point, but the most physically obvious one is yet to come. All three actors are turned into birds, an appropriate punishment for their crimes. Nonetheless, it is interesting that these two exiled women end up flying, an extremely mobile activity, and are made capable of leaving land at their pleasure and moving around in the skies as far as they like. The earlier act of leaving the fatherland is now taken one step forward when the women literally leave the earth.

"What do women see?" What can we know about women's gazes from this episode? Viewing and gender are central elements of the story and the tale gives a gaze to women, especially Philomela, who, from static object of a man's gaze to agent of revenge, can create images through textile and give her version of what has happened—against the false version narrated to Procne by Tereus. There are two general points which apply to

Philomela's tapestry and that are, at a more general level, qualities of the 'female gaze.' As seen in chapter 2, perhaps precisely because women cannot look 'straight,' they are forced to find alternative and 'oblique' ways of looking and knowing. This was exemplified in Juno's 'suspicion.' Philomela with her tapestry invites a 'suspicious' gaze in her sister. Her textile does not seem to provide straightforward information but rather to give hints that the sister needs to decode. Philomela also believes that "meaning is realized in the acts of reading and viewing." In this respect the insistence on *indicia* is relevant. First, it is said that Philomela's *os mutum facti caret indice* / "Her speechless lips could give no indication of what had happened" (*Met.* 6.574) and then that the tapestry provides an *indicium sceleris* / "indication of the crime" (*Met.* 6.578). The verb *indico* means to "show, indicate or point out," but *indicium* always suggests a signal, a warning or *indicator* that opens the doors to a discovery but which also begs for further decodification and illumination of a larger picture. The smoke coming out of a back yard is an *indicium* that someone is preparing a barbeque, or that the shed is on fire. But in any case this *indicium* invites us to forge a *phantasia* and complete the information in the imagination. This is in fact what Philomela achieves. She provides hints and indicators and stimulates a creative interpretation in her sister that forces her to 'suspect,' to see beyond the appearances. Just as Tereus severs Philomela's tongue and with it her power of speech, Ovid seems to suppress her capacity of visual representation, for he does not let the reader 'see' her tapestry directly—as he did with Arachne and Minerva—but dispatches her weaving in two lines. So Philomela's *indicia* are also hints to the female reader to arouse her curiosity and try to recover in her imagination the contents of Philomela's tapestry. Thus one quality of the 'female gaze' is this capacity to incite 'suspicion' and to stimulate viewers to complete visions from a few *indicia*. Women as viewers and creators construct visual imagery with a female audience in mind, an audience that, they know, will be able to 'suspect' and find what is behind the appearances.

The second point about the female gaze in the story has to do with a particular endowment: its capacity to 'witness.' Feminist critics, like Kaplan, hold that "women can return the gaze but they cannot act on it." But thinking of the gaze of women as being able to witness and record experiences effectively may offer an alternative to this statement. Philomela's tapestry gives testimony of what she has undergone and by bearing witness it provokes action in her reader. So, while the story does not have a very edifying ending for women, it still provides—if only momentarily—a female gaze. It allows Philomela to inscribe her story in the book of *Metamorphoses* and to incite a response in her sister to 'suspect' and interpret what cannot be seen. Philomela witnessing her story will be an important model that the gaze of other women in the poem will follow.

To conclude, just like Arachne, Philomela takes up weaving not to comply with ideals of femininity but to assume 'unfeminine' prerogatives: the power to signify through weaving and to articulate her own 'voice.' She is doomed, but like other weavers in the poem, she is able to leave an indelible mark in *Metamorphoses* and to give a glimpse of 'what women see.' Thus Philomela stands as a good example that can challenge the assumption that women can "return the gaze but cannot act on it." It might be true that faced with a man looking at her directly, a woman becomes passive, yet by being witness and communicating stories of women to others, especially other women, she always achieves some effect; in Philomela's case, a very concrete one: vengeance and punishment. While many males perform acts of violence in the poem and get away with impunity, women may not always get away with acting directly, as in the case of Procne and Philomela, but at least they can witness, record, and communicate.

CHAPTER FIVE

&

Women for
Women, Women
by Women

. . . facies non omnibus una,
non diversa tamen, qualem decet esse sororum.

They don't all have the same look, yet not dissimilar, as it should be for
sisters. (*Met.* 2.13–14)

M ost of *Metamorphoses* is narrated by a masculine authorial persona,
which for the sake of simplicity has here been referred to as
'Ovid.'[1] Nevertheless, Ovid's hexameter poem has several internal narrators and even third-degree narrators already included in an internal narration. This is a highly problematic issue, for much has been said about
the narrator of *Metamorphoses*. Some would argue that there is a single
narrator throughout the poem, while others would argue for many voices;
others try to find a middle ground. Readers have always found it difficult
to read embedded stories in *Metamorphoses* and other texts. The crucial
question seems to lie in deciding whether to see the internal narratives as
productions of a greater 'unique' and omnipresent authorial figure or to
give these narratives and their narrators independence and a value free
from the authority of the external author.[2] Again, the question is whether
to adopt a resisting or a releasing reading.

    Metamorphoses includes about forty internal narrators who narrate sixty
episodes. Of these numerous narrators only fourteen are female (Cornix,
an unnamed daughter of Minyas, her sisters Leuconoe and Alcithoe, the
Pierides, an unidentified muse, Calliope, Arethusa, Alcmene, Iole, Venus,
Galatea, the Sibyl, and Circe's *famula*), two are unidentified, and the rest

are male.[3] Statistics, however, may be deceiving, for female narratives occupy very large portions of the text (e.g., the Minyeides: half of Book 4, and Calliope: half of Book 5). While the weight of masculine voices is larger, occupying more lines than the discourses of women, women's voices are still very audible and their visual constructions very 'visible.' The main concern of this book is with women, and therefore this chapter will concentrate only on female narratives in the search for a female gaze and a female voice. Aspects of male narratives have been alluded to in previous chapters, but a full discussion of male-authored narratives is beyond the scope of this study.[4]

The debate over the interrelations, precedence, and independence between the main narratorial voice and imbedded narrators is particularly germane when dealing with stories told by female characters. As with *Heroides*: is it possible to separate the voices of women from the male authorial voice? In a resisting approach to the text, it is not. Female discourses will always be impregnated by the masculinity of the author. In a releasing reading, the reader is allowed to question his authority and consider female narrators as authorial figures in their own right.[5] While the ensuing discussion will try to avoid being completely one-sided, this chapter, by its very nature, is predominantly an exercise in releasing reading. Although it is undeniable that the author's voice is felt throughout behind the female voices, the very nature of the poem admits the possibility of shifting narrators; thus we can relieve women's utterances from the male authorial weight.

The *phantasiae* that women create with words presuppose a previous gaze, whether this is a 'real' vision evoked in the imagination or simply an imaginary experience. Women's production of visual images through discourse provides a way of entering the domain of the female gaze. This chapter studies the visual (and other) constructions that women create in their narratives as expressions of their gaze. However, the reader will note that although the primary focus is the gaze in relation to images woven with words, voice, and image will be constantly interlinked. Some episodes that were explored in previous chapters will now be assessed specifically as products of the female imagination. When women represent visually (whether on actual canvas or in their mind's eye), they usually do it for a female internal audience, although a few episodes, like the Sibyl and Venus, have male listeners. The audience of these images will also be a primary concern, since receptors of visual constructions play an important role both in the design and effects of the images and even provide hints about the reactions of external readers.

A Gathering of Weavers

Although weaving is a central aspect of the daughters of Minyas, their apparent means of expression is verbal, which is why they deserve a place in this and not the previous chapter. Nonetheless, as Rosati has shown, the visual and the textual are constantly interlaced in the tale: just as weaving is a metaphor for narrating, narrating can also be a metaphor for weaving.[6] Therefore both facets always need to be kept in mind when dealing with the stories of the Minyeides.

Book 4 begins with the daughters of Minyas who resist the divinity of Bacchus. While the whole town joins the Bacchic revel, these women stay at home weaving and telling stories. Their narratives expand through half of Book 4 and comprise the tales of Pyramus and Thisbe, Mars and Venus, Leucothoe and Clytie, and Salmacis and Hermaphroditus. As was mentioned in the previous chapter, behind every act of female speech and communicative weaving lies a latent subversive mode, for the female voice itself is felt as something both transgressive and inadequate. A woman's speech in itself, regardless of what she says, is often a claim to have a voice, a struggle for power. So the daughters of Minyas stay at home and weave believing that this is what 'proper' women do, but they deconstruct this 'virtue' by the very act of telling stories. One can then observe a contradiction and a gender struggle from the beginning of the tale. They want to stay in and be 'good women,' so they choose weaving, without realizing that this in itself is only a signifier of proper femininity if they remain silent (or chatter but without signifying). Instead, in their storytelling they claim a voice for themselves, speech being a masculine prerogative par excellence, as Telemachus indicates in the *Odyssey*. These interactions and battles between femininity and masculinity, activity and passivity, will be a constant undercurrent in the stories they tell and in the expression of their own visions. We will suggest here that one of the main characteristics of the Minyeides is fear of mingling, diversity, and change, which involves a conservative outlook that denies the power of Bacchus and which could be seen as the extreme opposite to metamorphosis (despite the fact that they are commonly seen as an alter ego of the poet). The gaze in these tales is not only a concrete act of seeing but also a way of knowing, understanding, and comprehending the world.

In these gender conflicts, the roles of the gods in the passage are meaningful. On the one hand, there is Bacchus, with all his sexual complexity; on the other hand, although she does not appear directly in the action, Minerva is also central. The text describes how when the women in town follow the Bacchic celebrations, they leave their weaving behind (*Met.*

4.9–10). By way of contrast, the daughters of Minyas stay at home weaving:

> . . . solae Minyeides intus
> intempestiva turbantes festa Minerva
> aut ducunt lanas aut stamina pollice versant
> aut haerent telae famulasque laboribus urguent.

> Only the daughters of Minyas stay inside, marring the festival with the untimely tasks of Minerva. They spin wool or turn the threads with their fingers, or cling to their webs and urge the slave-girls to work. (*Met.* 4.32–35)

Then when the stories are about to begin Alcithoe says:

> "dum cessant aliae commentaque sacra frequentant,
> nos quoque, quas Pallas, melior dea, detinet" inquit.
> "utile opus manuum vario sermone levemus."

> "While the other women are idle and celebrate a false festival," she said, "let us also, who worship Pallas, a better goddess, lighten the useful work of our hands with varied conversation." (*Met.* 4.37–39)

This antagonistic presentation of Dionysus and Pallas is significant. While Bacchus is the god of celebration, Minerva is identified with working and household tasks. Further, Minerva rules over things ἔνδον, while Dionysus's domain is the ἔξω. However, both gods are at some level sexually problematic. Dionysus is a male, but a very effeminate one, and Minerva is a goddess who is tightly linked with the father and masculinity in her role as warrior. The fundamental difference between them here is that Minerva is adamantly opposed to sexual mingling while Dionysus foments it. The alliance of the Minyeides with Minerva is also meaningful because it adds to the problematization of weaving as a feminine signifier. They, too, while striving to be purely feminine by staying at home like house-bound women, endeavor to have a voice and a gaze, which are not traditional feminine prerogatives.

PYRAMUS AND THISBE

The first tale that they narrate is the doomed love of Pyramus and Thisbe. All the stories of the Minyeides tend to support their decision to stay inside and be 'proper women.'[7] These stories, as Anderson recognizes, are also irreverent because they problematize the merits and dignity of gods and human beings.[8] Catherine Campbell Rhorer has shown how the color implications of red and white in the story of Pyramus and Thisbe stage erotic struggles between sex and purity.[9] For example, Thisbe arrives under the tree that bears snow-white berries (*arbor ibi niveis uberrima pomis*, Met. 4.89). One can see the white fruits as symbols of the young couple's virginity and sexual immaturity. Thisbe, while waiting for her love, escapes a lioness whose mouth drips blood from a victim (*venit ecce recenti/ caede leaena boum spumantis oblita rictus/* "Look, here comes a lioness, her foaming jaws dripping with the blood of recently slain cattle," Met. 4.96–97).[10] Abandoning the place, the heroine leaves her cloak under the mulberry. The lioness bites it and stains it with blood (*inventos forte sine ipsa/ ore cruentato tenues laniavit amictus/* "It so happened that she found the cloak without the girl and tore it to pieces with her bloody jaws," Met. 4.103–4). The light garment is an obvious synecdoche for the girl herself. Although the text does not give a precise color definition of the cloak, it conveys that it is 'stainable' and thus probably of a light hue— otherwise, it would not make such a horrifying spectacle in Pyramus's eyes (Met. 4.107–8). Still, it is described as *tenues amictus* and thus it is possible to envision an association with the hymen here.[11] In a somewhat fetishistic reaction, Pyramus grabs the cloak, takes it to the tree, and weeps on it. The white tree and the light cloth may be seen as symbols of the virgin. Tears are associated with ejaculation in male sexuality and there are cases when the *mentula* is said to weep.[12] Thus Pyramus's weeping on the light cloth, a metonymy for her white body, under the white tree is sexually charged. Even more significant is his desire to 'stain' the garment himself with his own blood (*"accipe nunc" inquit "nostri quoque sanguinis/ haustus!"/* "'Receive now a draught of my blood too,'" Met. 4.118). Here the drinking metaphor is linked to sexual imagery, as it is the case in the Ceres episode in Book 5. Now Pyramus's own blood has smeared the cloak, now he is the one to color 'her.' With this begins an aetiological story, that of the mulberry, whose fruits turned from snow-white to purple:

> arborei fetus adspergine caedis in atram
> vertuntur faciem, madefactaque sanguine radix
> purpureo tinguit pendentia mora colore.

> The fruits of the tree turn black with the sprinkling of the blood and the roots drenched in purple blood color the hanging berries. (Met. 4.125–27)

Purpureo colore is relevant because purple is associated with Bacchus in *Met.* 3.556. Most peculiar also is the commonly condemned (Segal calls it "bathetic"[13]) metaphor of the pipe bursting for Pyramus's self-performed wound where the verb *eiaculatur* is potent:

> ut iacuit resupinus humo, cruor emicat alte
> non aliter, quam cum vitiato fistula plumbo
> scinditur et tenui stridente foramine longas
> eiaculatur aquas atque ictibus aera rumpit.

> As he lies with his back on the ground, the blood spouts up high, just as when a pipe breaks due to rusty lead and spouts up long streams of water through a small hissing hole and breaks into the air with its jets. (*Met.* 4.121–24)

Anderson argues that because this, and possibly *Fasti* 1.270, are the first appearances of the verb, possible sexual connotations are misguided and anachronistic.[14] But if one thinks about the image of his body bursting in springs of blood in the erotic context of a story where the ultimate goal is lovemaking, the simile cannot but imply an unfortunately displaced sexual discharge. Besides, both Segal and Hinds believe that in the word *ictus* there is a latent idea of male ejaculation, reminiscent of the Lucretian passage where *ictus* is used in this sense (*DRN* 4.1049–53).[15]

This is a tale of errors, of love forbidden and displaced, where the protagonists, as Barkan affirms, suffer from "perceptual confusion" and where the object of love appears as metonymy in other objects.[16] Now when Thisbe returns to the place, the metaphoric sexual union in color is completed with her death. Her first realization of the situation is deeply significant in terms of color. The text reads: *quae postquam vestemque suam cognovit et ense/ vidit ebur vacuum . . . /* "After she recognized her own cloak and saw the ivory scabbard empty of the sword . . ." (*Met.* 4.147–48). The scabbard from which the sword has been drawn is of ivory, an epitome of whiteness. Pyramus's weapon, a metaphoric instrument of male sexuality, has been kept while inactive in a white case, which accords well with the imagery of sexual purity and virginity. Further in the story, Thisbe decides to share the sword "still warm with her lover's death" (*Met.* 4.163).[17] The text gives away the aetiological formula in Thisbe's words:

> at tu quae ramis arbor miserabile corpus
> nunc tegis unius, mox es tectura duorum,

signa tene caedis pullosque et luctibus aptos
semper habe fetus, gemini monimenta cruoris.

But you, wretched tree that now shade one body with your branches,
soon you will cover two. Keep the marks of our death and always have
your fruits dark, fit for mourning, a memorial of our double death.
(Met.4.158–61)

Thisbe's interpretation of the color of the mulberry is death, as she sees
it as black or very dark, and she associates the color with the imagery of
mourning and the funeral. However, the mulberry is not an absolute black
but rather a very deep dark purple, especially, as it has been tinted with
blood. It is outstanding at this point that the text identifies this as the
color of mature, ripe fruits: *nam color in pomo est, ubi permaturuit, ater* / "For
black is the color of the fruit when it is ripe" (*Met.* 4.165). This detail aids
in the interpretation of purple as the color of sexual maturity.[18] While at
the beginning of the story their affection may be said to be more immature, the desire and sexual implications of the metaphors at play mark a
clear, though doomed, passage to adulthood. In the tale of Pyramus and
Thisbe the combination of red and white functions as a metaphoric—
even displaced—form of sexual intercourse. The light cloak and the
white scabbard, the white tree before their encounter and their shedding
of blood by death act as a symbolic deflowering that stains the white.
Sexual maturity and the loss of virginity are finally embodied in the transformation of the fruits of the mulberry, from white to red.

Interestingly, it is their purity that the Minyeides strive to preserve
without mingling with the god of wine. Bacchus identifies with the deep
purple of the grapes (*uvae*, *Met.* 4.14) and the Minyeides with the white
of purity they pretend to have, thus making the name of the second narrator, Leuconoe, significant. In this sense, the change of the mulberry's
color from white to purple embodies what the Minyeides reject, the mingling with Bacchus and their own transformation into 'stained women.'
The tree is thus the visual emblem of the story. Its transformation is what
matters to the narrator, as it is exactly what the sister is set out to narrate
(*Met.* 4.51–52).

The meanings of the story of Pyramus and Thisbe go even further in
their links to the ideology of the daughters of Minyas. Both lovers, who are
confined to the house, and especially the girl, make a transgressive move
towards the outside, the wilderness.[19] First, the text insists on the impor-

tance of walls and dividing lines (*Met.* 4.57–58). City walls and the walls of the house are precisely what Pyramus and Thisbe will break through to be together. The emphasis on the house is also apparent in the repetition of the word *domus*; there is likewise a constant insistence on the semantic field of roofs and coverings, which Segal interprets as the shelter of childhood, away from which the lovers move.[20] This contrasts with the stubborn desire of the Minyeides to stay at home and not follow the passionate world of the god. Furthermore, the lovers cheat their guardian and traverse the doors, which are emblematic limits between inside and outside, chastity and sexuality, propriety and crime. The verb describing the exit from the house is *egredior* (94), which is the same verb used for Medea leaving her house in Book 7 (*egreditur tectis vestes induta recinctas /* "She leaves the house dressed in loose robes," *Met.* 7.182), in a line that bears profound echoes of deviancy as well as sexual openness. The lover, who goes out of the city and the house, will 'mingle' in symbolic sex and be doomed. With this story the Minyeides justify their closure inside the house.

What kind of gazes are present here? Whom does the narrator focalize with? There is not a 'straightforward' identification here as in the episode of Apollo and Daphne, for example. The narrator tells us that both youths were pretty (*iuvenum pulcherrimus alter,/ altera, quas Oriens habuit, praelata puellis/* "He was the most beautiful of all youths, she was the loveliest among the girls of the East," *Met.*4.55–56). But the narrator also does not stop and dwell on the physical description. This is a gaze that does not reify—at this moment—the image, but in fact lets the narration flow. While the lovers are finally fixed in the static metaphor of the mulberry, they are fixed together, preserving the sexual 'balance' that had been developed. To say that the gaze of this narrator is 'male' or 'female' would be rather reductive, for the gaze here shifts and fluctuates. The first narrator permits the flow of images and treats the female and the male in similar ways (in terms of power relations) and does not focalize specifically with any of the characters at all times, but rather sees the story as an observer who can look at the scene from varied viewpoints. This is a gaze that does not look from the conventional place of the male perspective that aligns with the male oppressive eyes; rather, it displaces and fragments the look toward a series of erotic objects. Male readers are forced to redirect their gaze and not align only with a unique male gaze, while women readers find a different place from where to view the scene which is neither identification with the male gaze, nor deprivation of aesthetic pleasure, but an appreciation of the scene from a plurality of viewpoints.

MARS AND VENUS

This brief tale by Leuconoe of the affairs of Mars and Venus also acts as a justification of the morality of the Minyeides. The Sun, the god who sees everything first, saw the lovers (*primus adulterium Veneris cum Marte putatur, / hic vidisse deus; videt hic deus omnia primus /* "It is thought that this god saw the affair of Mars and Venus first, this god sees everything first," *Met.* 4.172) and told Vulcan, Venus's husband. The Sun here recalls many telltale characters in the poem, such as the birds in Book 2. Vulcan fashioned a net of thin threads of bronze to capture the adulterous lovers:

> . . . at illi
> et mens et quod opus fabrilis dextra tenebat
> excidit: extemplo graciles ex aere catenas
> retiaque et laqueos, quae lumina fallere possent,
> elimat. non illud opus tenuissima vincant
> stamina, non summo quae pendet aranea tigno;
> utque levis tactus momentaque parva sequantur,
> efficit et lecto circumdata collocat arte.

> But his spirit failed him, and the work he was fashioning fell from his hands. Immediately he forges slender chains of bronze and bonds that can cheat the eyes. Neither the finest threads would surpass that work, nor the threads that the spider weaves from the ceiling beam. He made the web in such a way that it would yield to a slight touch and a small movement, and he spread it artfully around the bed. (*Met.* 4.174–81)

Vulcan's web unavoidably recalls the weaving of the Minyeides and their condition of being creators. He is the bringer of morality and nemesis for passionate crimes in the story. Like Vulcan, the Minyeides wish to 'catch' morality with their weaving. But Vulcan is a laughingstock, as in a way the Minyeides will be when they are transformed into bats. Vulcan has a sort of Cyclopean character in his problematic hypermasculinity. As Ernest Kris and Otto Kurz show, plastic artists in antiquity were looked down on as craftsmen, social inferiors, one of the likely reasons being that they worked with their hands. Therefore, "one must be prepared to assume, as Zilsel does, that all the insults, malign gossip, and mild contempt to which Homer's Hephaestus was subject are attributable to the fact that this highly artistic metal-worker labored with his hands."[21] In Ovid, Vulcan is the forger of metal, but he is often cheated by his beautiful consort in a way that recalls the relationship between Juno and Jupiter.

Likewise his epithet *mulciber*, "the softener," lends a somewhat delicate hue to his character. No matter how successful Vulcan's vengeance is, he still remains embarrassed by Venus and in this he suffers some sort of demasculinization, seen symbolically when his work falls from his hands (*Met.* 4.175–76). Finally, the intercourse of Mars and Venus that both Vulcan and the Minyeides oppose functions as an appropriate metaphor for all the mingling involved in the Dionysiac ritual.

While the narrator and the reader/viewer see the adulterous pair humiliated and trapped in the net, despite Vulcan's effort to turn the scene into a comic spectacle (*Met.* 4.185–86), we do not really see much because the lovers are not described in detail; instead we only hear that they were caught in their embrace (*Met.* 4.184). But curiously, by the very act of narrating how the Sun told the tale to Vulcan, the Minyeides are telling it to us and in this sense they become *delatores* as well.

LEUCOTHOE AND CLYTIE

The next story of the Minyeides involves precisely the vengeance of Venus: the Sun falls in love. As seen in chapter 3, the Minyeides identify with Leucothoe in her whiteness and fixation as a proper virgin who spins in a scene that alludes to Lucretia's purity in Ovid and Livy. The circle of the slaves weaving around Leucothoe (*Met.* 4.220–21) is a doublet for the Minyeides spinning and telling stories. Yet to this apparent innocence of Leucothoe, one passing comment is puzzling:

> at virgo, quamvis inopino territa visu
> victa nitore dei posita vim passa querella est.

> But the maiden, though terrified by the unexpected vision of the god and overwhelmed by his radiance, endured the god's violence without complaint. (*Met.* 4.232–33)

What does *posita querella* imply? Is this a voluntary act of surrender?[22] If so, perhaps the Minyeides are condemning her behavior. Leucothoe, who was before chaste like them, has willingly surrendered to the power of a god, while they still oppose one with strength. There is one further point of significance in the story. Leucothoe's defeat by the god is symbolized by the fall and loss of her weaving (*et colus et fusus digitis cecidere remissis*/ "Both distaff and spindle fell from her heedless fingers," *Met.* 4.229). The loss of power, as with Vulcan, is envisioned as something significant falling from a character's arms.[23] Leucothoe drops her weaving, thus showing defeat. In contrast, the Minyeides cling to their threads to the end and they even become part of their transformation (Met. 4.389–90 and 394–98).

Thus the Minyeides paint Leucothoe as an example of what a woman may suffer when she 'loosens' herself. Paradoxically, the ones who end up lost and completely overcome by Bacchus are the Minyeides themselves, although curiously they are not forced to participate in the Bacchic celebrations. The fate of a woman, again, "hangs from a thin thread"—a particularly apt metaphor for weavers. While complete sexual availability is condemned, a woman must know when to give in to the power of a male god. This is precisely the root of the Minyeides' transformation. They wish to impose their own vision and end up blinded. The gaze in the story seems to focalize partly with a male gaze, as both Leucothoe and Clytie are fixed as visual objects. But the very fact that Venus has provoked the god's love and that he is virtually impotent to save his beloved turns this male gaze into something more complex than it appears at first, where identifications are constantly shifting and often undermined.

SALMACIS AND HERMAPHRODITUS

This last story of the Minyeides is told by Alcithoe. Before she opens her tale, Alcithoe's femininity is asserted by the insistence on her weaving (*quae radio stantis percurrens stamina telae* / "who, running her shuttle through the threads of the upright loom . . . ," Met. 4.275). Again, she introduces a *praeteritio*, which includes several stories of metamorphosis. The first few that she mentions have to do with gender bending and gender reversal (Met. 4.277–89). This preoccupation with gender destabilizations and mingling appeared at the beginning of Book 4, where the text explained that all mothers and servant women alike join the festival (Met. 4.9) and that they dance with the satyrs (Met. 4.25); we hear the mixed voices of women and youths (Met. 4.28–29). The Dionysian orgy upsets gender and social boundaries by creating chaos in the eyes of the daughters of Minyas. What is more, in the first description of the Bacchic revel the participants are described as follows: *turba ruit, mixtaeque viris matresque nurusque/ vulgusque proceresque ignota ad sacra feruntur/* "A crowd rushes on, both mothers and daughters-in-law mingled with men, commons and nobles are driven to the unknown rites" (Met. 3.529–30). At last, Alcithoe decides to tell the story of the fountain of Salmacis (Met. 4.285–87).

What the daughters of Minyas fear is a mingling of the sexes. The irony is that what they fear is something that they actually represent because they weave *and* speak at the same time. In her description of Salmacis as an unvirginal nymph, Alcithoe also shows her novelty with regard to previous pictures of nymphs presented by Ovid; in this one may even note a certain irreverence toward and independence from the overarching author. But Salmacis' gaze is also problematic and complex; in a way, like Hermaphroditus, she mingles in her desire aspects of masculinity and femininity. While she actively sees and turns Hermaphroditus into the object of her eyes, she also looks at herself with a 'male gaze' when she regards her image in the mirror as well as when she desires to be looked at by the boy (*nec ante . . . /quam circumspexit amictus,/ et finxit vultum et meruit formosa videri/* "Not before she arranged her robes and composed her face, and deserved to look beautiful . . . ," *Met.* 4.317–19). Alcithoe introduces Hermaphroditus with a visual image of indefinition. Not only is he a *puer*, but also it is said that *cuius erat facies, in qua materque paterque/ cognosci possent/* "In his face you could recognize his father and his mother" (*Met.* 4.290–91). The fact that Hermaphroditus bears the marks of mother and father in his face, points to the forthcoming mingling of masculinity and femininity in the story. His very name is also a conflation of his father's and mother's (Hermes and Aphrodite).[24] Gender instability marks the boy long before the introduction of Salmacis into the story; indeed, his feminine characteristics are notable from birth.[25] Furthermore, the effeminacy of a male is a visual mark of Bacchus who is said to be an eternal *puer* (*Met.* 4.18) and to have a "virginal face" (*tibi, cum sine cornibus adstas,/ virgineum caput est/* "Your head is virginal when you stand without your horns," *Met.* 4.19–20), a feature already introduced by Acoetes in Book 3 (*utque putat, praedam deserto nactus in agro,/ virginea puerum ducit per litora forma* / "Having found a prize (so he thought) in a deserted field, he brings with him a boy of virginal beauty to the shore," *Met.* 3.606–7) and in the very words of Bacchus referring to himself (*quae gloria vestra est?/ si puerum iuvenes, si multi fallitis unum?/* "What is your glory if being young men you cheat a boy, if, many in number, you deceived just one?" *Met.* 3.655). The whole Bacchic celebration is viewed in *Metamorphoses* and other contexts as effeminate and devirilizing. In Book 3 Pentheus wonders why youths have left their arms to take up the thyrsus (*Met.* 3.541–42). Likewise, the virility of Bacchus himself is traditionally questionable, a trait expressed in *Metamorphoses* through the eyes of Pentheus, the 'macho' proud of his masculinity (*Met.*3.553–56).

Spencer believes that Pentheus must be about thirty years old, for in his dispute with Bacchus he assumes the position of an elder against a *puer*.[26] There is, however, no concrete evidence to maintain that

Pentheus is thirty years old; his immaturity, his almost adolescent eager-
ness to see in Euripides, and his inexperience in handling these matters
make him look younger. We may argue that Pentheus tries to show himself as a grown-up by treating Bacchus like a *puer*. The fact that both Bacchus and Hermaphroditus are called *puer* and that attention is drawn to
the beauty of their faces creates identification between them. For her
part, Salmacis represents all the visual sensuality identified with the
Dionysian revel that the Minyeides strive to avoid in their stubborn
'matronhood.' Everyone in town is seduced by Bacchus's beauty, and he
becomes an object of visual admiration: *tu formosissimus alto/ conspiceris
caelo/* "You shine the fairest in the lofty sky" (*Met.* 4.18–19). It is precisely this visual fascination that seduces the other women, but not the
Minyeides. In the same way, Salmacis, the hypersensuous female, is
seduced by the beauty of the *puer* Hermaphroditus (*Met.* 4.316). Salmacis
succumbs to what the daughters of Minyas will not.

But just like the Minyeides, Salmacis is a sexually ambiguous character
who wavers between being an object of the gaze—she tries to make of
herself an attractive visual object (*Met.* 4.318–19)—and having an intrusive gaze. The reactions of Hermaphroditus to the nymph's declaration of
love are those of a modest, blushing virgin (*Met.*4.329–30).[27] His blush
may be assimilated to the color combination in the mulberry, which
emblematized the Minyeides' fear of mingling with Bacchus. The red of
the blush is viewed as the color of apples, but more poignant is the reference to the painted ivory. It is the boy here who is 'painted': he is the
white board to be colored by the thought of love and by the gaze of a
desiring woman. The image is enhanced by the reference to his *eburnea
colla* in line 335 (cf. Narcissus in *Met.* 3.422), which Salmacis strives to
embrace. Then Hermaphroditus persuades her to retire and she leaves the
pool for his enjoyment. But when the boy, having disposed of all his
clothes, jumps naked in the fountain, the nymph cannot control her
desire at the sight of his naked body. It is here that a most eloquent simile
takes place:

> desilit in latices alternaque bracchia ducens
> in liquidis translucet aquis, ut eburnea si quis
> signa tegat claro vel candida lilia vitro.

> He jumps in the water and, swimming with alternating movement of his
> arms, he shines through the clear water, as if someone were to encase
> ivory figures or white lilies in clear glass. (*Met.* 4.353–55)

The body of the *puer* has the whiteness of ivory or lilies and it is this image that arouses Salmacis' desire. One may again think of the fragility of white, the 'stainable' character of ivory, and the 'virginal' weakness of flowers. But the image of ivory looks forward to Pygmalion's maiden and in some sense converts Hermaphroditus into an artefact. The end of the story is well known: Salmacis violently wraps herself around the boy like a serpent and they become one forever—a mixture of man and woman, neither one nor the other. This is precisely what the daughters of Minyas fear, yet, paradoxically, in the very act of telling Hermaphoditus's story they assume a nonfeminine stance, because they not only 'speak,' they also 'look.'

The story portrays a woman who is seduced by the world of sensuality and beauty. She cannot resist the attraction of a *puer* with a beautiful face. Salmacis and Hermaphoditus are a sort of doublet for the Minyeides and Bacchus. Bacchus is also a beautiful boy whose gender definition is problematic and who merges in himself the female and the male. To fall into such a passion is dangerous and entails the loss of proper gender and sexual boundaries, which the Minyeides so wholeheartedly strive to preserve. Salmacis' doom and disintegration as a woman confirm and support the decision of the Minyeides to stay in the house and not to succumb to Bacchus's charms.

Focalization in the story seems to be achieved through Salmacis who reifies the boy. She appears to have a 'male gaze.' Therefore, the narrator who looks with Salmacis also possesses a 'male gaze.' In this she once more transgresses the limits of traditional femininity that in appearance she tried to defend. But in view of the failure of Salmacis' gaze, one is allowed to question whether this is the right way of looking for a woman. Likewise, this failure of Salmacis' gaze may be telling the reader that we should not look at the *puer* Bacchus either or we will get 'lost' like Salmacis.

The narrative gathering of the daughters of Minyas ends with their transformation into bats, a change that displays their stubbornness to an extreme. They reject leaving the house, and there they will stay forever (*tectaque, non silvas celebrant lucemque perosae/ nocte volant seroque tenent a vespere nomen/* "They frequent the houses, not the woods, and hating light they fly at night; and have the name of the late evening," *Met.* 4.414–15). They are also fixed as creatures of the night. The setting of the scene of transformation at twilight stages the liminality of the new beings they have become (*Met.* 4.399–401), a liminality that may also express their gender instability. Interestingly, they cling to their weaving to the end, but in their transformation they lose their capacity for articulate speech, emitting only a thin squeak (*levi stridore*, 413). Transformation not only silences these women, but also leaves them in the dark. The metaphorical incapacity to recognize Bacchus as a god is extended to the fact that bats prefer the darkness of night. This visual rejection of Bacchic visual imagery is well exemplified when they escape from the phenomenon that is overtaking their house: *diversaeque locis ignes ac lumina vitant,/ dumque petunt tenebras/* "In various directions they flee the light and fires, while they seek darkness "(*Met.* 4.406–7). Relevant as well is the transformation of their weaving. Ovid does not tell what the Minyeides weave, whether it is some kind of clothing or a tapestry. It is, however, purple and Ovid uses the same language that he employs later for Philomela's, Arachne's, and Minerva's cloths (*telae, fila, stamina*):[28]

> resque fide maior, coepere virescere telae
> inque hederae faciem pendens frondescere vestis;
> pars abit in vites, et quae modo fila fuerunt,
> palmite mutantur; de stamine pampinus exit;
> purpura fulgorem pictis adcommodat uvis.

> A greater thing than you would believe: their threads began to turn green and the hanging cloth was covered by leaves and acquired the appearance of ivy. A part becomes grape-vines, and what were once threads turned into tendrils. From the warp shoot vine leaves and purple adapts to the radiance of colored grapes. (*Met.* 4.394–98)

The text does not actually say whether the weaving had images or whether it was a more conventional 'silent' cloth, but its transformation into grapes together with the loquacity of the daughters of Minyas supports the possibility that the sisters wove pictures and thus expressed their voices through that means as well, and that weaving was not only a 'futile' activity as Anderson calls it, but a deeply communicative one, like Arachne's.[29] But whatever they weave is appropriated by Bacchus, who turns the textiles into hanging grapes.[30] If what they wove were images, he then would be robbing them of a gaze by turning the weaving into Bacchic imagery. Unlike Arachne, who at least preserves a skeleton of her old weaving art, the Minyeides lose it completely, for there is nothing connected with weaving in the newly formed bats. Perhaps the problem of the Minyeides is that they do not accept that human beings are a combination of feminine and masculine aspects, and that despite their adamant rejection of masculinity, they are themselves more complex in a gender perspective than they want to be. As Ovid's poem constantly shows, nothing is stable and identity is proved precisely in the process of change.

For all the transformative power of Bacchus, we can still imagine a struggle by the Minyeides for preservation of their voices and their gaze. First, they are not completely silent, and although their new squeak cannot articulate human words, it can be viewed as a last cry of the inner self. Even as bats, they try to speak and narrate. Likewise there is a curious meaning in their new form. Ovid alludes to the Latin *vespertilio* (from *vesper*, "evening"). In technical terminology, they are called *chiroptera*, meaning "hand-winged." Ovid alludes to this characteristic in line 411 with *perlucentibus alis* ("transparent wings"). The preservation of this sort of metamorphosed hand can also be viewed as a reminiscence of the hands that the Minyeides used for weaving, which constitute such a central part of their story. Their weaving, however, is lost to them, and with it the capacity to narrate stories and create visual imagery. The eternal darkness in which the Minyeides are wrapped forever clearly symbolizes their lack of knowledge and understanding of the divine order and place in the world. The insistence on the loss of light stresses, in a manner akin to what happens in most metamorphoses, a literalizing fixation of a characteristic that was already there. Also, while the Minyeides try to be 'feminine,' they actually appropriate endowments that are traditionally masculine because they have a 'voice,' they have a 'gaze,' and they create visual images.[31]

Every story of narrators in the poem may be linked to the main narrator, 'Ovid.' Paradoxically, Ovid, being a male author, has often been identified with women authorial figures to display personal poetics, which suggests perhaps that *Metamorphoses* itself is a mixture of 'masculine' epic and 'feminine' fluidity and that strict gender definitions are doomed to failure. The metamorphic stories of the Minyeides also approximate to the art of the poet in that, as Wheeler suggests, they believe in a Callimachean type of poetics in their search for the rare mythological tale instead of dwelling on trite and common stories.[32] Another parallel between these women and the main narrator is that their stories are a form of opposition to the power of a god, which proves significantly suggestive for those who want to see in Ovid an 'anti-Augustan.' The final silencing and symbolic blindness of the Minyeides can also be linked to the exiled poet, who claims to have been robbed of his capacity to sing.[33] However, the Minyeides could be read as embodying the opposite end of the critical spectrum. They reject the blurring of boundaries that is so kin to *Metamorphoses*. In this way, they are punished readers, for they do not appreciate this 'Bacchic' poetics. They see a world where mingling and transformation are dangerous; thus they resist change, personifying a rather conservative literary stance, more keen on Minerva's poetics and Augustan ideology. One could see the Minyeides as the embodiment of Ovid's literary critics and a proof from 'Ovid' that trying to separate categories—gender and other— is an impossible task. It is not enough to tell obscure stories of transformation to be Callimachean and Ovidian when all the Minyeides do is reject fluidity of identity and condemn the outcomes of the stories they present.

  What the Minyeides see is a world of corruption and temptation opposite to the image they wish for themselves. But their very doom is due to their incapacity to see that there are other possibilities for women beyond seclusion—although one may see that the Bacchic revel does not offer a particularly edifying context for femininity if we understand that celebrants are possessed by Bacchus and do not have a mind and a gaze of their own. But in the stories that the Minyeides tell there are alternative roles for women, which despite being doomed, can be taken as alternatives to traditional seclusion. The Minyeides see a world where separation of gender categories is desirable, yet their very gender complexity undermines this view. Despite the recuperative readings of their voices, the sisters are not good models for feminist readings, for in their stubbornness they almost oppose sisterhood, unlike Arachne and Philomela.

Calliope's Gaze

Book 5 presents the singing contest between the Pierides and the Muses, with the palm going to the Muses.[34] The story presents an enormous complexity in its narratorial and visual levels. In a Chinese-box fashion we hear the voices and perceive the gazes of the external narrator, the muse who tells the story of the contest to Minerva, the Pierides, and Calliope. Within Calliope's narrative we see and hear what Arethusa experiences.[35] The story begins with Minerva's curiosity. The goddess has heard about the new spring created by Pegasus's hoof and wishes to see it:

> fama novi fontis nostras pervenit ad aures,
> dura Medusaei quem praepetis ungula rupit.
> is mihi causa viae; volui mirabile factum
> cernere; vidi ipsum materno sanguine nasci.

The reputation of the new spring has come to our ears, which the hard

hoof of Medusa's winged son created. This is the reason for my visit. I
wanted to see the marvelous deed, I saw him being born from his mother's blood. (*Met.* 5.256–59)

The phrase *volui mirabile factum/ cernere* stresses the goddess's desire to see
and to know. At the same time, she asserts herself as viewer and witness,
affirming that she has actively seen (*vidi*) Pegasus's birth. But the episode
will bring her more visual spectacles than just the spring. Urania is very
perceptive and understands Minerva's visual desire ("*quaecumque est causa
videndi/ has tibi, diva, domos, animo gratissima nostro es*"/ "'Whatever the
reason that brought you to see this house, goddess, you are most welcome
to our hearts,'" *Met.* 5.260–61). She soon leads her to the site where the
goddess can look around and admire the scene:

> quae mirata diu factas pedis ictibus undas
> silvarum lucos circumspicit antiquarum
> antraque et innumeris distinctas floribus herbas.

> She admired the spring made by the stroke of Pegasus's hoofs for a long
> time and gazed around at the ancient woods, the grottos, and the lawns
> spangled with numerous flowers. (*Met.* 5.264–66)

The scene recalls other stories of characters coming to *loci amoeni*, especially Actaeon, Narcissus, and Hermaphroditus. First the goddess admires
the waters of the spring, which are highly significant symbols in the
poem.[36] Then she looks around and, unlike Actaeon, is allowed to look at
the *antra* (cf. *antrum nemorale* in *Met.* 3.157). We may suggest, then, that
although a female, Minerva's divinity (and presumably her masculine
aspects) allows her to look and not be punished. What is interesting is that
the muses understand well the visual hankering of their guest and will tell
stories that are highly visually charged. But the first thing one of the
muses narrates is that they would be completely happy if only fierce
Pyreneus had not harassed them:

> sed (vetitum est adeo sceleri nihil) omnia terrent
> virgineas mentes, dirusque ante ora Pyreneus
> vertitur, et nondum tota me mente recepi.

> But (to such level has the crime come) all things terrify our virginal
> souls. And cruel Pyreneus appears before our eyes, and I have not yet
> recovered from this. (*Met.* 5.273–75)

The story of how Pyreneus hassles them is important, for it foregrounds the major themes to come in Calliope's song. The Muses are concerned about their virginity (*virgineas mentes*) and it is a *phantasia* of Pyreneus that threatens their virginal minds. The Muse goes on to relate how once they were, as guests, trapped in Pyreneus's house and offered violence (*vimque parat*, Met. 5.288).[37] This euphemism unavoidably alludes to rape and, one must recall, entrapment is also a common metaphor for sexual violence, as in the episode of Philomela. It is, then, the personal experience of the Muses that will influence the choice of narrative material in Calliope's song. But the figure of Pyreneus offers further connections with other characters, for he is a human who offends deities (the Muses), just like the Pierides, who challenge the Muses, and Arachne, who offends the godhead of Minerva. Here Minerva comes to see the *locus 'amoenus* in a somewhat masculine (and arguably intrusive) attitude, but she soon finds herself the witness of a feminine story of rape. It is curious, though, that while here she seems receptive to this kind of feminine testimonies, she rejects the theme of rape presented from a woman's perspective in the following book, when she engages in the contest with Arachne. Minerva's defeat in the following book may reveal that she has not been a successful gender-sensitive reader of Calliope's song. On one level, Minerva seems to read theodicy correctly and tries to enact it in Book 6 in her contest with Arachne, but she does not appear successful in understanding how gender works and how female audiences read gender issues.

The Muse's story is interrupted by the sound of the magpies, which is "quasi-human" (Met. 5.296–97) and an aetiological tale follows. The Pierides vied with the Muses in the art of singing, but were defeated and transformed into garrulous birds. The voice of the human women, however, is somewhat silenced by the narrating voice of the unidentified Muse, who does not give their account more than fourteen lines. The Pierides relate the battle between gods and giants, giving supremacy to the giants and mocking the cowardice of the gods. Their speech alludes to the gods' capacity for transformation, not taken, as in Arachne's tapestry, as a device for deceit, but as a resource of the coward. The story seems like a simple offense to the power of the deities and represents *en abîme* the defying attitude of the Pierides toward the Muses. As presented, the story does not show much artistry, yet the Pierides' voices are censured by the Muse narrator and we only hear some aspects of an abridged version of their tale.[38] The Pierides lose the contest and are transformed into magpies who can imitate any voice but have lost their own (*imitantes omnia picae*, Met. 5.299). Garrulity seems to be a feature of the magpies, yet they cannot sing or narrate their own stories, like the Minyeides whose voices are reduced to a thin squeak and like Echo who can only repeat fragments of others' voices. We may suppose that, as in the case of the Minyeides, it is not only hubris against a divine power that causes their doom, but the very desire to have a voice, which is in itself subversive of gender norms. In this sense, the Pierides' 'unsignificatory' garrulity parallels the 'uncommunicative' patterns of the textiles of 'good women' and the squeaking of the Minyeides turned into bats. This meaningless chatter of the Pierides agrees with a common ancient accusation against women, namely, that they talk a great deal but don't say anything.

Minerva's reading of the story is peculiar, for in Book 6 she chooses for her tapestry a more epic theme—the divine order and the punishment of humans who defiled the divinity of the gods. Minerva thinks that by putting divine authority back in its place she will win the weaving contest. But, it appears, she does not read the contest between Pierides and Muses well, for what actually triumphs is the very feminine theme of rape from the victim's viewpoint. Minerva is so tied up in her own image and her struggle for authority that she loses the artistic sensitivity to produce an image that will move the audience.

By contrast, the Muses are very sensitive to the concerns and tastes of their audience. They manage to show deference to Minerva's mood and at the same time to create intrigue by asking her if she would care to hear the rest of the story (*Met.* 5.333–34). To the song of the Pierides Calliope responds with the story of the rape of Proserpina. From the beginning, Calliope reasserts the divine power, affirming that "all things are the gift of Ceres" and thus she should be celebrated (*Met.* 5.343–44). She also views the feminine as the principle of all things. Calliope relates how Venus, disturbed by the rejection of love by Minerva and Diana, worried that, left to her own devices, Proserpina would adamantly remain a virgin. Interestingly, Venus mentions that both Diana and Minerva have rejected her power (*Met.* 5.375–76). It is worth inquiring how Minerva reads this allusion to herself in Calliope's narrative. She might be pleased to hear the emphasis on her virginity, which is an astute move on the narrator's part. The muses strive for virginity, Proserpina and Ceres for the preservation of maidenhood, while Minerva is emblematized as a virgin goddess. The narrator in this way forges an alliance with the reader and attracts her sympathy. But Venus urges Cupid to incite a desire for Ceres' daughter in the god of the Underworld by piercing him with an arrow of love—one finds again, as with Apollo in Book 1, the image of the lover that is penetrated by Cupid.

The introduction of Proserpina begins with an interesting ekphrasis:

> haud procul Hennaeis lacus est a moenibus altae,
> nomine Pergus, aquae: non illo plura Caystros
> carmina cycnorum labentibus audit in undis.
> silva coronat aquas cingens latus omne suisque
> frondibus ut velo Phoebeos submovet ictus;
> frigora dant rami, Tyrios humus umida flores:
> perpetuum ver est. quo dum Proserpina luco
> ludit et aut violas aut candida lilia carpit.

> Not far from Henna's walls there is a lake of deep water by the name of
> Pergus. Not Cayster with its flowing waters hears more swans' songs than
> this pool. Woods crown the water surrounding its banks and with its
> foliage as an awning it protects from the rays of the sun. The branches
> provide coolness and the moist earth produces purple flowers. There is
> eternal spring. In this grove meanwhile Proserpina plays and plucks vio-
> lets and white lilies. (Met. 5. 385–92)

The phrase *lacus est,* as in other ekphrases, marks the visual and narratological boundaries and frames the image of Proserpina, but there are many
layers of intrusive gazes and readers. The obvious male intruder (physically
and visually) is Pluto, who comes up from his realm to inspect the land of
Sicily. He sees Proserpina and becomes instantly infatuated with her. But
many other internal audiences 'view' the scene with their minds' eyes, and
they are all female: the Pierides, the nymphs who judge the contest, the
other Muses, the Muse who narrates the tale to Minerva, and Minerva
herself. So at this middle level, the viewers and visual intruders in the
ekphrasis are women. In the external audience, one assumes, as usual,
both male and female readers. Curiously, the picture that Calliope presents
not only provides a testimony of rape, but in a metaphoric way, also allows
women to intrude in a female *locus amoenus* and assume, momentarily,
some sort of Actaeon-like stance. This would go well with Mulvey's
model of trans-sex identification. One may also suppose that they identify with the victim and, from a monolithic male viewpoint, lose all possible empowerment and enjoyment. The problem here is that the Muses and
Minerva are also striving to preserve their virginity. They do find enjoyment in the viewing and gain power because they gain knowledge. So this
is a different kind of empowerment that Mulvey's model cannot conceive.

Flowers in general "are traditionally associated with virginal purity and also with its vulnerability,"[39] while the act of picking flowers may be seen as sexual violation.[40] These remarks are very appropriate for our passage, and they are enhanced by the fact that when she is carried away by Pluto, Proserpina's flowers fall from her bosom. The text here is explicit in making the connection between the loss of the flowers and the loss of Proserpina's virginity:

> collecti flores tunicis cecidere remissis,
>
> tantaque simplicitas puerilibus adfuit annis,
>
> haec quoque virgineum movit iactura dolorem.

> The gathered flowers fell from her loosened tunic. Such was the innocence of her childish years. Even this loss caused pain to the maiden. (*Met.* 5.399–401)

The *dolor virgineus* can also be interpreted as the physical pain of deflowering. The flowers Proserpina collects are noteworthy because they are not just any flowers, but "violets and lilies." As with purple, the color of the mulberry, this combination of white and a purplish color conveys the symbolism of sex. The idea of death, which is always linked to the violence of rape, also surrounds the episode, as Dis is involved and the couple is headed toward the Underworld.[41]

There is also a play on gazes in the story. On the one hand, the reader seems to witness the rape through Pluto's lustful eyes (*visa est dilectaque raptaque Diti/* "She was seen, loved, and taken away by Dis," *Met.* 5.395). Proserpina's position as visual object may be enhanced by Hinds's idea that the *locus amoenus* is a place of performance and could be physically assimilated to an amphitheater. Proserpina is then "forced to 'play' (*ludit*, 392) out 'the spectacle' of her own violent abduction."[42] Finally, unlike the story of Daphne, this rape is a *phantasia* of a woman narrator; as such it may be understood in the same way as the weaving of Philomela, that is, a denunciation of rape and a search for sisterhood. As with Philomela, the color implications of rape in the combination of white with red or purple are present. Calliope's *phantasia* can be seen as an imaginary tapestry where rape is inscribed through visual imagery. The female reader has a choice: to align with the male gaze of Pluto (and the overarching male narrator), in which case she would gain power in a transsexual way. She can also identify with the female victim as sufferer, but the problem with this option is that Proserpina is not really given a gaze in the text and this type of identification would be a passive one. But the female reader can also read the story as a whole, not focalizing with the rapist but finding an alternative, more holistic viewpoint from where to appreciate the complete story. She could also adopt shifting viewpoints and thus acquire a more complex understanding of the scene that surpasses the constraints of focalization.

On their way to the Underworld, Pluto and Proserpina encounter the nymph Cyane in her own pool. The text introduces the scene with another ekphrastic formula, which becomes meaningful for the sexual overtones of the story:

> est medium Cyanes et Pisaeae Arethusae,
> quod coit angustis inclusum cornibus aequor.

> Between Cyane and Pisaean Arethusa there is a bay confined by thin points of land. (Met. 5.409–10)

Here again, the reader needs to perform a metaphorical penetration of the text to read and view what is inside an ekphrasis. As in the Actaeon episode, water is an image of femininity and the verb *coit* is quite 'consequential' as it brings overtones of sexual penetration, for *coeo* means both to "come together or assemble" and to "copulate." This image of an intrusion into a feminine space may also be strengthened by the idea that the bay symbolizes a vagina enclosed and centered between the legs. [43]

Cyane tries to impede the rape with a speech that wants to bring Pluto to his senses and points to the uncivilized aspect of rape, but to no avail, as her voice fails to be heard. Pluto does not hold his wrath, but smites the pool with his scepter. The smitten earth opens up and the couple plunges down to the Underworld. Some sort of metaphoric rape can be inferred from the god's violence toward her pool, after which the symbolism of her *vulnus* (Met. 5.426) becomes clearer. Cyane laments the fate of Proserpina and the disrespect shown to her pool, and through her tears dissolves into water. The description of her transformation is detailed:

> at Cyane, raptamque deam contemptaque fontis
> iura sui maerens, inconsolabile vulnus
> mente gerit tacita lacrimisque absumitur omnis
> et, quarum fuerat magnum modo numen, in illas
> extenuatur aquas: molliri membra videres,
> ossa pati flexus, ungues posuisse rigorem;

primaque de tota tenuissima quaeque liquescunt,
caerulei crines digitique et crura pedesque;
(nam brevis in gelidas membris exilibus undas
transitus est); post haec umeri tergusque latusque
pectoraque in tenues abeunt evanida rivos;
denique pro vivo vitiatas sanguine venas
lympha subit, restatque nihil, quod prendere possis.

But Cyane, lamenting the rape of the goddess and the contempt for the
rights of her spring, silently bears an inconsolable wound in her soul and
is entirely consumed by tears. And she dissolves into those waters whose
great deity she had recently been. You would see her limbs softening, the
bones bending, the nails having lost their hardness, and first of all melt
the slenderest parts, the bluish hair, her fingers, legs and feet—for the
change is small from tender limbs to cool water. After these, her shoulders, back and side, and her frail chest dissolve into soft streams. Finally,
water creeps through the weakened veins instead of living blood. Nothing remains which you could grasp. (*Met.* 5.425–37)

Cyane's watery nature is worthy of attention, for transformation into
water is a particularly feminine phenomenon in *Metamorphoses*.[44] The
origin of Cyane's transformation lies in her tears. In general, tears are particularly feminine and associated with women's debility and inconti-
nence. Granted, there are numerous examples of men who cry in *Metamorphoses*, but tears may still carry feminine overtones in men. Cyane has
tried to be hard and assertive but has been vanquished by Pluto. Defeated
by Man, she has proved to be *mollis* to such an extent that it leads her to
liquefaction. Cyane tries to stop the rape and oppose Pluto but is defeated and vanquished; likewise, violence—even metaphorical rape—is
exerted on her and all she can do about it is cry. In a sense Cyane is
already *mollis* before her actual physical mollification.

Is Cyane, then, only an example of female powerlessness and dissolution? While this is partly true, the story finds a way to be narrated and to
leave a mark and testimony in *Metamorphoses*. Cyane has not only lost
her body, but also her voice. She has now become another silent character through rape and dissolution. Yet when Ceres later comes searching
for her daughter, Cyane is able to communicate through visual imagery:

venit et ad Cyanen. ea ni mutata fuisset,
omnia narrasset; sed et os et lingua volenti
dicere non aderant, nec, quo loqueretur, habebat.

> And she came to Cyane. If she had not been transformed, she would
> have told her everything, but, although she wanted to talk, she had nei-
> ther mouth nor tongue, nor any means to speak. (*Met.* 5.465–67)

The choice of *muto* in line 465 is a remarkable one. The verb means "to
change," but through sound play it also recalls the idea of silencing and
muting implied in *mutus*.[45] The raped nymph has lost her voice and needs
to find an alternative form of expression: Proserpina's *zona* lies on the
pool. Cyane is able to give an *indicium* of what has happened. As with
Philomela's and Arachne's tapestries, female visual communication is
accomplished through hints that invite the female reader to 'suspect,' to
see behind the appearances. The silent code of imagery replaces words:
Ceres sees Proserpina's *zona*, a most potent symbol of what has been loos-
ened and lost. Thus, Cyane can perform sisterhood in an alternative way
and, though silenced, can still be a witness of what has occurred.

After Cyane's dissolution, the narration returns to Ceres' search for
Proserpina. References to food and drink are central to the story. The
episode presents a thirsty Ceres who has not yet touched water (*Met.*
5.446–47). At this moment in the story line the key conflict that has
been developed is a struggle between the preservation of virginity and
sexuality—already present in the conflict of the muses and Pyreneus.
Food and drink are in ancient poetry—and beyond—linked to sex.[46] The
act of not drinking may be linked with the desire on Ceres' part for the
preservation of her daughter's virginity. Now the goddess arrives at a hut
and is given water. While she is drinking the barley water she has been
offered, a rude boy laughs at her and calls her greedy: *dum bibit illa datum,*
duri puer oris et audax/ constitit ante deam risitque avidamque vocavit (*Met.* 5.
451–42).
   This scene may have meaningful implications for the gaze. Although
no verb of seeing appears in the text, the phrase *constitit ante deam* most
likely implies that the boy stood looking at her, especially considering the
implications of stopping in other episodes.[47] The goddess's reaction is
interesting. She throws what she has not yet drunk in his face and turns
him into a lizard:[48]

> offensa est neque adhuc epota parte loquentem
> cum liquido mixta perfudit diva polenta.

The goddess was offended and as he spoke, she poured on the boy's face
the barley mixed with the liquid which she had not yet drunk. (*Met.*
5.453–54)

The scene recalls Diana throwing a splash of water on Actaeon, Athena's
punishment of Tiresias in Callimachus, and, indirectly, the Homeric
Hymn to Aphrodite. The boy's transformation is here, too, a punishment
for seeing and intruding into the privacy of a goddess. Further, the boy is
referred to as *loquentem*, the speaker. In this the reader is reminded of
Diana's fears that Actaeon will tell others what he has seen and of
Aphrodite's warning to Anchises in Homer. Could something similar be
posed? The act of drinking avidly, which in the story may be concurrent
with sexuality, is a private one for Ceres. Having been turned into a lizard,
the boy will be impeded from intruding into the private acts of the goddess and also from narrating what he has seen. In contrast with the fate
of Cyane, where water implies *mollitia* and powerlessness, water is used
here as a vindictive element with the power to change.[49] But while Cyane
can still 'speak' through symbols, the boys are eternally silenced.

After searching all over and not finding her daughter, Ceres returns to
Sicily and comes to the pool of Cyane, where she finds a hint of what
happened. Infuriated, she destroys the crops and all sources of food on
Earth. Then comes the story of Arethusa who is witness to the rape of
Persephone (*ergo dum Stygio sub terris gurgite labor,/ visa tua est oculis illic
Proserpina nostris* / "Therefore while I was gliding in my Stygian stream
under the earth, your Proserpina was seen there by my very eyes," *Met.*
5.504–5) and informs Ceres that her daughter has been made queen of
the Underworld and spouse of Dis. Arethusa uses the passive *visa* and not
the more emphatic and performative *vidi* that Minerva does, for example,
when she says that she saw the birth of Pegasus. Arethusa's gaze poses the
same implications as other female gazes. Although she cannot actually
prevent or fight sexual violence, she can still be a witness and, in an indirect and oblique way, she can act upon her gaze by telling the story and
stimulating others—like Ceres here—to take action.

When Ceres looks for help in Jupiter, he gives the male-oriented
answer that justifies his own rapes in *Metamorphoses*: *non hoc iniuria factum,/ verum amor est/* "This deed is not a crime, but true love," *Met.*
5.525–26). The condition upon which Proserpina shall be returned to her
mother in the upper world is, significantly, that she has tried no food in
the Underworld (531–32). The connection between food and sex here is
again meaningful. In the words of father Jupiter, the implications of eating
and sexual purity are present: "She can only return if she is still sexually

untouched." But this is not the case, as Proserpina has eaten, and what she has eaten bears multiple symbolisms: a crimson fruit (*puniceum pomum*, 536). The meaning of the fruit as temptation is well extended in western ideology, with its most paradigmatic example in the Bible. The deep purple fruit has the color of love, passion, and, as seen before, of sexual maturity. Proserpina is no longer a maiden. She has lost the innocence of the simple child that she was (*cultis dum simplex errat in hortis,/ puniceum curva decerpserat arbore pomum/* "While, simple girl as she was, she wandered in the tended gardens, she had plucked a crimson pomegranate from a bending bow," *Met.* 5.535–36). In this issue of fruits as symbols of virginity lost, one is reminded of the golden apples, gifts of Venus, which Atalanta picks up during her race with Hippomenes and which will cost her her maidenhood. Hinds is probably right in pointing out that Proserpina has not learned from her mistake and has twice failed to learn that there are dangers in plucking earth's fruits in a *locus amoenus*.[50] But what seems to be key in the story is not so much that the girl ate from the pomegranate, but that somebody reported the incident. It is the boy Ascalaphus who saw it:

Ascalaphus vidit . . .
. . . .
vidit et indicio reditum crudelis ademit.

Ascalaphus saw it . . . he saw it and by his disclosure he cruelly prevented her return. (*Met.*5.539 and 542)

Ascalaphus has actually performed what Actaeon was prevented from doing; in his case also, water proves to be the weapon of transformation. The issue of the *indicium* is again poignant. The queen of Erebus throws a splash of water in his face (his eyes) and transforms him into an ill-omened bird.[51] The new bird possesses big eyes (*grandia lumina*, 545) in a literalizing metaphor for someone who sees too much. The text also emphasizes that his punishment is due to his tattling tongue (551–52).

After a brief inclusion of the story of the Sirens, who preserve their voices though partly turned into birds, Jupiter resolves to divide the year in two halves, thus reaching a compromise between Ceres and his brother Pluto. Proserpina will spend part of the year on Earth and part in the

Underworld. After this comes the story of Arethusa followed by Ceres' transformation of king Lyncus into a lynx after he committed a murder to become himself the bearer of Ceres' gifts. With this concludes Calliope's tale, which, not surprisingly, wins the contest.

Before concluding this reading of the episode, a few words about Arethusa's tale and *phantasia* shall be offered. Ceres asks Arethusa why she is now a sacred spring and an aetiological tale follows. After lifting her green locks from the pool, what Arethusa tells is a story of love and violence, how she was chased by the river-god Alpheus. She used to be a virgin who delighted in hunting:

> "pars ego nympharum, quae sunt in Achaide," dixit,
> "una fui, nec me studiosius altera saltus
> legit nec posuit studiosius altera casses.
> sed quamvis formae numquam mihi fama petita est,
> quamvis fortis eram, formosae nomen habebam,
> nec mea me facies nimium laudata iuvabat,
> quaque aliae gaudere solent, ego rustica dote
> corporis erubui crimenque placere putavi."

> "I was one of the nymphs who live in Achaida," she said, "and no other chose the woodlands more eagerly than I, no other set the nets more keenly. But although I never sought the fame of beauty, though I was brave, I had the name of beautiful. Neither did I enjoy that my beauty was praised too much. I, a country girl, blushed at the gifts of my body, which often gives pleasure to other girls, and deemed a crime to please." (*Met.* 5.577–84)

Although Arethusa rejects her beauty, she nevertheless loads her discourse with allusions to it. Her virginity is stereotypical and responds to the mold of other wild virgins in *Metamorphoses*. Curiously, for a virgin who dreads being desired, her description seems to be tailored for a male viewer by setting the scene with a description of her beauty.[52] What follows responds to the same patterns of female reification; however, the ekphrastic description of landscape and her interaction with it add complexity to the gender implications of the passage:

> aestus erat, magnumque labor geminaverat aestum:
> invenio sine vertice aquas, sine murmure euntes,
> perspicuas ad humum, per quas numerabilis alte

calculus omnis erat, quas tu vix ire putares.
cana salicta dabant nutritaque populus unda
sponte sua natas ripis declivibus umbras.

It was hot, and the effort had doubled the great heat. I found a stream
without eddy, flowing without a sound, crystal-clear to the bottom,
through which every pebble could be counted, which you would scarcely
think was flowing. Silvery willows and poplars fed by the water provided
natural shade to the sloping banks. (*Met.* 5.586–91)

The verb *invenio* signals Arethusa's intrusion into the landscape and
recalls Narcissus's and Hermaphroditus's intrusion into their respective
loci amoeni. The reader here is invited to focalize with Arethusa as she
enters this virginal landscape, and the text creates an odd gender positioning for female viewers and readers. The clear transparency of the pool
also recalls Hermaphroditus's desire to swim in a similar pool, which
incites this same desire in the nymph:

accessi primumque pedis vestigia tinxi,
poplite deinde tenus; neque eo contenta, recingor
molliaque inpono salici velamina curvae
nudaque mergor aquis. quas dum ferioque trahoque
mille modis labens excussaque bracchia iacto.

I approached and first I wet my foot, then I dipped up to my knee; and not
content with this, I disrobed and left my soft garment on a bending wil-
low. Naked I dived in the waters. I tossed my arms around while I beat
them, drawing them and gliding in a thousand ways. (*Met.* 5.592–96)

The insistence on her nudity, which is repeated in lines 601–2 ("*sicut
eram, fugio sine vestibus [altera vestes/ ripa meas habuit]*") / "'As I was, I fled
without my robes [the other bank had my robes]),'" seems designed for the
gaze of a male who is seduced by the naked body of the nymph. It evokes
the naked body of Hermaphroditus viewed by Salmacis and Daphne in
her flight (*nudabant corpora venti* / "The breeze unrobed her body,"
*Met.*1.527),[53] and it even has a hint of Diana in her bath. One could say
that Arethusa is, at least partly, looking at herself with a male gaze, as a
man would see her. The complication is that she does not enjoy being
looked at.

    Although Arethusa is at all costs trying to convey the image that oth-
ers have of her exemplified by *formosae nomen habebam*, she is the only

testimony that this is the 'gaze of others.' But couldn't her picture of herself also convey autoeroticism? As virginal nymph who rejects contact with others, Arethusa is absorbed in herself and cannot achieve interchange with the other sex. The poetic coincidences with Narcissus and Hermaphroditus are striking. Moreover, water is an important signifier of self-eroticism and self-absorption notable in *Met.* 5.586–89, quoted above.

In *Met.* 5.586 there is a strong intertextual allusion to the beginning of *Amores* 1.5 (*Aestus erat, mediamque dies exegerat horam*/ "It was hot, and the day had passed its mid-point"), perhaps one of the most erotically charged poems in the collection, where a scene of lovemaking is insinuated. Further, the gradual description of Arethusa's body recalls the very cinematographic (or perhaps pornographic) description of Corinna in *Amores* 1.5. In such a clear stream, given the antecedents of the poem, one may even suppose that Arethusa, like Narcissus, sees her own image reflected. Indeed, the very act of jumping in the river embodies awkward gender complications, where she penetrates the waters that belong to/are a male deity. We may compare this scene to Hermaphoditus's pool, which is also described as so clear that you could even see the bottom (*Met.* 4.297–98). It is noteworthy that the word *perspicuus* (588) is only used twice in Ovid, here and for Hermaphroditus's pool in *Met.* 4.300. The connotations of self-absorption conveyed by crystal-clear pools in *Metamorphoses* are most clearly revealed in the episode of Narcissus. Both Narcissus and Hermaphroditus are immature boys who cannot grow up and engage in the societal and sexual interchange of adults. In a way, Arethusa, fixed in the delights of the pool and rejecting sexual contact, represents an analogous case of a girl who cannot grow up and distance herself from herself. Her gaze is fixed on her own image, which coincides with the male gaze of Alpheus. Arethusa's autoerotic gaze could be taken as a 'male gaze' and what she 'objectivizes' is herself, as Elsner suggests for Narcissus. Nevertheless, Arethusa, by the very act of narrating her story, achieves some maturity and thus grows up in a different way. Although she still rejects the contact with males, she does however develop the skill to interact verbally with a female audience. Arethusa grows out of autoeroticism and can even be sensitive to the needs of others, as when she delays her narrative to accommodate Ceres' feelings. One could also suppose that her self-construction as object of the gaze represents the price that she must pay to escape rape and preserve her voice. Thus for the male 'external' viewer/reader, she offers a somewhat voyeuristic reifying picture of herself. The experience of the 'female gaze' is more difficult to decipher. As in other episodes, at this point in the narrative the female reader may either align with the male gaze or acknowledge the difficulties involved in the pleasure of viewing and remain outside of it.

Although at first it can be said that Arethusa's portrait feeds male voyeuristic desire, soon her visual construction will be aligned with virginity and she will change the focus to complain about the violence and intrusion of the male gaze. There is already a transformation in her from intruder and viewer to object of the gaze. Unlike episodes such as Daphne's where the focalizer seems to be Apollo all the time, here Arethusa switches from the male gazer to the experience of the young virgin. There is an interesting play of powers in the narratorial layers. The fact that she can narrate the story as a victim represents a new development that departs from the figure of the mute Daphne. The voice of the sufferer is now heard. After the river-god discovers her, Arethusa begins to run away. In the description of the chase, the text shows for the first time the perspective of the running virgin. Arethusa tells us that she cannot see Alpheus but only his shadow (*"vidi praecedere longam/ ante pedes umbram"* / "'I saw his long shadow stretching out before my feet,'" *Met.* 5.614–15); nor can she see a clear image of her persecutor. She even doubts whether she has really seen him: *"nisi si timor illa videbat;/ sed certe sonitusque pedum terrebat et ingens/ crinales vittas adflabat anhelitus oris"* / "'Unless it was fear that made me see these things—but surely the sound of his feet terrified me and his panting breath fanned my braided hair'" (*Met.* 5.615–17). Arethusa thus reconstructs a *phantasia* of Alpheus through the fragments and *indicia* that she perceives. This may be linked to the oblique female gaze and the possibility of seeing beyond what is apparent.

Soon Diana responds to Arethusa's cries for help and surrounds her with a cloud. Alpheus, after looking for her for a while and finding the cloud, fixes his gaze on it (*servat nubemque locumque* / "He watched the cloud and the place," *Met.* 5.631). Arethusa begins to disintegrate in blue drops. We may compare the function of the cloud here with that in the Io episode in Book 1. Although Juno looks at the cloud, she cannot penetrate it and can only 'suspect' what is behind. Alpheus, although he is not even sure of what lies behind it, can still visually penetrate the cloud and affect the girl to the point of metamorphosis, thus displaying the performative power of the male gaze. His gaze disintegrates her and provokes her dissolution.

Now Arethusa witnesses her own transformation and this is the *phantasia* that she constructs:

> occupat obsessos sudor mihi frigidus artus,
> caeruleaeque cadunt toto de corpore guttae,

quaque pedem movi, manat lacus, eque capillis
ros cadit, et citius, quam nunc tibi facta renarro,
in latices mutor.

A cold sweat pours over my beleaguered limbs, and blue drops fall from
my whole body. Wherever I move my foot, a pool is formed and dew falls
from my hair; and faster than I retell these events to you now, I am
turned into water. (*Met.* 5.632–36)

It is not tears, as in other episodes, but *sudor* that leads to her transformation into water. Man here is stronger ("*nec me velocior ille;/ sed tolerare
diu cursus ego viribus inpar/ non poteram*" / "'Nor was he faster than I, but
I, ill-matched in strength, could not bear the race for long,'" *Met.*
5.609–11) and change is the only possible way out of rape. Like Cyane,
Arethusa tries to resist with her own means, but they prove fruitless. She
is weakened and overpowered by Alpheus. Already *mollis*, she becomes
running water. *Latex* is a curious word, as it may mean simply "water" but,
more commonly, it indicates "running water," a spring or stream. Paulus
Ex.Fest. 118.23–24 defines it as "*profluens aqua.*"Arethusa's fluidity is sup-
ported by *manat* in line 634. In this sense, the running virgin is now running water; her capacity to escape is maintained.

Arethusa also compares herself to a dove fleeing from a hawk, a lamb
escaping from a wolf, and a hare running from dogs. This well-known
hunting imagery adds to the equivalence between Alpheus and Actaeon
the hunter; the word *aestus* also adds to the erotic connotations of the midday heat. The paradox here, as in other episodes, is that the huntress is
now the prey herself. In part, Arethusa constructs her story on the model
of the episode of Actaeon and Diana in Book 3, told directly by the main
narrator. The comparison with prey also recalls Daphne fleeing from Apollo in *Met.*1.533–34. Like Daphne, Arethusa sees herself as weak and incapable of surpassing Alpheus without divine help (619–20). The difference
is, however, that now the prey can tell the story. Although Arethusa
begins to sweat with fear and is soon transformed into a pool, the god recognizes her in the water and mingles with her as a river, which insinuates
an actual rape. Diana opens the earth and Arethusa plunges into its
depths. She resurfaces in Ortygia where she now lives happily as a pool.

The picture that Arethusa presents of herself is not much different
from other portraits of virgins in episodes narrated by male authorial figures, but Arethusa can escape, 'speak,' and give a female perspective.
Arethusa has 'read' Ovid, but has learned how to—or has been lucky
enough to—avoid the fate of the Ovidian virgin-victim. While, on the

one hand, there is an overarching authorial voice that caters to the male viewer-reader, on the other hand, this masculine gaze is juxtaposed with the autoerotic gaze of Arethusa herself. But when Arethusa starts running and does not concentrate on her image, there is a more 'feminist' cry for camaraderie among women and denunciation of rape. Her salvation is of a passive nature, through the pity and help of a 'sister,' yet her narrative power is doubtless active. Arethusa's construction of herself as a visual object is therefore intricate and may serve different purposes simultaneously. On the one hand, it attracts the eye of the male reader who delights in reifying the female. On the other hand, Arethusa may be denouncing the suffering of women and the crime of rape. Both readings can coexist in the juxtaposed voices of male and female (Arethusa, Calliope, the unnamed muse, and 'Ovid').

The attempted rape of the nymph Arethusa appeals to the sensibility of the judges of the contest between the Muses and the Pierides because they have frequently experienced the sexual violence of males in *Metamorphoses*. But the primary audience of the story is the goddess Ceres, whose daughter has also been raped. The first time that Arethusa is heard, she does not tell her story, but prays that Ceres not devastate the land with hunger, claiming that the land has no guilt. In fact, it had saved Arethusa by opening a path through which she could escape from Alpheus (*Met.* 5.501–2), and by offering itself as home for her. In this first intervention by Arethusa, she delays the narration of her story by saying that she will tell it later in happier circumstances for the goddess ("*veniet narratibus hora/ tempestiva meis, cum tu curaque levata/ et vultus melioris eris*"/ "'There will come a time more propitious to tell you, when you, once your pain is relieved, will be in better spirits,'" *Met.* 5.499–501). This is quite wise of Arethusa. Given the irritable temperament of Ceres in the tale, she may well withhold the story of her salvation for a moment when it may not cause envy in Ceres and when she can empathize with her. Therefore, once Ceres has recovered her daughter and a compromise has been reached, Arethusa can speak safely. Like Proserpina, she has suffered sexual violence (perhaps even figurative rape) and has been saved by the mercy of a deity. In this way, Arethusa becomes a sort of daughter to mother Ceres. Finally it is worthy to note that, as Patricia Johnson puts it, all the audiences of the story of the rape of Proserpina and, ultimately, of the contest between Muses and Pierides, are women who fight against the power of Venus and detest the crime love has performed on the goddess's daughter. This opposition to Venus makes sense if one thinks of Venus as the embodiment of male desire, which explains why Venus often seems to be on the male side. The song of Calliope is directed to the judgment of the nymphs who have suffered Venus's power in many other episodes. Ultimately, it is the virgin Minerva who listens to the story of the contest.[54] Venus in Book 5 complains about deities who wish to remain virgin; she refers directly to Minerva, Proserpina, and Diana. The first two have an obvious role in Book 5. The third appears in a veiled way through identification with other characters.

One finally wonders why Calliope has chosen the story of the rape of Proserpina, and what the effects of her *phantasia* on her audience are. The judges of the singing contest are the nymphs. Eleanor Winsor Leach suggests that it is not surprising that the nymphs vote for the Muses' song given the honorific place they are given in the story of Ceres.[55] But it is more than the honor of a prominent place that the story offers them. The violence perpetrated by Pluto in his rape of Proserpina mirrors the many rapes of nymphs in episodes throughout *Metamorphoses*. With her story, Calliope appeals to the empathy of the nymphs through a feeling of sisterhood because they understand well the experience of sexual violence. The story not only gives a voice to women, even if it is an alternative voice as in Cyane, but it also punishes male speech. The two boys who talk too much suffer silencing and transformation. The song of Calliope offers women an opportunity to reverse the typical silencing of rape victims. It is, like Philomela's tapestry, a web of *phantasies* that represents the fate of women for other women.

So, what do women see? How do they see? What can Calliope's song tell us about female gazes? Again, 'female gaze' or 'what women see' involves more than a physical gaze. It also refers to a more metaphoric gaze connected with capacities such as 'understanding,' 'realizing,' 'knowing,' and 'perceiving.' To begin with, there is a general concern by the Muses with virginity, explicit in their own personal story, in the tale of the rape of Proserpina, and in the internal audience. Calliope's song is also highly visually charged because it is, in part, designed to respond to the visual cravings of Minerva and to the nymphs who are judges of the contest—and the reader knows well from the episode of Minerva and Arachne how much the nymphs delight in viewing. Calliope places herself as narrator and witness of a story of rape, which both allows women to be spectators and places the female as origin of all things. The interesting point about Calliope's song is that she lets other women assume the narrating voice and express their gazes. Cyane embodies another instance of women's silencing. What she has seen is the rape of Proserpina; thus she has become a witness who can potentially narrate what has occurred. But unlike Actaeon, she finds a way to tell what has happened through visual images. The *zona* floating on her pool is a clear *indicium* of the crime, which invites Ceres to reconstruct the story. Cyane's gaze, just as in the episodes discussed in chapter 4, captures the feminine qualities of the gaze: to witness and to incite an oblique and alternative viewing.

Arethusa is likewise a witness of Proserpina's fate, but she is a witness of her own attempted rape and her own story as well. First, Arethusa sees herself as a man would, thereby recapturing the essence of rape stories like Daphne or Syrinx, but soon the focalization shifts and she shows us a female perspective. While Arethusa is not allowed to look directly at Alpheus, she still reconstructs him from fragments and hints of his image that she perceives. Like Juno, her 'female gaze' is oblique and calls for an extra effort to decipher the meanings of the images.

Interestingly, Calliope's song does not offer any instances of how and what males see. While Pluto may be seen to embody the typical mono-lithic male gaze, his viewing is destabilized by the fact that Venus insti-gates his erotic gaze. The two boys—with all the sexual problematization that surrounds boys in the poem—are silenced and transformed by Ceres and Proserpina. Their gazes are antagonistic toward the female and threaten to utter female secrets, but are dismantled. What the two boys see are secrets of women's lives and interiority that should not be exposed. They suffer a fate similar to Actaeon's.

Stealing the Cyclops' Eye

Affairs between goddesses and mortal men offer a whole new set of possi-bilities for the gaze. As Stehle puts it, "one reason for the popularity of the mythic pattern of goddess with young man is that it opened space for fan-tasies of uncodified erotic relationships."[56] Galatea herself narrates her story to Scylla. The text presents another speech of lamentation and self-pity that, in appearance, represents man as monster and woman as victim. As Tissol indicates, the figure of Galatea narrating the story is an Ovidian innovation with respect to the model in Theocritus' poem 11.[57] This actu-ally provides a feminine perspective. The stress on Galatea's voice is seen in *Met.* 13.745 where she is defined as speaker who can speak until tears run down her cheeks (*et lacrimae vocem inpediere loquentis*). There is a curi-ous trick in the tale. All we know about the Cyclops and Acis is what we hear through Galatea's focalization. She begins by expressing her love for Acis and defining him as a young boy on the verge of masculinity, an image that assimilates him to other *pueri* like Narcissus, Hermaphoditus, and Adonis (*pulcher et octonis iterum natalibus actis/ signarat teneras dubia lanugine malas /* "He was beautiful and, at sixteen, his soft cheeks had been marked by an undefined down," *Met.* 13.753–54). The adjective *dubia* is particularly meaningful for Acis' instability.

Galatea continues with her construction of Polyphemus's image and imagines him as a spectacle horrible to the sight (*nempe ille inmitis et ipsis/horrendus silvis et visus ab hospite nullo/impune)/* "Indeed he was rough and horrible to the woods themselves, and looked upon by no guest with impunity," *Met.* 13.759–60). The same idea of hardness in the adjective *inmitis* will later define Galatea in Polyphemus's speech. But Galatea soon moves to paint a picture of the Cyclops as somewhat effeminate in a way that recalls the self-adornment of Salmacis in front of her pool:

> iamque tibi formae, iamque est tibi cura placendi,
> iam rigidos pectis rastris, Polypheme, capillos,
> iam libet hirsutam tibi falce recidere barbam
> et spectare feros in aqua et conponere vultus.

> And now you care for your appearance, now you care to please, now,
> Polyphemus, you comb your stiff hair with a rake, now you like to trim
> you hirsute beard with a sickle; and to gaze upon and compose your fierce
> features in a pool. (*Met.* 13.764–69).[58]

Polyphemus—or rather the *phantasia* of him that Galatea gives—is following the advice of *Ars Amatoria* 1.518: *sit coma, sit trita barba resecta manu/* "Let hair and beard be cut by a practiced hand." In this process, Galatea turns the tables and makes Polyphemus the object of the gaze. In this sense the gender destabilization and feminization of the elegiac lover that Polyphemus embodies is taken to the extreme that visually reifies him, like a woman. Likewise, the scene of self-admiration and *cultus* in front of a mirror recalls both Salmacis and Narcissus, whose sexuality is unstable and undefined, offering both male and female aspects. Personal care and self-admiration in the mirror are particularly feminine in ancient conceptions of sexuality.[59] In men, personal *cultus* is necessary as affirmation of citizenship and definition of their place in society. It includes keeping the hair and beard well cut, washing, and eating adequately in order to stress the difference between the civilized man and the savage. In women, adornment before the mirror aims at self-construction as a visual object of desire for men. It has to do more with eroticism and less with self-definition in society.[60] In the case of Polyphemus above, the comic effect lies in the incongruence of the image, that is, a hypermasculine character who nonetheless looks at himself in the mirror as a woman would. Hypermasculinity tends to be problematic. Indeed, it seems that, like femininity, masculinity can barely avoid falling into excess. The gaze of Polyphemus looking at his own image in the pool resembles the case of women 'making themselves pretty' for men, in which case we say that the gaze is male although the eyes are female. This is probably what Galatea wishes to exalt: the instability and incongruity of the Cyclops, and the kind of power over him that this gives to her.

We suggest here that an important part of the Cyclops' feminization and lack of power has to do with his incapacity to see. When Telemus predicts that one day Ulysses will take his one eye, Polyphemus responds, "*altera iam rapuit [lumen]*" / "'Another has already stolen my eye'" (*Met.* 13.775). This pun, as Tissol recognizes, is based on a double-entendre that links epic with elegy. While talking about Ulysses' enterprise, it plays on the common elegiac expression of the lover being robbed of his eyes, as in Ovid's *Amores* (*nostros rapuisti nuper ocellos*/ "Recently you stole my eyes," *Am.* 2.19.19) and Propertius (*oculos cepisti*, 3.10.15).[61] But this 'stealing' of Polyphemus's eye has more profound implications for the narrative. The reader never really hears Polyphemus's voice or perceives his gaze directly; his vision is always mediated by Galatea's gaze as narrator. Thus in a way, Galatea has actually robbed him of his power to see and leave his own testimony in the poem, or rather, she lets him have a gaze but only sieved through her own feminine narrative. The reader, however, is also allowed to think that it is not only Galatea who has deprived the Cyclops of his gaze, but the very narrator of the *Metamorphoses* who lets Galatea command the gaze and the story. In regard to gender, Galatea as thief of eyes aligns with Perseus and Ulysses in the poem and thus acquires some prerogatives of the epic hero.

Soon, however, 'blind' Polyphemus becomes a singer and the situation turns extremely intricate. The episode proposes a komastic reading, though less obvious than those discussed in chapter 2.[62] This hypermasculine giant bound to land woos Galatea, a creature of the sea. It would be possible to read the boundary between land and water, the solid and the liquid, as a metaphoric barrier to be crossed by the lover, who begs that Galatea lift her head up from the sea: "*iam modo caeruleo nitidum caput exere ponto,/ iam, Galatea, veni, nec munera despice nostra!*" / "'Now raise your shining head from the blue sea, Galatea, come now and do not despise my gifts!'" (*Met.* 13.838–39).[63] In any case, Polyphemus is clearly an excluded lover, both spatially and figuratively. What approximates the episode to a paraclausithyron situation is Polyphemus's song. Ovid presents here a sort of poet-lover who serenades his beloved and begs for acceptance with a surprisingly long *carmen* (789–869).[64] As in the elegiac paraclausithyron, the man is mollified and feminized while the woman remains hard, obstinate, and intransigent.

Now Galatea says that she was lying with Acis (*Met.* 13.786–87) while she heard Polyphemus's song, which in part describes her own image. So Galatea offers a construction of herself as she is seen through the eyes of the Cyclops.

> candidior folio nivei Galatea ligustri,
> floridior pratis, longa procerior alno,
> splendidior vitro, tenero lascivior haedo,
> levior adsiduo detritis aequore conchis,
> solibus hibernis, aestiva gratior umbra,
> mobilior damma, platano conspectior alta,
> lucidior glacie, matura dulcior uva,
> mollior et cycni plumis et lacte coacto,
> et, si non fugias, riguo formosior horto.

> Galatea, whiter than the leaves of the snowy privet, more full of flowers than the meadows, taller than an alder, more radiant than crystal, more playful than a tender kid, softer than shells smoothened by constant waves, more pleasing than the winter sun and the summer shade, more nimble than a doe, more beautiful than a lofty plane-tree, clearer than ice, sweeter than ripe grapes, softer than a swan's down and milk curd, and, if only you would not flee from me, more beautiful than a well-watered garden. (*Met.* 13.789–97)

The game of narrators and narrated, viewers and visual objects, is somewhat circular. One should remember that Galatea makes fun of Polyphemus in an effort to preserve her hold on the gaze and its power. Galatea relates what Polyphemus said about her image. In Polyphemus's speech there is a male-oriented discourse where the gaze is male because it reifies Woman; in this sense, therefore, Galatea looks at herself with a male gaze. Soon she changes roles and Polyphemus is evaluated by his physical appearance and placed as the visual object. Curiously, Polyphemus is more an object of the gaze than Acis, the boy subjected to Galatea's domain. But there is more to the description of Galatea in the Cyclops' song. The long list of comparisons that defines the *puella* tends to assimilate her to landscape, which has much to do with femininity in the poem.[65] First, the adjective *niveus* alluding to Galatea's whiteness recalls the color of such eroticized virgins as Pygmalion's maiden (note the use of *niveus* in that passage), Atalanta, Daphne, and Andromeda. Then she is *floridior pratis*, which literally assimilates her body to a pleasant landscape open to violation—an image so common in *Metamorphoses*. *Splendidior vitro* recalls the transparent pools that are so visually and erotically attractive to Narcissus, Hermaphroditus, and Arethusa.[66] The reference to the pleasant climate is, as is well known, particularly apt to *loci amoeni*; trees and swans also appear in the imagination of landscape in the poem. There are two points to be made about this. First, Polyphemus (or rather Galatea's construction of Polyphemus) has 'read' *Metamorphoses* well and makes up the image of Galatea as a pastiche of Ovidian *topoi* used in the poem. Likewise, the fact that Polyphemus describes Galatea with images of landscape and nature may also have to do with the fact that this is the world he, an uncultivated and rustic character, knows best. But perhaps it is this lack of originality that fails to seduce the intended object. Second, descriptions of landscape in the poem commonly preannounce 'real' or figurative rape and the possibility of violation. Galatea, as goddess and independent woman, does not enjoy being fixed in this *topos*. Galatea is, then, symbolically the landscape and surface of the poem, into which the narrator and reader intrude. But the gaze of Galatea rejects this reading of *Metamorphoses* and its fixation of women. Galatea can be seen as a critical reader of the gender stereotypes that *Metamorphoses* proposes. In this respect it is worth pointing out that this episode takes place almost at the end of the poem, after conventional gender patterns have been so well established that criticism is allowed. It must be said that Polyphemus never attempts to rape Galatea, and so we are led to think that he is actually less 'bestial' than Galatea wants us to believe. Paradoxically, while she presents him as a monster, Galatea sees him as effeminate and develops the image of the Cyclops as elegiac lover and slave of love (note *serviet* in line 820).

Soon Galatea turns to the description of Polyphemus by narrating how the Cyclops sees himself:

> certe ego me novi liquidaeque in imagine vidi
> nuper aquae, placuitque mihi mea forma videnti.
> adspice, sim quantus: non est hoc corpore maior
> Iuppiter in caelo, nam vos narrare soletis
> nescio quem regnare Iovem; coma plurima torvos
> prominet in vultus, umerosque, ut lucus, obumbrat;
> nec mea quod rigidis horrent densissima saetis
> corpora, turpe puta: turpis sine frondibus arbor,
> turpis equus, nisi colla iubae flaventia velent;

pluma tegit volucres, ovibus sua lana decori est:
barba viros hirtaeque decent in corpore saetae.
unum est in media lumen mihi fronte, sed instar
ingentis clipei. quid? non haec omnia magnus
Sol videt e caelo? Soli tamen unicus orbis

Surely I know myself and lately saw my image on the surface of a pool, and I liked what I saw. Look how large I am: Jupiter in the sky does not have a body bigger than this, for you often say that some Jupiter or other reigns there. Much hair grows on my fierce face and it covers my shoulders like a forest. And do not deem me ugly because my body is thick with hard bristles. The tree is ugly without foliage, the horse is ugly if a mane does not veil his golden neck. Birds are covered with feathers, their wool is becoming to the sheep, a beard and thick hair on the body suit men. There is only one eye in my forehead, but as big as a huge shield. What? Doesn't the mighty Sun see all these things from heaven? Yet the Sun has only one eye. (*Met.*13.840–53)

The search for self-identity in the mirror here obviously recalls Narcissus, but in a comic way. Just as Narcissus could not really 'know' himself, one could suppose that if Polyphemus sees himself as 'pretty,' he cannot know himself either and that his capacity to see is distorted. There is also another peculiar problem. At the beginning of the tale Polyphemus recognizes that he has been robbed of his gaze. Thus, when he mentions that he has one big eye like the Sun, this eye could be taken to be an empty and blind one; therefore, the construction of his own image is undermined by his lack of 'eye.' In fact, in terms of narrative and focalization, Polyphemus's gaze in the mirror may not only be distorted by his visual impairment by love, but also tainted by Galatea's visual control.

The Cyclops soon emerges from his feminization and becomes 'manly' (or possibly 'beastly'). Galatea now confesses that she has seen his wrath and, as witness, gives away the fact that the whole story is tainted by her own gaze (*"talia nequiquam questus (nam cuncta videbam),* / *surgit"* / "'Having thus lamented in vain (for I saw everything), he rose,'" *Met.*13.870–71). It is the visual discovery of Galatea in the arms of Acis that infuriates the Cyclops (*"cum ferus ignaros nec quicquam tale timentes*/ *me videt atque Acin videoque exclamat et ista*/ *ultima sit, faciam, Veneris concordia vestrae"* / "'When the savage creature saw us, Attis and myself, unaware and fearing nothing like that, he exclaimed, 'I see you. Let this be your last amorous embrace,'" *Met.*13.873–75). Polyphemus also tries to show his strength and sexual power in the image of the violence exercised against Acis:

sentiet esse mihi tanto pro corpore vires!
viscera viva traham divulsaque membra per agros
perque tuas spargam (sic se tibi misceat!) undas.

He'll find that I have strength matching my size. I will tear apart his living entrails and scatter his rent limbs over the fields and over your waters
(thus he will be joined with you!). (Met.13.864–66)

The phonic effect of -vi-, which recalls vis, is at play in vires, viscera viva, and divulsaque. The sparagmos that Polyphemus wishes to perform relates Acis to the dismemberments of Pentheus and Orpheus, which, as dis-cussed, involve the dissolution of masculine integrity. Tissol points out that this final violence in the story constitutes a narrative disruption and that it provides the reader with a surprise, because while the reader is pre-pared to follow the Theocritean and Virgilian versions of a rather peace-ful and inoffensive Cyclops who finds a cure for love in song, the story concludes with a violent act typical of the Homeric picture of Poly-phemus.[67]

Galatea herself relates much more about the Cyclops than Polyphemus includes in his song. This is particularly relevant if one compares the male narrator of Theocritus's Idyll 11 and Galatea as a female narrator in Meta-morphoses. Farrell already notes this point, although he does not dwell on its gender-specific weight.[68] What Galatea, like the Sibyl in her story, will do is offer a female perspective to a well-established masculine version. In her narrative, the Cyclops describes himself as a huge male, hairy and with one eye. The depiction that the Cyclops creates of his own image intends to convey a mighty masculinity comparable even to that of Jupiter, the most truly masculine god in Metamorphoses. Nevertheless, it is in Galatea's discourse that Polyphemus is mocked and seen as an effemi-nate lover who pays too much attention to his image. The information given by each character is slightly different; in fact, there is nothing about the Cyclops' toilette in his own speech. Thus Galatea knows more than what she hears in his song. But where did she learn this? She must have looked at him with some attention to be able to display such a complete picture. Or is she simply imagining it? The gender destabilizations in the episode, where Man is feminized like an elegiac lover and Woman is iden-tified as a dura puella (cf. durior annosa quercu/ "harder than an aged oak," Met.13.799) were mentioned before. To this inversion will correspond the reification of Polyphemus as a visual object.

Ovid and Galatea play with some element of surprise with the intrusion of Acis, who was probably an unknown character to Ovid's audience.[69] The jealous Cyclops throws a part of a mountain in an attempt to kill him (an obvious allusion to *Odyssey* 9.537–40); blood runs from under it and Galatea then transforms him into water (*"fecimus, ut vires adsumeret Acis avitas"*/ "'We caused Attis to assume his ancestral powers,'" 886).[70] There are two possible ways of interpreting this transformation. On the one hand, the word *vires* may seem to point at virility and the fact that Acis gains strength, becomes a man, and therefore grows bigger through his transformation (*maior*, Met.13.895). On the other hand, the lengthy description of his change seems to be open to a different reading:

> puniceus de mole cruor manabat, et intra
> temporis exiguum rubor evanescere coepit,
> fitque color primo turbati fluminis imbre
> purgaturque mora; tum moles iacta dehiscit,
> vivaque per rimas proceraque surgit harundo,
> osque cavum saxi sonat exsultantibus undis,
> miraque res, subito media tenus exstitit alvo
> incinctus iuvenis flexis nova cornua cannis,[71]
> qui, nisi quod maior, quod toto caerulus ore,
> Acis erat, sed sic quoque erat tamen Acis, in amnem
> versus, et antiquum tenuerunt flumina nomen.

> Crimson blood was trickling from the mass, and soon his ruddy color began to fade away. His hue became like that of a river swollen by early rains, but it cleared in a while. Then the mass that had been thrown split and through the cracks a tall green reed rose. The hollow opening in the rock resounded with leaping waves, and, a miracle, suddenly, a youth stood waist-deep from the water, his new-sprung horns woven around with winding rushes. He was Acis, except bigger and all blue in his face. But still he was Acis, turned into a river, and his waters kept their former name. (Met.13.887–97)

In comparison with the stories of Cyane and Arethusa, the description of Acis' transformation does not stress the dissolution of each part of his body into water, but rather focuses on the transformation of his blood. The transformation concludes with an assertion that Acis is the same but bigger and blue (*caerulus ore*). But the passage is interesting from a gender standpoint, because the one who seems to hold the power is the woman. First, Acis is no more than a sixteen-year-old *puer* (like Narcissus)

(*Met*.13.753–54), whose power and masculinity are dubious and *tenues*, like his down, and weak in comparison with the hypermasculine Cyclops. He cannot fight them with his own means and needs the help of Galatea. Liquefaction seems to be somewhat feminine, and thus it is not an unbecoming end for a *puer*, in contrast with Galatea who is *dura* for her rejection of Polyphemus's love (798–807). Acis was *mollis*, and as such, he is easily mollified. But by this very softening, that is, liquefaction, of his limbs and blood he becomes a man, unlike Narcissus and Hermaphroditus. We may also observe that normally males are transformed into rivers (*in amnem*, 896, and *flumina*, 897) while women become only pools or streams.

Up to now we have pointed out two possible readings of the passage. Either Acis matures as a man and achieves masculinity in his transformation into the river god or else he becomes *mollis*, like Arethusa. Though apparently contradictory, both interpretations can be easily reconciled. As noted, Acis is a sort of hybrid, not yet defined in his masculinity. This gender struggle is well illustrated in the partition of his body, his flowing water symbolizing the feminine and the half-body with its new horns (*Met*.13.893–94) his masculine part. The solid element, the body that does not disintegrate, embodies the masculine, while the female dissolves. The *phantasia* that Galatea constructs of Acis is ambivalent. While in principle he is the object of the gaze and Galatea seems to look at him with a 'male gaze,' Acis is not exactly eroticized in his transformation. His fluidity seems to evade the fixation typical of the male gaze.

The audience of Galatea's personal story is Scylla and other nymphs. It all starts with a reference to the monster Scylla who torments sailors. In a flashback, Ovid tells us that she was once a virgin nymph who fled from many suitors. This gives place to Galatea's tale. The narrative circumstance is a reunion of nymphs in which Galatea is letting Scylla comb her hair. This detail is poignant when one thinks about Polyphemus combing his hair and arranging his beard. Galatea's tale wishes to prove, as in various episodes of female narratives, that she suffered more than her interlocutor did. Her story of wooing by the horrid giant is expected to provoke sympathy in Scylla and the nymphs who will pity her. A witty paradox is likewise played out in the story. Scylla, who has listened and 'seen' the monster Polyphemus in Galatea's, tale ends up as a monster herself, probably exemplifying, in an extreme situation, how stories can affect, modify, and change the reader.

To sum up, the story told by Galatea, like that of Arethusa, shows another instance of female perspective. There is a sense of gender destabilization in the tale, whereby Galatea tries to arrogate a powerful gaze for herself. But while she tries to feminize the pictures of both Polyphemus and Acis, she can only do it halfway, because Polyphemus, despite his hinted effeminacy, still has the strength of the hypermasculine. Acis, in his transformation becomes a river god in whose *phantasia* Galatea fuses masculine solidity and feminine fluidity. Finally, although Galatea tries to create a picture of herself as a *dura puella*, she can only do so in an oblique way, appropriating the discourse of Polyphemus to describe herself.

So what and how does Galatea see? As a reader of *Metamorphoses*, she sees a world where women are reified and transformed into landscape. She rejects such fixation, but, at the same time, she regards Polyphemus as effeminate. Galatea strives to have her own gaze and, at some level, to possess a somewhat masculine gaze that can objectify the male. Nonetheless, she is never completely successful, for her own creation—Polyphemus (just as in Pygmalion's story)—comes alive and ceases being an object and becomes masculine and active. At the same time, her lover Acis, while a spectacle to be looked at, still becomes mobile and achieves a certain level of masculinity and, with that, independence.

Pregnant with Words

Hercules' mother, Alcmene, finds a confidante in Iole, who is herself pregnant, and tells her the story of her sufferings at Hercules' birth. The interrelated stories of Alcmene and Dryope are particularly rich for the study of women in *Metamorphoses*, but they have suffered from an almost complete lack of critical interest.

ALCMENE

Alcmene's is a story of pregnancy, childbirth, and creativity. When she was ready to give birth to Hercules, she called for the help of Lucina, but it was obvious that jealous Juno was set on preventing the delivery. In her self-depiction as a pregnant woman, Alcmene emphasizes her heaviness and effort:

> namque laboriferi cum iam natalis adesset
> Herculis et decimum premeretur sidere signum,
> tendebat gravitas uterum mihi, quodque ferebam,

tantum erat, ut posses auctorem dicere tecti
ponderis esse Iovem. nec iam tolerare labores
ulterius poteram. . . .

The birth of the labor-enduring Hercules was at hand and the tenth
month was pressed on by its star. The weight of my womb was great, and
what I was carrying was so huge that you could tell Jupiter was the father
of the unborn baby. I could not bear the pain of labor any longer. . . .
(Met. 9.285–90)

Pregnancy is felt as a pressure and a weight. Stephen Wheeler suggests
convincingly that "Alcmene's *labores* (Met. 9.289) directly compete as
subject matter for narrative with Hercules' canonical labors (cf. Met.
9.277). Moreover, the narrator Alcmene concludes with an image of
Juno's wrath that supersedes the goddess's better known persecution of
Hercules."[72] Let us remember that Juno's hatred toward Hercules is
expressly stated by Achelous earlier in Book 9 ("*tantum ne noceat, quod me
nec regia Iuno/ odit . . .*" / "'Let it not be to my disadvantage that queen
Juno does not hate me,'" Met. 9.21–22) and that she is addressed by
Hercules at the time of his death (Met. 9.176ff.). The word *auctor* is here
significant as it foregrounds issues of authority and authorship in the story.
Hercules is a creation of Jupiter, yet woman as vehicle is needed to give
birth to the hero and to the story as well. But although Jupiter is talked
of as *auctor*, the voice we hear is a female one. The retrospective narration of Hercules' birth right after his death may be read as an account of
woman as creator both of the hero and of the story just narrated. In this
sense a releasing reading of female voices does not necessarily imply
women's independence or that her voice is perfect, yet the alternative
would be silence and the view that the only author is masculine. This
episode is good to think with in these matters. Alcmene recognizes
Jupiter as author, but she still has the narrating voice; in this way, she
could be compared with a prophetess like the Sibyl. Although inspiration
comes as an intrusion on the woman's body and she becomes the 'mouth'
of the god's voice, the medium is always part of the expression, her mouth
a vital element in the creative process. But Alcmene is more than a simple instrument like Syrinx. Although Jupiter seems to be envisioned as
author, which may agree with ancient conceptions of sexuality and reproduction, Alcmene as a body and a mouth becomes essential in the creative
process of giving birth to the hero and to the story. Alcmene is, then, an
author, though a constrained one. A contrast with Plautus's version of
Hercules' birth is thought-provoking. In the *Amphitruo*, the divine inter-

vention of Jupiter is marked precisely by the absence of pain and ease of delivery (1091–97 in particular). Juno is never mentioned in the parturition except for a very early reference (831–32) by Alcmene stating simply that Juno is a goddess to be revered by her. In a generalizing way, Alcmene is less active and less distinguished in Plautus than in Ovid. In Plautus the events seem to be controlled by Jupiter, while Ovid pays more attention to Alcmene's sufferings and participation in the birth of her son.

Alcmene's discourse stages a battle between the unborn hero and the hateful goddess Juno. Now, most critics, like Wheeler, think that Alcmene's sufferings respond to Juno's hatred of Hercules. But it is possible also to think that Alcmene, as concubine of Jupiter, is already the object of her anger, and it is because of this that Hercules is loathed by the goddess. This reading would prioritize the role and importance of women in the story rather than the figure of Hercules.

The whole episode proposes a struggle between openness and closure. Lucina sits at the door of the house with arms and legs crossed, an action that by sympathetic magic affects Alcmene's body:[73]

> utque meos audit gemitus, subsedit in illa
> ante fores ara, dextroque a poplite laevum
> pressa genu et digitis inter se pectine iunctis
> sustinuit partus. tacita quoque carmina voce
> dixit, et inceptos tenuerunt carmina partus.

> And as she heard my complaints, she sat on the altar before the doors and crossing her right knee over her left, with fingers interlocked, she prevented my delivery. In whispering voice she chanted charms and the songs stalled the birth as it began. (*Met.* 9.297–301)

This closure and binding of Alcmene's body embodies Juno's desire not only to prevent Hercules' birth but also the possibility of his life being narrated and incorporated in *Metamorphoses*. Similarities and parallelisms between mouth, female pudenda, and doors are well attested in classical literature.[74] This appears clearly in the story. Alcmene's only possibility of being creative is to open up and the house with its door acts as a clear metaphor for the female body. In this, the character of Galanthis is key, as this faithful attendant of Alcmene suspects that some injustice is being done by Juno. When entering and leaving the house through the door, she surprises Lucina by saying that Alcmene has given birth and provokes her to unbind her arms and legs:

> . . . ea sensit iniqua
> nescio quid Iunone geri, dumque exit et intrat
> saepe fores, divam residentem vidit in ara
> bracchiaque in genibus digitis conexa tenentem,
> et "quaecumque es," ait "dominae gratare. levata est
> Argolis Alcmene, potiturque puerpera voto."

> She sensed that something was being plotted by unfair Juno, and while
> she was going in and out of the doors, she saw the goddess sitting on the
> altar, with her fingers linked and her arms crossed over her knees and
> said to her: "Whoever you are, congratulate my mistress. Alcmene of
> Argos has been freed from suffering. Her prayers are answered and her
> child is born." (*Met.* 9.308–13)

Doors are a central element in the story. The goddess sitting with closed
arms and legs at the door implicates closure. What is more, Galanthis'
coming and going seems to be the first step in the final opening of
Alcmene. Galanthis crosses the passage of the door. Then she opens her
mouth to speak, and by opening her mouth she unchains the bindings of
the goddess, an act that will lead to Hercules' birth and ultimately to the
possibility of his inclusion in *Metamorphoses*. By narrating the story,
Alcmene has decided to 'open her mouth' like Galanthis rather than keep
silence in a more conventionally feminine stance. The tale of Alcmene
and Galanthis stages the struggle of women to create, a desire that Juno
strives to impede. Because Galanthis has cheated the goddess with her
mouth, she is changed into a weasel, condemned to give birth through her
mouth (*quae quia mendaci parientem iuverat ore,/ ore parit/* "Because she
had helped the woman in labor with her liar's mouth, she now gives birth
through the mouth," *Met.* 9.322–33).[75] The equivalence between speech
and opening of the body is then finalized and completed. Nevertheless,
sisterhood and women's triumph always have their limits. Some trade-off
is always expected, which is why Galanthis loses her human condition and
is fixed in an animal behavior.

   The audience here is Iole, also pregnant by Hyllus, Hercules' son. Segal
recognizes that Ovid "may be writing with an awareness of an audience of
women readers."[76] This story demonstrates the sisterhood and help of one
woman to another, and Alcmene's words stage a moment of intimacy and
confidentiality between women. It also asserts the magnitude of childbirth as a creative act that empowers women to—in a somewhat askew
fashion—be co-authors of stories. Alcmene thus sees herself as a medium.

As such she is a participant in the creative process. Likewise, in her self-representation, Alcmene develops the visual metaphor of the locked house for her body, which needs to be opened. While the functions of speech and childbirth are merged in Galanthis, Alcmene narrating her story also opens up her female 'interior,' which could function as an encouragement to Iole to both give birth and narrate.

DRYOPE

Now Iole responds with another tale: her sister Dryope. This odd story exemplifies most clearly the role of women's gaze as 'witness.' A witness of woman's tragedy and arborization, Iole is at the same time a partici-pant in the story (*"spectatrix aderam fati crudelis, opemque/ non poteram tibi ferre, soror"* / "'I was there, a witness of your cruel fate, and could not offer you help, sister,'" *Met.* 9.359–60). The tale begins with a remarkable ekphrasis:

> est lacus, adclivis devexo margine formam
> litoris efficiens, summum myrteta coronant.
> venerat huc Dryope fatorum nescia.

> There is a lake, whose shelving sides form sloping shores. Myrtles crown
> the top. Here Dryope had come, ignorant of her fate. (*Met.* 9.334–36)

Est lacus recalls the lake of Enna in Sicily in *Met.* 5.385. As in other cases, *forma* is here playing with the double meaning of beauty and 'shape.' The circularity of the space is well signaled by the verb *coronat*, indicating how myrtle surrounds the pool. All these elements point again to a femi-nine space. But what is surprising is that, unlike the ekphrases of Actaeon or Thetis, which contain a woman as the central object of the gaze, what the reader sees here is a woman entering the space of the description, as in Arethusa's story and like Minerva entering the space of the Heliconian fount. Most significantly, she enters into the closed space of the pool, which itself bears meaningful connotations in *Metamorphoses*. While in the first books of *Metamorphoses* it is only males who perform visual and spatial intrusions in ekphrastic landscapes, the poem gradually lets women enter these types of spaces. This 'masculine' act of intrusion will be important for the development of the story. Dryope is a mother bear-ing her young child in her bosom, and to please him, she plucks a flower standing by the pool:

haut procul a stagno Tyrios imitata colores
in spem bacarum florebat aquatica lotos.
carpserat hinc Dryope, quos oblectamina nato
porrigeret, flores, et idem factura videbar—
namque aderam—vidi guttas e flore cruentas
decidere et tremulo ramos horrore moveri.

Not far from the pool a water lotus-tree of color like Tyrian dye was blos-
soming in hope of forthcoming fruit. Dryope had picked some of these
flowers to please her child. I was about to do the same, for I was there,
when I saw blood dripping from the flower and the branches moving
with shivering horror. (*Met.* 9.340–45)

In this passage the narrator asserts her role of witness (*vidi*), which makes
explicit the purpose and meaning of her narrative. There is also an interesting play on activity and passivity in terms of viewing. Iole affirms that
she seemed/was seen to be about to do the same (*et idem factura videbar*).
Videbar makes Iole not only grammatically passive but also turns her into
an object of the audience's gaze. However, it is an immediate act of active
seeing that changes the course of her life, saves her from transformation,
and gives her a gaze, which she can then transform into narrative (unlike
Actaeon) so as to become an author of stories and of human life—let's
remember she is pregnant. As discussed before, the very act of picking a
flower symbolizes defloration in other contexts in *Metamorphoses* and
Latin literature more generally. The color of the flower is also significant
as it emblematizes the blood that will soon be spilled.[77] Up to now, the text
has presented a woman who has infringed on the limits of an ekphrasis
and exerted some violence on a flower that begins to bleed. But it
becomes more meaningful when Iole relates that the lotus tree was in
actuality the virgin Lotis who had taken refuge in that form to evade rape
by Priapus:

scilicet, ut referunt tardi nunc denique agrestes,
Lotis in hanc nymphe, fugiens obscena Priapi,
contulerat versos, servato nomine, vultus.

Certainly, as the slow rustics indeed now say, the nymph Lotis, fleeing
from Priapus's sexual advances had changed into this form, transforming
her appearance but keeping her name. (*Met.* 9.346–48)

Segal believes that Dryope's action "involves no sexual violence," although he recognizes that there are sexual implications in the landscape of the scene.[78] But one can disagree with Segal in that there is no sexual violence in the plucking of the flower, at least at the symbolic level if not at a concrete level. Likewise, while Segal's observations about sexuality and violence in landscape were eye-openers, he often seems rather vague in his discussions of sexuality. What we have here is a woman who—unwillingly—destroys the integrity of a virgin. The dripping blood clearly symbolizes the loss of Lotis' virginity and performs, figuratively, the act of rape from which she was escaping.[79] By the violence she exerts on the flower, Dryope becomes like Priapus. As a 'punishment' (we are not sure from whom), Dryope is turned into a tree. Underscoring this episode there is again Daphne in Book 1 as a model. However, this 'arborization' is curious because, unlike the case of Daphne, it is not a welcomed and happy transformation. In fact, it is a negative outcome as it deprives Dry-ope of her role of mother and family life. In a sisterly wish that recalls Anna's desire to die with her sister in the *Aeneid*, Iole desires to join in the creeping bark that is enclosing her sister (*Met.* 9.362). This contrasts with the kisses later applied by men to the tree that eroticize the transformed body (365). When Dryope is about to disappear under the bark she delivers a speech declaring that she has lived and died innocently (*Met.* 9.371–73). But she has accidentally committed a sort of figurative rape and for this, she is to be punished. Ovid tells us that when Andraemon married her, Dryope was no longer a virgin, having suffered the violence of Apollo:

> . . . quam virginitate carentem
> vimque dei passam Delphos Delonque tenentis
> excipit Andraemon, et habetur coniuge felix.

> Andraemon took her after she had lost her virginity and suffered vio-lence from the god that holds Delphi and Delos; and he was counted happy in his wife. (*Met.* 9.331–33)

Another version of Dryope's myth is recorded in Antoninus Liberalis' *Metamorphoses* 32, and adjudicated to Nicander in the first book of his *Metamorphoses*. This version records that Dryope was a daughter of Dryops, a former companion of the Hamadryades who taught her to sing and dance. Apollo, seeing her dancing, transformed himself first into a tortoise, then into a serpent, and finally raped her. However, the girl said nothing to her family about the crime and married Andraemon. Soon, she gave birth to the boy Amphissus, who later built a temple to Apollo. One day as Dryope was approaching the temple, the Hamadryades abducted her and hid her in the woods; in her place they caused a poplar tree to grow out of the ground and made a spring gush forth.[80] The oak as mark of rape (an odd sort of rape by women) suggests the hardness of the tree (*robur*), which is normally a mark of masculine sexual potency, contrasting sharply with the delicacy of the lotus flower. While it is clearly not the dryads who abduct Dryope, their act may function as a reminiscence of her previous rape by Apollo. Although Ovid gives a different angle to the story, he may still be playing on this other version, where the rape by Apollo is given greater weight. The personal rape suffered by Dryope lends a paradoxical twist to the symbolic rape that she is performing on the flower, and even perhaps implies a sort of vengeance. Both Lotis and Dryope have suffered the same toils—although Lotis escapes—but instead of sisterhood, the episode shows violence, even if unintentional, among women. One more question concerns the significance of Dryope's transformation into a tree. In *Metamorphoses*—it is not told exactly why this occurs—it seems clear that this is a punishment, while in Antoninus's version it actually becomes the source and emblem of her life. In Ovid, Dryope's transformation closely echoes that of Daphne, something with which Apollo may have had something to do. In this way, he keeps his mistresses in the form of a tree, which is in other contexts a clear symbol and fixation of rape and possession by a god.

There are two ways of reading this embedded tale. From a female-oriented perspective, one can see that it is one of sisterhood and denunciation of rape. The women in the story all lose something: Lotis her virginity and her humanity, Dryope her humanity and her family, Iole her sister. This is also a clear example of how a woman can actually 'act upon her gaze,' for she can definitely do something with it, by transforming what she has seen into story and by giving other women the possibility to enjoy and learn from her own experience. Kaplan may object that Iole cannot "act upon her gaze" in the same violent way as the male gaze does. That is precisely the point. If she could, Iole would be another Salmacis whose gaze is almost a 'male gaze.' A female gaze is not actively violent, yet she can still produce and perform in a different, alternative way. Here the monolithic 'male gaze' should again be deconstructed, as it is not sufficient to explain the power relationships in the episode. The importance of Iole's gaze is that of being a witness. She sees herself as a sister who can remember and tell. Although hers is a 'helpless' gaze that cannot modify the images it sees and the facts of her sister's fate, *Metamorphoses* allocates room for Iole's testimony, her point of view, and her narrative, for it is precisely in her story that she can modify, influence, and act upon what she has seen. For all the personal loss in the tale, there is some gain in the possibility of telling what has happened: to communicate with a female audience, to fix it as a testimony of female suffering, which strengthens bonds among women. Now, if one resists the text and assumes the author as male overall, one can see punishment for two women who have defied male authority. Lotis has tried to avoid possession and ends up symbolically raped; Dryope has tried to hide her rape and ends up losing her humanity and committing violence. The male power finally imposes his authority and prevents sisterhood. But thanks to a woman we can still read the story and reflect on its visual wealth.

Warning Adonis

In Book 10 of *Metamorphoses*, Venus advises her young lover Adonis to fear wild beasts. and to illustrate her hatred of them the goddess narrates the story of Atalanta and Hippomenes while lying comfortably under the shade of a tree.[81] To take Venus's narrative as an example of women's creation and *phantasia* is problematic because not only is Venus a goddess and not a human female, but also, at some level, she actually embodies a male ideal of what the erotic female is. This problematic character of the goddess of love and passion makes her often act against sisterhood and justify male desire. But the episode here discussed is particularly engaging because the goddess and her own desire are involved.

As with the Sibyl's story, the audience of Venus's narrative is masculine—though problematically: the boy Adonis, Myrrha's child.[82] One can recognize some identification between the goddess and Atalanta. In the erotic relationship, both Venus and Atalanta are women in power. Venus clearly overmasters the *puer*, being herself a goddess. Now, although Atalanta is really not free to choose and 'fate' is imposed on her, her physical strength surpasses her contestants' in the race. In a way, she still holds the power of life and death over Hippomenes. Like Venus in love with a young boy, Atalanta says that what truly attracts her about Hippomenes is that he is still a boy: "*nec forma tangor, (poteram tamen hac quoque tangi)/ sed quod adhuc puer est; non me movet ipse, sed aetas*" / "'I am not touched by his beauty (though this could also touch me), but by the fact that he is still a boy. He himself does not move me, but his age does'" (*Met.*10.614–15). This is an intriguing statement, followed by praise of Hippomenes' *virtus*

and *mens interrita* (Met.10.616). It is somewhat odd that Atalanta is enam-
ored of this *puer* who has virile qualities, but the situation serves as a model
of a woman in power that mirrors Venus's relationship with Adonis. She is
also a more powerful woman who is finally vanquished by an inferior man.
Despite the anachronism—Atalanta and Hippomenes are previous to
Venus's affair with Adonis—this background permits the reader to link
Venus's inclination to help Hippomenes to her own sympathetic feelings
for boys in general and for Adonis in particular. Venus's choice of narrative
material is appropriate to her present narrative circumstances. One could
even think of Venus as a sort of lover/mother figure to the boy, thus invert-
ing and reenacting the incestuous sexual story of Adonis' family.

At first Venus shows herself a benevolent and assisting goddess. She
describes how the prayers of Hippomenes touched her heart (*motaque
sum*, Met.10.643—note here that Atalanta is also moved by the boy's age
and beauty). She also appears as a teacher who instructs Hippomenes on
how to use the golden apples. Yet soon the story turns into one of revenge
on impertinent humans for neglecting the gods. It is remarkable that
Venus destroys the lovers with the very element she cherishes so much:
love and sexual passion. Hippomenes, inspired by the goddess, feels an
uncontrollable lust and has sex with his wife in a sacred temple. They are
punished with transformation into lions, beastly animals that Adonis
should fear. But why tell this story to Adonis? Obviously, it is a warning to
him that he should fear these uncontrollable beasts, but also an assertion of
Venus's power and the consequences of defying it. Perhaps with this story
Venus wishes to scare and control Adonis, though with the loving purpose
of protecting him.[83] Furthermore, she wishes to preserve him as a *puer*,
since daring to fight and defeat wild beasts would imply a manly enterprise.
All to no avail. Venus's narrative is not effective and she does not manage
to impress upon her lover the perils of disregarding her or the danger of
wild beasts. Adonis dies trying to fight a huge boar, for he is not ready for
manhood. Venus preserves Adonis' memory forever as a flower, the
anemone, and perhaps with this image she also keeps him eternally a boy.

Venus's gaze should be considered in different terms from the gaze of
other females because, as stated above, she is a powerful goddess who
often embodies a male conception of desirable woman. Nevertheless,
some common features can be observed. Venus's story acts as testimony to
her power. She is a witness of her own success and vengeance, and by
transforming this vision into narrative she hopes to do something productive for the fate of Adonis. In this sense, like other women, Venus wishes
to 'act upon' her gaze. But the reception of her story is not successful, for
Adonis cannot 'read' the *phantasia* in a productive way and loses his

humanity and masculinity. Perhaps, as a product of incest, this *puer* is, with so many others in the poem, stuck on the threshold of masculinity but unable to achieve full manhood. Having Venus as lover, a more mature, protective, almost motherly figure, he wishes to revert to the incestual relationship that gave him origin, unable to trascend the limits of the self needed for sexual maturity.

The Last Testimony

We end with a discussion of the Ovidian Sibyl, who has commonly been relegated by the critics to a place behind the traditional Virgilian prophetess. Here her voice, her gaze, and her testimony are brought to the spotlight, for she is not only the last woman to narrate a story in the first person in the poem but she is also, in a metanarrative way, at the end of her life.[84] It is true that the Sibyl still has to live three hundred years. In this sense her life is not finished, but she identifies herself as an old woman and her voice can be taken as an expression of the concerns of the aged (*"sed iam felicior aetas / terga dedit, tremuloque gradu venit aegra senectus, / quae patienda diu est"* / "But now the more joyous time of life has gone by, and weak old age to be endured for a long time comes with its unstable step,'" Met.14.142–44). The Sibyl is also given a voice and a gaze in *Metamorphoses*. Whether this voice is a personal endowment or simply a tool, a 'mouth' of the god Apollo remains a matter of discussion, but against other accounts of the Cumaean Sibyl, especially Virgil's version, the Ovidian prophetess is allowed a voice and a gaze of her own. In Book 14, Ovid reworks the Virgilian scene by presenting a new interaction between Aeneas and the Cumaean Sibyl. This is an attractive story because the audience is here a man, and not any man but the legendary father of Rome. After she assists him, the hero wonders whether the Sibyl is human or a deity, to which she responds, *"nec dea sum"* / "'I am not a goddess'" (130) and goes on to tell her personal story. Apollo, trying to persuade her to join him in love, offers precious gifts and even asks her to "choose anything" and he will give it. The voice of the prophetess narrates:

> . . . ego pulveris hausti
> ostendens cumulum, quot haberet corpora pulvis,
> tot mihi natales contingere vana rogavi.

> Pointing at a gathered heap of sand, I vainly asked to live as many years
> as the grains of sand in the mount. (Met.14.136–38)

Ovid compresses the Virgilian story of Book 6; yet what is truly remarkable is that Aeneas' descent to the Underworld, which plays such a decisive role in the *Aeneid* and in Roman history, is only given about fourteen lines, while the personal yarn of the Sibyl is allocated twenty-three. This is all we have of the Virgilian scene in *Metamorphoses* because after the hero's encounter with the Sibyl he swiftly continues his journey. To the overwhelming weight of masculine stories in Virgil's *Aeneid*, the feminine voice prevails in *Metamorphoses* 14. It is also noteworthy that in the *Aeneid* the Sibyl tells the stories of others, while in *Metamorphoses* she centers on her own fate. Segal argued that in the narrative art of *Metamorphoses*, one salient characteristic is 'humanization' of the characters.[85] He refers to Apollo, Pyramus and Thisbe, Andromeda and Perseus, and other characters, but he does not mention the Sibyl, which, following Galinsky, represents one of the clearest examples of Ovid's tendency to introduce the human side of his characters. The effect of this humanization is the undermining of the epic and propagandistic aspects of *Aeneid* 6. Nonetheless, as Galinsky suggests, Ovid still preserves the Sibyl's respectfulness and serious status.[86] Furthermore, issues of divine possession and oracular inspiration have been long discussed from a gender perspective. In particular, women prophetesses are seen as 'mouths' of the god that act as media for his own expression and messages to the world.[87] It is also well established that 'mouths' are 'female things,' an analogy favored by sexuality and female anatomy.[88] A direct comparison with Virgil's *Aeneid* is required here. Book 6 of the Virgilian epic presents the Sibyl mainly as a 'mouth' of Apollo and thus her divine possession and inspiration are highlighted:

> ventum erat ad limen, cum virgo, "poscere fata
> tempus" ait: "deus, ecce, deus!" cui talia fanti
> ante fores subito non voltus, non color unus,
> non comptae mansere comae, sed pectus anhelum,
> et rabie fera corda tument, maiorque videri
> nec mortale sonans, adflata est numine quando
> iam propiore dei. . . .

> They had come to the threshold, when the maiden said: "It is time to ask the oracles, the god, look, the god!" Having said this suddenly before the doors, neither her countenance nor her color was the same, her hair did not remain braided, but her chest heaves and her wild heart swells with madness. She is taller to behold and does not sound mortal when the spirit of the god is nearer and breathes in her. . . . (*Aen.* 6.45–51)

The Sibyl here is entirely possessed and dominated by the god. Let us now compare her brief description in Ovid: *at illa diu vultum tellure moratum / erexit tandemque deo furibunda recepto /* "But after fixing her eyes on the ground for a long time, she lifted them at last and possessed by the god's mad inspiration" (*Met.* 14.106–7). To the six-line detailed description of divine madness in Virgil, Ovid opposes three words (*deo furibunda recepto*). While her eyes fixed on the ground could be taken as a sign of possession, they could also be seen as a mark of sadness, given the general character of the Sibyl that Ovid proposes. Likewise, it is noteworthy that while in Virgil the prophetess is described as something horrific and fearful (*horrenda Sibylla, Aen.*6.10), Ovid humanizes her character. The focus of Ovid's story is not so much her divine possession by Apollo, but the sufferings of an old woman who expressly avows that she "is not a goddess." Furthermore, while in Virgil she only performs the prophetic commands of the god, in *Metamorphoses*, she takes time to tell her personal story in her own voice without any divine intervention.[89] It is also a story much like that of plaintive women who lament their own suffering. Likewise, the Sibyl tells a story of attempted sexual possession by Apollo, which recalls many other human and semi-divine maidens in Ovid's epic. But the Sibyl escapes rape, though like Daphne she loses something. She has become old and powerless, losing her youthful beauty. A peculiar trade-off is seen in the passage. The Sibyl preserves her voice and is able to narrate her own testimonial story, but she loses her body in a way that recalls Echo, although Echo—one could say—really loses her voice as well, as she cannot utter her own words but simply repeats the speech of others. The humanity of Ovid's Sibyl is seen also in her intimate conversation with Aeneas. It gives her a personal voice and the possibility of recalling her sad fate and her relationship with Apollo.

Greek and Roman writers often portray older women in a negative light. What the gaze of the Sibyl offers is a perspective rarely found in classical literature, that of an old woman for whom youth and beauty are lost and who finds herself disintegrating and banished from the erotic gaze of others (". . . *nec amata videbor/ nec placuisse deo, Phoebus quoque forsitan ipse/ vel non cognoscet, vel dilexisse negabit:/ usque adeo mutata ferar nullique videnda/ vocem tamen noscar"/* "'And now I will not seem to have been loved, neither to have pleased the god; perhaps even Phoebus himself will not recognize me or will deny that he loved me. To such an extent shall I change and, though nobody may recognize me when they look at me, I will be known by my voice,'" *Met.*14.149–52), but who is not presented in negative terms.[90] The Sibyl is left in an uncodified and marginal place for women in antiquity, in which elder women are usually inscribed. However, as Anastasios Nikolopoulos suggests, storytelling may be a way for old women to cope with their invisibility.[91] It is interesting that Ovid does not register any response from the audience (Aeneas) which could point to the isolation of the Sibyl's life and story. Despite this displacement, loneliness, and isolation, her story still has a point: to leave a testimony of her life and sufferings as emblematic reflection of the lives of old women.

This chapter was a search for a female gaze, or at least, an attempt to find *indicia* of what a 'female gaze' might be. We cannot and do not want to establish any restrictive definitions, for we would fall into the same short-comings as the theorists of the monolithic male gaze. However, the journey undertaken has been in itself productive. One thing to consider is the variety of female gazes and that the female gaze is not a homogeneous entity. Ovid's *Metamorphoses* gives testimony of women not only as erotic objects but also as mothers, goddesses, and aged human beings. Likewise, assigning a voice and a gaze to women does not necessarily mean that they will be perfect or unproblematic, as they can even be 'unsisterly.' Overall, this and the previous chapter have shown that Kaplan's argument that women cannot 'act upon' the gaze is valid only if taken in a very restrictive sense. While it is true that women like Cyane cannot return the violence of the male gaze, they can, however, find a more 'feminine' and alternative gaze, by turning what they have seen into narrative and visual testimony for other women to read, to decode, and to learn.

POSTSCRIPT

❦

Sideways Glances

I began this study in search of the gender-specific meanings of images and gazes in the complex mosaic of pictures woven in text that is Ovid's *Metamorphoses*. I found myself in the intersection between two critical movements: the mainly male-dominated Ovidian criticism and the mostly female-centered gaze theory. While the first has fallen short of recognizing the rich gender implications of looking in the poem, the latter, though enlightening, has likewise shown itself insufficient to account for the complexities that *Metamorphoses* has to offer.

Feminist film theory has proved useful for reading the Ovidian epic, for it has promoted productive readings of its episodes and has stimulated us to look at amply discussed episodes in an 'oblique' way. It has also encouraged us to 'suspect' both traditional views and feminist views of the poem. Yet our discussions have also shown the shortcomings of feminist gaze theory, for Mulvey's model can only conceive of successful male viewers and cannot properly account for all the unsuccessful, feminized, and problematic males or for the gaze of women. Likewise, Kaplan's idea that women's gazes are completely passive and that females cannot 'act upon' their gazes, has been deconstructed, as female narrators prove to be witnesses who can give *indicia* of what and how their gazes see. This also offers an answer to the crucial question of whether the masculine position is the only possible position of power for women. By narrating their stories and transmitting their gazes to other women, they not only leave their imprint in the world of *Metamorphoses* and in Latin literature, but they also stimulate other women to forge cooperative and personal readings from a feminine perspective.

Using feminine film theory has also illuminated aspects of both male and female gazes which have much to do with narratological issues. The penetrative, active, and intrusive male gaze of both readers and characters can intrude on the 'visual' and textual representation of 'landscaped' women. Its fixing power is also capable of detaining images and actions and of fixing eroticized female figures. Yet to all this male power, we saw that females like Diana and Ceres can return the gaze and affect the male viewer with paralysis or transformation. Likewise, sometimes like Andromeda tied to a rock, the very image of detained females can paralyze and disturb the mobility and independence of the male viewer. We also saw how gender has meaningful implications for narratology, for the active and advancing Narrative may be seen as a masculine aspect of the text, while 'static' and 'passive' Description may be taken as female. Thus, as Blake once said, "Man is Time and Woman is Space."

Do we know more about female gazes than we did before? I offered ideas of how and what some women see in the poem. Again, there is no definite formula because women's gazes are varied and complex and fluctuate from conservatism, to sisterhood, to rebellion. Nonetheless, I hope to have revealed that there is a gaze behind every female textual and visual production and that the journey in search of those gazes is in itself worthwhile.

In the history of Ovidian criticism the mainstream concerns about *Metamorphoses* have had to do with narrative questions, structure, humor, aetiology, and Alexandrian tradition among other things. With few exceptions, male readers have created the bulk of this tradition. Yet this book, alongside other recent attempts by feminist readers, has shown that there is much room for alternative views, from alternative readers. Philip Hardie ends a recent piece by saying: "I hope to have shown how readily the *Metamorphoses* opens itself to a reader, such as Petrarch, possessed of a sense of alienation and strangeness, of not being at home."[1]

To conclude, I would like to echo Hardie's words to describe my readings of *Metamorphoses*, for, as a woman and an exile, I am placed in a doubly oblique spot from where to cast sideways glances at the poem. I hope that I have challenged male and female readers and viewers to find their own slanted standpoints from where to create ever-changing readings of this ever-changing poem.

> ultima pars telae, tenui circumdata limbo,
> nexilibus flores hederis habet intertextos.

> The edges of the tapestry, surrounded by a slender border, have woven flowers intertwined with ivy. *Met.* 6.127–28

NOTES

❦

All abbreviations of classical texts are those of LSJ and Lewis-Short.

Chapter One

1. See Rosati (1983), xxxi and 136, who refers to the visual sensitivity of the poem, to its ekphrastic and descriptive character, to its tendency to visualize scenes in plastic images, and to its "spectacular language." See also Wilkinson (1955), 172; Mariotti (1957), 626; Tissol (1997), 64–88; Spencer (1997), 7–8; and Galinsky (1975), 179–84, who refers to the "visual over-explicitness" of the poem. Barkan (1986), 17, likewise asserts that "the art of metamorphosis is the art of the image" and he states that "one comes to understand that Ovid's stories are visual or 'photogenic' because the power and drama are expressed in the objects themselves, in their physical shape. This holds true not only for persons undergoing metamorphosis—it is hardly surprising that a man with a stag's head will be visually arresting—but for the whole range of Ovidian concerns" (88). Solodow (1988), 36, also stresses the importance of visuality in the poem and suggests that "the stories strive towards a kind of pictorial realization, which is usually found in metamorphosis." Even recent discussions on the body in *Metamorphoses* deal constantly with visual description. See Segal (1998).

2. See Rosati (1983), 137 n80; Laslo (1935); Viarre (1964), chapters 1 and 2; and Sharrock (1996). This strategy, however, has been criticized by, among others, Laird (1993), 19, who, with some reason, remarks that "it is often a fault of classicists to insist on pinning literature down to known facts and artefacts, giving little credit to poetic imagination."

3. On reading itself as a metamorphic process, see Sharrock (1996), 107.

4. See notes 1 and 2, except for Sharrock (1996).

5. On the genre of *Metamorphoses*, see Hinds's review (1987), 99–114, and Farrell (1992), *passim* and especially 235–45. On the issue of reading the poem as a whole, see the discussions in Wheeler (1999), 4 and Barkan (1986), 20: "we must follow the changes but not forget that it is a *carmen perpetuum*. Without a sense of the poem's wholeness, we shall not grasp the metaphor," and, 52, "one of the traits that makes Ovid's work a *perpetuum carmen* is that every major episode, however resolved it may

seem, has important links with and depends for its meanings upon the episodes that follow. Hence the impossibility of satisfactorily dividing the poem into discrete chunks."

6. This is a problem that goes beyond Ovid and *Metamorphoses* and is attached to every act of reading. Sharrock (2000), 2, observes: "Breaking off chunks is just what critics sometimes try to do—or have to do, in order to read. . . . We need to compartmentalise, to make our texts in bite-sized chunks, in order to read at all, but in doing so we also tend (and ought) to resist the compartmentalisation: 'tend to,' because we all read for unity, in that we look for ways of putting things together; 'ought to,' because the rigidity of unified reading (which tends also to be univocal) desensitises us to the richness of texts. Reading inevitably involves some kind of movement or drive towards some sort of unity, because that is how we make sense of things." Reading is in essence a constant process of dividing and rejoining.

7. Finding a unifying element in Ovid's *Metamorphoses* has been problematic and most efforts, though useful in some ways, seem to confine the poem to too rigid concepts. Stephens (1958) thinks that the unifying principle is love; Buchheit (1966) proposes that the unifying theme of the poem is the relation between *cosmos* and *imperium*; Schmidt (1991) sees 'Man' as the central concern; Ludwig (1965) and Otis (1970) strive to find structural "plans" for the poem; and Solodow (1988), 14ff., maintains that the unifying concept is 'metamorphosis.' Altieri (1973) proposes 'flux' as a unifying principle and Segal (1969) refers to landscape as offering a pervasive theme in several episodes. But all these attempts seem to fail in one way or another to account for the multiphase nature of *Metamorphoses*. For a good discussion see Liveley (1999b), 10–14.

8. See note 45 below.

9. Fredrick (2002).

10. Ibid., 3.

11. Barkan (1986), 9.

12. See Elsner (1995), 24 and the full discussion of ekphrasis on 23–27.

13. On *phantasia* see Panofsky (1968) and Schweitzer (1934). For *phantasia* in *Metamorphoses*, see discussions in Rosati (1983), 81–84 and Tissol (1997), 61–72.

14. Elsner (1995), 25.

15. On constructionism and essentialism, see Fuss (1989), especially xi–21. Kennedy (2000) discusses some of these issues in Lucretius.

16. Rosati (1983), 81, explains that *phantasia* "liberates the artist of his role of truthful imitator, of scrupulous copyist of reality and recognises his autonomous creative faculties." This more idealistic theory is found in the writings of Philo, Dio of Prusa, Maximus of Tyre, and Philostratus, but it achieves philosophical systematization with Plotinus.

17. Tissol (1997), 64.

18. Rosati (1983), 83–84.

19. On synchronicity and diachronicity as qualities of writing and pictures, see Sharrock (1996), 103 and 106.

20. See Lacan (1998), 67–119, on the gaze and Evans (1996), "mirror stage," for an overview of the question.

21. Mulvey (1975), 10.

22. Ibid., 12. For the above ideas see Mulvey (1975), 9–12. For a thorough analysis of Mulvey's ideas in ancient looking, see Fredrick (1995).

23. On the distinction between sex and gender, see Butler (1990), chapter 1.

24. Kaplan (1983), 311.

25. For a full treatment of female spectators, see Pribram (1988) and Gamman and Marshment (1988).

26. For reflections on the absence of criticism of women as spectators see Pribram (1988), 1–11.

27. Mulvey (1989), 29.

28. Ibid., 37. See Freud (1986a), 228.

29. I will use the term *focalization* for what was traditionally termed *point of view* to refer to a particular perspective by either authors or characters. For further discussions of the term, see Fowler (1990), 40–42.

30. Kaplan (1983), 318.

31. Ibid., 324.

32. Snow (1989), 31.

33. Ibid., 38.

34. Devereaux (1990), 337.

35. Ibid., 40–41.

36. Ibid., 343.

37. Ibid., 345.

38. See Bing's review (1999).

39. See Fish (1980b), 181–83, with Tompkins (1980), xxi.

40. Sharrock (2002a), 269. For an overview of the development of discussions surrounding the 'male gaze' see Sharrock (2002a), 267ff., and Fredrick (2002).

41. See Caws (1985), 269.

42. Sharrock (2002a), 287.

43. Stehle (1990), especially 107–8.

44. Other important studies are Doane (1987), Penley (1989), de Lauretis (1984), Studlar (1988), and Armstrong (1989).

45. Fränkel (1945); Wilkinson (1955); Due (1974); Galinsky (1975); Solodow (1988); Otis (1970); Hinds (1987); Barkan (1986); Tissol (1997); Myers (1994b); Wheeler (1999); and Hardie, Barchiesei, and Hinds (1999). See also the less well-known studies by Davis (1983), Glenn (1986), Schmidt (1991), Spencer (1997), Wheeler (2000), Jouteur (2001), Hardie (2002a and b), and Liveley (1999b).

46. Otis (1970), 103.

47. See note 2.

48. Segal (1969).

49. Hinds (2002) follows Segal's lines in his study of landscape in *Metamorphoses*.

50. Barkan (1986), 18.

51. Ibid., 52–54.

52. Tissol (1997), 64. For *prosopopeiae* see 64–88.

53. Sharrock (1991a).

54. Elsner (1991), 154 n7, quoting Bauer (1962), 13. Narcissus has also been seen as the myth of the artist and poet who creates metamorphosis. Leon Battista Alberti (1972), 61—quoted in Barolsky (1995), 255—thinks that Narcissus was the first painter and asks: "what is painting . . . but the act of embracing by means of art the surface of the pool?" See Barolsky (1995) on Narcissus as author of transformations.

55. Winsor Leach (1974), 106–7.

56. Elsner (1991), 155–66.

57. Sharrock (1991b), 169.

58. Liveley (1999a).

59. Elsner (1996), 247.

60. Ibid., 249–55.

61. Nugent (1990), 165–72.

62. Richlin (1992).

63. Segal (1994), 260.

64. Ibid., 266.

65. Segal (1998), 23.

66. For a good overview of the different facets of reader-response criticism, see Tompkins (1980).

67. Ibid., ix.

68. This is mainly Iser's (1980) point of view, but reader-response criticism is by no means homogeneous and while concentrating on the reader, it assigns to him various roles and degrees of participation in the literary process.

69. Tompkins (1980), xv.

70. Iser (1980), 50.

71. This issue was already at the center of the polemics between Due and Otis. Due distrusts the "plan" of the poem that Otis so adamantly tries to formulate precisely because he believes that there cannot be *one* plan but many and that the meaning is realized in the eyes of the readers and not by the critic who strives to provide parameters on how to understand *Metamorphoses*. See Due (1974), 135. Due (1974), 134, also responds to Wilkinson's view of *Metamorphoses* as an elaborate picture with a clear chronological organization of themes that the reader perceives as a finished totality, by saying that "such diagrams give the impression of something static, like a façade of a building . . . The perspective of a reader is not like that of a bird who looks down upon a landscape in its totality, but bears a closer resemblance to that of a wanderer to whom the landscape reveals itself in constantly changing views as he moves along."

72. Tompkins (1980), xvi–xvii and Fish (1980a).

73. Fish (1980a), especially 82ff.

74. Segal (1994), Sharrock (2002a), and Elsom (1992). For audience-oriented studies of *Metamorphoses*, see Konstan (1991); Tissol (1997), especially chapter 2; and Wheeler (1999).

75. See the discussion in Tompkins's introduction (1980), xxiv.

76. Fish (1980a), 83ff. and (1980b), 181–84. The notion of "community of interpreters" or "interpretative communities" is used in slightly different ways by different critics. For an overview see Tompkins (1980), xxi–xxii.

77. Due (1974), 11 and 14.

78. Ibid., 9–14.

79. See Culler (1982), 65–66, for criticism of the Fishean model.

80. Ibid., 43.

81. See Culler (1982); Showalter (1971); the essays in Mills (1994); and the readings in Eagleton (1996), chapter 5, among others.

82. Fetterly (1978).

83. Richlin (1992), 161, and Devereaux (1990), 346–47.

84. Sharrock (2002a), 271–72.

85. See Spentzou's (2003) work on the *Heroides*.

86. Richlin (1992), 179: "We can appropriate; we can resist. The old stories await our retelling." Cahoon (1996), 46: "Both Calliope and Hinds make me a 'resisting reader' (Fetterly 1978) with a vested interest in daughters (and in mothers when they seek to help their daughters)."

87. Shaw Hardy (1995), 145–46.

88. Joplin (1984).

89. Liveley (1999a).

90. Marder (1992), 162–63.

Chapter Two

1. The performative power of the eye is particularly "visible" in Egyptian hiero-glyphics where an eye is contained in expressions connected with the performative verb "to do." See Gandelman (1991), 1–2.

2. For a thorough discussion of Varro's passage see Fredrick (2002), 1–3. For *phal-logocularcentrism* and the connection between the phallus, representation, and the eye in Western thought see Jay (1993), chapter 9.

3. See "*vir*" in Maltby (1991).

4. See Glare, *OLD* (1997), "*acies.*"

5. Gandelman (1991), 1 and chapter 9.

6. Richlin's work on rape (1992) is of course essential here. See also Curran (1978). On rape in antiquity in general, see Deacy and Pierce (1997).

7. The point of gazing and desiring is pervasive and present in the embedded story of Syrinx (*Met.*1. 699) and later in Book 2 with Mercury raping Corone (*Met.* 2.574), in Mercury and Apollo's violence against Chione (*Met.* 11.305), in Pluto's abduction of Proserpina (*Met.* 5.395) and in Aesacus's desire of Hesperia (*Met.* 11.769–71). Tereus looking at Philomela pre-announces her rape (*Met.* 6.455).

8. Segal (2001), 81, observes that the contrast with *Met.*1.263 and *Met.*2.308 where Jupiter brings clouds with a noble purpose, reminds the reader here of Jupiter's "less noble motives and his less exalted behavior." For a thorough study of Jupiter in *Metamorphoses*, see Segal (2001).

9. Kirk (1985), on Homer, *Iliad* 1.551.

10. For the term "informed reader," see Fish (1980a), 86–87.

11. On the story of Callisto, see W. R. Johnson (1996), O'Bryhim (1990), and Wall (1988).

12. For this and other puns concerning the names used for Io, see Ahl (1985), 146–47.

13. Davis (1983), 55 and n. 60, suggests that there is a paradox in the fact that Callisto avoids being pretty but her very name, derived from *kalliste* ("very beautiful") exalts her beauty. With her transformation into a bear she finally loses her beauty (see especially *Met.*2. 474 and 481).

14. The verb that Ovid uses is *tingo* (*ne puro tinguatur in aequore paelex!* / "Let not the concubine bathe in your pure stream!" (*Met.* 2.530), which plays with its double meaning of "bathing" and "dyeing/staining" and recalls the pollution of Diana's pool. Cf. *tinxit* in *Met.* 4.388 for Salmacis' pool. O'Bryhim (1990) believes that Callisto's "pollution" of Diana's pool has to do with the impurity associated with pregnancy in ancient ritual. By denying her the right to bathe in pure waters, Juno is depriving her

of a place where Callisto can ritually purify herself.

15. Wheeler (1999), 1. See also Konstan (1991); Ahl (1985), 154; and Nagle (1988c), 99–100. Konstan (1991), 19–20, suggests that the story of Pan and Syrinx puts Argus to sleep and not the reader because Ovid is playing here with two kinds of readership. Argus is the 'detached,' almost philosophical reader, who is "all eyes," the perfect witness but who cannot empathize with the story. On the other hand, the 'external reader' is someone who can empathize with the characters and desires to know the conclusion. There may be some difficulties in seeing that Argus's way of reading is "philosophical." Rather, as Konstan himself recognizes on page 18, one imagines that he falls asleep because of the repetitiveness of the god-nymph rape story (only lines before we heard about Daphne). This last interpretation assumes that Argus has also been 'reading' *Metamorphoses*.

16. Konstan (1991), 20, describes the erotic chase in terms of the eroticism of reading, but draws differences in the reader's identification: "The passion that generates the plot and terminates with its conclusion corresponds to the reader's need to undo the tension of the narrative and find repose or satisfaction in the completed myth, to the extent, at all events, that the reader's empathy is aligned specifically with the masculine desire of Pan. If, alternatively, it is an identification with Syrinx's desire to escape that involves the reader in the narrative, then the relation between audience and text will be figured curiously in an anti-erotic movement within the narrated tale."

17. On the Apollo-Daphne episode see Nicoll (1980), Nagle (1988b), Wills (1990), Knox (1990), and Laguna Mariscal (1989).

18. For the range yellow-golden as epithets of Venus and Cupid or their attributes cf. *Met*.10.277, *Met*.15.761–62, *Her*.16.35, *Am*. 1.2.42, *Am*. 2.18.36, and *RA*. 39. The dispute between Apollo and Cupid is probably an Ovidian invention. See Due (1974), 183 n100.

19. See especially Halperin (1990), 29–38; Veyne (1985), 26–35; and Skinner (1997). It is worthy of note that, as Sharrock (2002b) recalls, it is the very elegiac lover who in *Amores* 1.1 begins to write love elegy after he is wounded and penetrated by Cupid's arrows.

20. Due (1974), 114, says that "Daphne had run at the sight of Apollo." But his own quotation of the text contradicts this point: *fugit ocior aura/ illa levi neque ad haec revocantis verba resistit /* "She flees faster than a light breeze and does not stop at these words of the god who calls her back" (*Met*.1.502–3). There is no obvious interaction between gazes here and Daphne's reaction seems based on what she *hears* rather than what she *sees*. Yet the text gives no evidence that she ever turns round or actually looks at the god.

21. Davis (1983), 45, takes this detail of the hair as part of the 'neglect' of her appearance typical of nymphs who hunt, which is also a sign of the rejection of love. However, Daphne may not actually be 'neglecting' her appearance, but carefully choosing a look. She is 'dressing up' for the hunt and for her character. On the general traits of the type of the 'virgin huntress,' see Davis (1983), chapter 3.

22. See Hardie (1999) on presence and absence in transformation. Farrell (1999), 135–36, notices that the implied 'consent' of Daphne (her nodding) to become Apollo's tree may be no more than a fantasy of the focalizer Apollo, while she might be actually expressing rejection. Farrell's is a releasing reading that assigns agency to the female subject.

23. For these metacritical questions in connection with the plays on bark/book see Farrell (1999), 133–35, and Hinds (1985), 14 and 29 n2, for the interplays between *liber* "book" and *liber* "free." See Hardie (1999), 257–58, for Daphne as inscription. On the textuality of the elegiac mistress, see Wyke (1987).

24. This companionship between the lovers in goddess-boy relationships is particularly appreciated in the act of reclining together in a *locus amoenus*. Venus and Adonis recline together by a poplar in Met.10.554–59 and Galatea peacefully rests in Acis' arms in Met.13.786–87.

25. In Met.14.349–50 Circe also presents a masculine and penetrative attitude with the gaze when she beholds Picus in the woods, who is made a spectacle, and wishes to possess him. However, though she ends up dominating the man in his transformation into a woodpecker, penetration is not as close as with Salmacis.

26. Keith's (1999), 219–20, contention that the Minyeides destabilize the image of the 'epic hero' by turning him into a *semi-vir* also gives pre-eminence to the female subjectivity of the narrator.

27. There is also a desire to see in the boy as he wanders around new lands avid to see new things: *ignota videre/ flumina gaudebat/* "He enjoyed seeing unknown rivers" (Met. 4.294–95). On Hermaphroditus's travels and the contacts of the story with epic heroes, namely Odysseus and Aeneas, see Keith (1999), 216–17.

28. Nugent (1990), 169. As Nugent observes the similarities between the Freudian phrasing and Ovid's articulation of Salmacis' desire are truly uncanny. Or, the coincidences may not be so striking if we recall that Freud probably 'did' *Metamorphoses* at school!

29. This issue of separating deities from the natural phenomenon they belong/identify with or 'are' is a difficult one. In this case, Nugent (1990), 165, insists that Ovid tries to distinguish the nymph and the pool as sharply as possible, but the play of identities is still present. But one wonders why the master of fluidity would want to draw clear distinctions between categories. On Salmacis' identification with landscape see Keith (1999), 218, and Segal (1969), 25ff., in particular.

30. Anderson (1997) on Met. 4.346–47, believes that the mirror actually "suggests the frustration of contact between nymph and the object of her eager gaze."

31. See Nugent (1990), 163.

32. Ovid uses *unda* twice before in the story (285 and 312), twice *fons* (310 and 287), and once *liquor* (300) for Salmacis' waters.

33. Lively's (1999b), 156, observation of Tissol's (1997) index: "*Echo. See Narcissus*" is particularly good. Interestingly, Davis (1983), 89, finds in the story of Echo a 'digression' from the main story and on page 92 when he himself discusses the episode he feels that he is 'digressing' as well.

34. Lively (1999b), 158–59.

35. Line 401, as Bömer observes, is rather disconcerting—how can a sound live 'in her' if she has no body? See Bömer (1969) on Met. 3.401.

36. See Reed (1995), 343–45, on Adonis.

37. On the box and the jar in connection with female interiority see Mulvey (1996), 57–62, and Zeitlin (1996), 65–66. On Pandora in Western tradition and art, see Dora and Erwin Panofsky (1956).

38. Mulvey (1996), 55.

39. Pandora has also been compared to Eve in her desire for knowledge that brings doom to the world. See Mulvey (1996), 6.

40. See also *Met.* 9.177, where Hercules burning addresses Juno: *"et hanc pestem specta, crudelis, ab alto"* / "'Look at this plague from the sky, cruel goddess.'" What is more, the direction of the human gaze is exactly the opposite to that of the gods and it is what distinguishes men from animals. In Book 1 the poet speaks about the creation of Man: *finxit in effigiem moderantum cuncta deorum,/ pronaque cum spectent animalia cetera terram,/ os homini sublime dedit caelumque videre/ iussit et erectos ad sidera tollere vultus/* "He molded [the earth] into the form of the gods who control everything and though the rest of the animals are prone and look downwards at the earth, he gave Man an uplifted face and ordered him to look at heaven and to raise his up-facing head to the stars" (*Met.*1.83–86).

41. The opposite of unruly Aglauros is suggested by the story of Pygmalion, where the submissive and ideal wife created by the artist looks up to him as soon as she comes to life: *oscula virgo/ sensit et erubuit timidumque ad lumina lumen/ attollens pariter cum caelo vidit amantem/* "The maiden felt the kisses and blushed, and lifting her timid eyes to the light, she saw the sky and her lover at the same time" (*Met.*10.293–94). Pyramus looking up when he dies in Thisbe's arms can also be taken as an image of his loss of power and masculinity: *ad nomen Thisbes oculos a morte gravatos/ Pyramus erexit visaque recondidit illa/* "To the name of Thisbe Pyramus raised his eyes heavy with death and, having seen her, he closed them again" (*Met.* 4.145–46).

42. For the connection between Aglauros, "informants," and Actaeon, see Heath (1992), 76–87.

43. On the function of *invidere* and *invidia* in the episode, see Keith (1992), 126–27.

44. Cf. *OED* (1989), 5: 316, "envy" 3.

45. See references in Dickie (1993a), 64. For Baokavia Βασκανία and the evil eye, see Dickie (1993b).

46. Freud (1986b), 124–30, maintains that the influence of the penis envy is drastic in the development of women and that jealousy and envy play, due to this influence, a larger role in women than in men. This is adequate only if one thinks of the phallus as a metaphor for power, and Freud's words should not be taken to refer specifically to a part of the male body.

47. In his elegiac poetry, Ovid insists that *Livor* will not be able to destroy his work as a poet and that his fame will survive (*R.A.* 389; *Am.* 1.15.39–42).

48. See Tissol (1997), 67.

49. Tissol (1997), 67, observes that here Ovid is using the language of criticism and that the passage has metaliterary resonances, for he introduces a "process of visualization in his characters that recalls the critics' accounts of how readers experience a poet's vizualisations." "Our experience as readers mirrors that of Aglauros, in that we have, just before, witnessed the personification of Invidia as a richly detailed *imago* before our eyes, so to speak. Ovid has more to achieve with us than Invidia with Aglauros—to engage us in the power of the narrative while also permitting us to witness its operations."

50. For discussion of this pun see Tissol (1997), 35. For humor in this episode, see Galinsky (1975), 164–68. For a good overview of the stone image and petrifaction in *Metamorphoses* see Bauer (1962), 1–2.

51. On ekphrasis see Rosand (1990); Bartsch (1989); Perutelli (1978); Fowler (1991); Winsor Leach (1988); Zeitlin (1994a and b); Laird (1993); Elsner (1995), 23–28; Hinds (2002), and the essays in Goldhill and Osborne (edd.) (1994) and

Elsner (ed.) (1996).

52. A wonderful example cited by Gubar (1982), 76, is found in Ismael's Reed, *Mumbo Jumbo* (1978, 208–9): "He got good into her Book tongued her every passage thumbing her leaf and rubbing his hands all over her binding."

53. Gubar (1982), 77.

54. On the text as a unit with boundaries, see Sharrock (2000), 24.

55. Barthes in *The Pleasure of the Text* (1975), 11–12, comments on the pleasure experienced by the reader: "Thus what I enjoy in a narrative is not directly its content or even its structure, but rather the abrasions I impose upon the fine surface: I read on, I skip, I look up. I dip in again." Part of the pleasure of reading is derived from the sense of penetrating and marking the text.

56. For Ovid's episode see Brown (1987).

57. For these types of *formulae* as boundary markers of description, see Hinds (1987), 36–38ff.

58. For enclosure in *locus amoenus* in *Metamorphoses* see Segal (1969), 17 and n. 40. On *loci amoeni* in general and in *Metamorphoses* see Hinds (1987), 26–28.

59. Thetis' story stages a female type of "The Taming of the Shrew," where a rebellious woman is finally tamed and submits to her husband's power. In Devereaux's words (1990), 340–41, she "undergoes a process of re-education into proper femininity."

60. There are two other combined episodes that show this pattern of penetration into a natural ekphrasis: the rape(s) of Proserpina and Cyane in Book 5.

61. For sources and other versions of the story, see Spencer (1997), 16–22. For an excellent overview of the myth of Actaeon in classical literature see Heath (1992).

62. Intertext with the Homeric *Hymns* in *Metamorphoses* has been the subject of recent scholarly interest. See specifically Hinds (1987), Part II, and Barchiesi (1999).

63. Feldherr (1997), 27–30. Although Feldherr is aware of this reversal in the Theban Cycle, he does not relate it to the gender implications of looking.

64. This type of verbal word play recalls *Ars Amatoria* 1.99: *spectatum veniunt, veniunt, spectentur ut ipsae/* "They come to watch, they also come to be watched themselves."

65. Barkan (1986), 43. Hardie (1990), 225–27, also relates the serpent to Cacus in the *Aeneid*, both being savage forces that the founder needs to defeat in order to build the city and establish civilization.

66. Shlain (1998), 24. In the human eye there are both *rods*, in charge of a more comprehensive and holistic vision, and *cones*, which help us visualize sharply and in detail and are responsible for the perception of color and clarity. Shlain (1998), 26, tells us that "women have more rods in their retinas than men, and as a result, have better peripheral vision. They can see better in the dark and take in more at a glance than men. Men have more cones than women, allowing them to see a segment of the visual field in greater detail and with better depth perception than women." See Shlain (1998), 24–26.

67. In an odd way, the story of Io discussed before is set within an ekphrasis that includes the presence of a *nemus*. Ovid begins to describe the meeting of the river deities around Peneus and frames the scene with the phrase *est nemus Haemoniae /* "There is a vale in Thessaly" (*Met*.1.568). He goes on to explain that Inachus was absent because he was lamenting his daughter Io who had disappeared. The story of Io is in a way included in the ekphrasis through her father's absence.

68. For caves in the poem, see Segal (1969), 20–23.

69. Adams (1982), 82–85, mentions "fields" and "caves" as metaphors for female pudenda. One use of *antrum* is recorded but for "*anus.*"

70. Barkan (1986), 45.

71. The 'innocence' or 'intention' of Actaeon's gaze is much discussed. Otis (1970), 133–34, believes that Ovid strives to present an innocent picture of Actaeon, accentuating the goddess's cruelty. Heath (1991), 241–42, and (1992), 62–64, believes quite "blindly" in Actaeon's innocence. See also the discussion in Wheeler (1999), 107–8.

72. See for example Apollo's chase of Daphne and her description as a prey in *Met.*1.532–38. Note that Narcissus has also been hunting before falling in love with his own image reflected in the pool. See Elsner (1996), 253, and Sharrock (1996), 112. For the complex interplays between *amor* and *venatio* see Davis (1983), *passim* and especially chapter 1. The practical absence of Actaeon in Davis's book, which is entirely dedicated to love and hunting in *Metamorphoses*, is most surprising.

73. On midday in *loci amoeni*, see Segal (1969), 4, and Heath (1992), chapters 1, 2, and 3 *passim*.

74. On Ovid's reversal of the placid connotations of *loci amoeni* in contrast to Virgil's and Theocritus's use, see Spencer (1997), 21, and Segal (1969), 82. While Spencer (1997), 25, seems to bend towards Actaeon's innocence, he agrees with Glenn that "the successful hunting should have been a clue to Actaeon that Diana was present; but he stumbles on her unawares. He may not have planned to intrude on her, but neither was he alert to her presence—and he a hunter!" See Glenn (1986), 31.

75. Characters rebelling against the will of the author are often found in literature, like Unamuno's character in *Niebla*, who turns up at the writer's office and expresses that he refuses to die in the fiction according to the author's narrative intentions.

76. Heath (1991), 242.

77. Diana's stance and reaction have been linked to the attitude of the prudish Roman *matrona* in her bath, attended by a group of servants with designated tasks. See Solodow (1988), 87, and Spencer (1997), 19. But it is dubious whether this is appropriate or adds much to our understanding of the episode. Are critics saying that Diana is some sort of Lucretia here? The *pudor* of a *matrona* should be distinguished from the *pudor* of a virgin.

78. Also relevant are *Tr.* 4.10.90, *Tr.*1.3.37–38, and *Tr.* 3.5.47–50.

79. For this connection see Pohlenz (1913), 11–12, and Heath (1992), 95–97 n51.

80. For the possible causes of Ovid's exile, see Thibault (1964).

81. One can think of this incongruence between self and image as 'carnivalesque' in Bakhtinian terms, a quality that according to Segal (1998), 11, is a crucial trace of *Metamorphoses* with its dissolution of bodily boundaries and upsetting of hierarchies. For problems of identity and recognition in the Theban cycle, see also Feldherr (1997), 29–33.

82. For Narcissus's self-delusion as a key to being a perfect viewer of art in the mode of naturalism, see Elsner (1996), 249. Curiously, Spencer (1997), 22 and 33, does not mention the contrast viewer/object of the gaze in his list of contrasts in the story of Narcissus and he does not see this either in Actaeon.

83. Barkan (1986), 45–46, suggests that both Diana and the stag he has become are mirror images of Actaeon, one divine, the other beastly. On page 45 he also argues that because Actaeon and Diana are both hunters, in perceiving the naked goddess,

he looks in a sort of mirror and sees a "transfigured, sacred form of his own identity."

84. On the reader's alliances here see Feldherr (1997), 37–55.

85. Callisto, the huntress, is also said to be chased away by hunting dogs: *a! quotiens per saxa canum latratibus acta est/* "Oh, how often was she driven through rocky places by the barking of dogs!" (*Met.* 2.491).

86. Barkan (1986), 46.

87. Ibid., 44.

88. Ibid., 299 n31.

89. Heath (1992), 65–71, suggests that the silencing of Actaeon is a particularly cruel punishment because Actaeon appears as a young man who is very gifted in language and commands speech, which is seen in the clever naming of his dogs and in the fact that his companions respond to his orders.

90. Note this same paradoxical outcome of transformation in Callisto's episode: *venatrixque metu venantum territa fugit/* "And the hunter flees terrified with fear of the hunters" (*Met.* 2.492).

91. On focalization and its shifts, see Fowler (1990) with his bibliography.

92. For sources and intertextual links to other versions of the story—especially Euripides' *Bacchae*, Theocritus's *Idyll* 26, and the Homeric *Hymn to Dionysus*—see Spencer (1997), 41–44.

93. Here again, Spencer (1997), 44, overlooks the contrast between viewer and object of the gaze. For a connection between the *spectabilis* place and public spectacles in Rome see Feldherr (1997), 36 and 42–43.

94. The eyes of the onlooker as polluting and elements of disruption of a rite also appear in Medea's episode in *Met.* 7.256.

95. The idea that Dionysus acts "through" Pentheus's mother and aunt is also perceived in Book 4 when Bacchus is said to have killed Pentheus: *Penthea tu . . . mactas/* "You kill Pentheus" (*Met.* 4.22–23). See Anderson (1996) on *Met.* 4.22–25.

96. Spencer (1997), 56, notes that Tiresias prophesied that Pentheus would defile the woods, his mother, and his aunts with his blood (*Met.* 3.522–23). Spencer takes this as an indicator that perhaps Tiresias' prophetic vision is not infallible because there are actually no trees at the scene of the crime (*purus ab arboribus . . . campus/* "a field without trees" (*Met.* 3.709). According to Spencer, this makes "the readers wonder if the black-and-white characterization of Pentheus and Tiresias might not have a flaw to it, necessitating a re-thinking (deconstruction) of the entire episode."

97. See Segal (1982), 204–5. Segal (1969), 83–84, also recognizes a Virgilian echo (*Aen.* 6.309–12) in Pentheus's tree.

98. Spencer (1997), 60.

99. See especially Elsner (1996), Rosati (1983), and Barolsky (1995). See also Brenkman (1976) and for Narcissus's tale and its reception in the Middle Ages, see Knoespel (1985).

100. In Callimachus's *Hymn* 5 the boy was blinded for having seen the goddess Pallas naked, yet he is granted the power to predict the future in return. Both versions however are based on the question of knowledge allowed and forbidden.

101. See Davis (1983), 95. Segal (1969), 47, believes that the pool is a metaphoric extension of Narcissus himself in its isolated, unproductive, and self-contained nature. On pools and the erotics of water in the poem see Segal (1969), 10 and 23–33.

102. Elsner (1996), 249 and 255.

103. Miller (1986), 290 n.9.

104. On the border as signature see Miller (1986), 273 and 290 n9.

105. The fact that tapestries are actual textiles and could physically "wrap us around" may help the metaphor here.

106. See Copley (1978), 1. On the paraclausithyron in general and in Latin elegy see Copley (1978), Yardley (1978), and Cairns (1975). On the threshold and its erotic connotations in elegy, see Pucci (1978).

107. For the komastic elements in the episode and Ovid's innovations see Copley (1978), 134–39.

108. Adams (1982), 89, affirms that the external female pudenda may be likened to doors and the vagina to a path or passage. See Isidore's remarks at *Etym.* 8.11.69 and Auson. *Cent. Nupt.* 112. p.216 P, where *limen* is made to mean "entrance to the vagina."

109. See Copley (1978), 136.

110. Borghini (1979), 159, notes that Iphis and Anaxarete represent the social asymmetry of the two castes that lived in Cyprus. The Greek group, to which Anaxarete belonged, represented the noble class with social prestige and political power. The other group was of Phoenician origin and constituted the lower class, which was probably striving to occupy positions of higher power and prestige. Iphis belonged to this second group. The story, according to Borghini, stages a battle between endogamy and exogamy.

111. Liveley (1999a), 202. See also Bauer (1962), 9.

112. Wilson (1964), on *Met.* 14.760–61.

113. See Borghini (1979), 149, and his bibliography. She is found as *Aphrodite Parakuptousa* in Plut. *Amat.* 20.766c.

114. Borghini (1979), 153–54. It is noteworthy that the figure of *Aphrodite Parakuptousa* has parallels in the epithets that the Sumerians and Assyrians applied to the Babylonian goddess Kililu, and implies something like "the one that leans forward through the window."

115. Davis (1983), 70, believes that Pomona surrenders to Vertumnus on her own accord and yields "gracefully to the charms of Vertumnus. She unexpectedly 'falls in love' with the youthful god and reciprocates his ardour." Davis never refers to the fact that Vertumnus narrated the story of Iphis and Anaxarete, which is fundamental to understand why Pomona surrenders. Gentilcore (1995), however, shows that there is much sexual violence through symbolism in the episode, and Segal (1969), 70, although he talks about a "happy ending" in the tale, does actually recognize some violence. On Vertumnus's shifting shapes, see Tarrant (2000).

116. A large part of the story of Pyramus and Thisbe is an Ovidian innovation. Nonnos alludes to another version of the legend, which we find in Nikolaos, where Thisbe becomes pregnant and kills herself and so does Pyramus. The gods pitied them and transformed her into a fountain and him into a river. See Due (1974), 125 and 185 nn 12 and 13. For modern bibliography on the episode, see Fowler (2000).

117. Note the insistence on the separation between the lovers in Narcissus: "*quoque magis doleam, nec nos mare separat ingens/ nec via nec montes nec clausis moenia portis;/ exigua prohibemur aqua!*" / "'And to make me grieve even more, it is not a mighty ocean that separates us, nor a road, nor mountains, nor a wall with closed doors: it is thin water that keeps us apart'" (*Met.* 3.448–50). The presence of doors is also included in Konon's version of the myth of Narcissus, where the boy rejects a lover, Amenias, who kills himself at Narcissus's door and begs Eros to avenge him. See Spencer (1997), 30. On Narcissus as rejected elegiac lover, see Spencer (1997), 34.

Chapter Three

1. Fowler (1991), 25–26.

2. Bal (1997), 36–43. On narrative and description see also Genette (1982).

3. Mulvey (1975), 11.

4. Shlain (1998), 23. Shlain suggests that the invention of writing, which involves a more sequential, *one-at-a-time* perception of the world, brought a more masculine outlook to humankind and replaced the more female-oriented world of the image, which involved a more holistic, *all-at-once* type of perception.

5. William Blake, *A Vision of the Last Judgement*, 91. See Keynes's edition (1966), 614. Blake, both a poet and a visual artist, often combined image and text in his work.

6. It is also possible to suggest that "we could read the sculptor's loathing of these latter [the Propoetides] as itself a defensive reaction to repressed desire." See Gross (1992), 72–73.

7. See especially Sharrock (1991a and b), Elsner (1991), Elsner and Sharrock (1991), Liveley (1999a and b), and Rosati (1983).

8. Sharrock (1991b), 170 and 174. See also Segal (1998), 18, who sees that her only function is to give Pygmalion a child and that her existence depends only on her love for her creator.

9. Liveley (1999b), 71ff.

10. Elsner (1991). For an overview of critical positions on the Pygmalion episode see Elsner (1991), 154–55 with footnotes.

11. Ibid., 155.

12. See a critique of Elsner in Liveley (1999b), 59–60.

13. Elsner (1991), 160 and 164.

14. Liveley (1999a), 202–3, shows that the reader is invited to focalize through Pygmalion's male eyes and thus acquire a male-oriented impression of the Propoetides.

15. Elsner (1991), 155.

16. *Formam* (cf. *mutatas formas* in Met. 1.1) and *operis* are metacritical pointers. We also recall instances of *corpus* for the work of art (255, 289). On metaliterary uses of parts of the body in Ovid, see Farrell (1999).

17. In this section a contrast between the perfect and the historic present in the episode will be developed. While the present can be used to replace a perfect in narrative, they are not always interchangeable and the present produces different effects. See Pinkster (1990), 224–25. However, because the present belongs to the tenses of the *infectum*, it always conveys the idea of something unfinished and still in progress and thus, implies a detention of time and gives an impression of less activity. The perfect and the tenses belonging to the *perfectum* indicate that the action is completed, which can be linked to the performativity typical of the masculine.

18. On how a work of art is formed out of a combination of several models/readings/viewings, see Kris and Kurz (1979), 61, on an anecdote about Zeuxis: "Painting his picture of Helen, he selected the most beautiful feature of five different girls and incorporated each into his portrait. The conception on which this anecdote is based views the task of the artist, in accordance with Plato's theory of art, as surpassing the model of nature and, by improving on nature, to realize an ideal beauty in his works."

19. This is the current critical assumption. See references in Wheeler (1999), 216 n45.

20. I find it more difficult to see the ivory maiden behind the construction of Lucretia.

21. Later visual representations of Lucretia tend to show a woman with very light skin, though one needs, of course, to bear in mind that these representations also correspond to the canons of beauty and purity of the respective periods. See images in Donaldson (1982).

22. For further discussions of Lucretia's rape and chastity see Jed (1989), especially chapter 1.

23. Liveley (1999b), 74–75.

24. See Sharrock (2002a), 273–75, and Elsner (1991), 156–57.

25. For an in-depth overview of this statue, see Mitchell Havelock (1995).

26. Ibid., 14. For discussions of the statue's stance and gesture see ibid., 20–37.

27. For Pygmalion in love with Aphrodite cf. Clemens Alexandrinus, *Protrepticus* 4.57.3. See discussion in Bauer (1962), 15.

28. It is unclear whether the intruder is conscious that he is actually raping a statue or if in his delusion he thinks of it as the goddess herself, but he surely sees her as a living being capable of being loved.

29. Lucius's intruder ends up throwing himself off a cliff and vanishing completely, thus enacting the typical punishment that falls upon those who have sex with the goddess. One can compare the fate of the intruder with Anchises, although Anchises' physical defects are traditionally attributed to the fact that he divulged his affair.

30. Note that Elsner (1991), 160, sees here a sublimation of Pygmalion's own desire projected on the image: "His (and our) desire, for it becomes its desire to move, its desire to be moved by him (both these meanings—active and passive—being implied in *velle moveri*, 251)." Sharrock (1991), 171, on her part draws a link between *moveri* and the ritual moving of cult-images, as she believes that the ivory maiden has strong connections with the goddess Venus. This could go well with the view that the ivory maiden is a doublet for Aphrodite. But then Sharrock also acknowledges the possible overtones of prostitution implied in *moveri* and further discusses the verb on 172ff.

31. The connection between sex and movement impregnates a set of metaphors which pervade many erotic passages of Latin literature. For extensive references, see Adams (1982), 136–38 (specific verbs for sexual movement) and 193–94 (metaphors). Further, Lucretius in his prescriptions for women in sexuality says that wives have no need to move in bed and that their function of motherhood and pregnancy is better achieved by passivity and immobility (Lucretius, *DRN* 4.1263–77). See Brown (1988) on Lucretius, *DRN* 4.1268 for comparative references.

32. For a good discussion of the intertextual links of Ovid's version and Virgil's tale of Orpheus in the *Georgics*, see Spencer (1997), 99–116.

33. See Prop.3.2.3–6.

34. Heath (1996), 364–65. For general discussions on Orpheus see Hardie (1999), Knox (1986), Segal (1989), and Anderson (1982) with their respective bibliographies.

35. Heath (1996), 368–70.

36. Ibid., 363–64.

37. Janan (1988) and Hardie (1999) recognize that each story in Orpheus's song is meaningful for the bard's own history, identity, and desire. Janan (1988), 124, suggests that "the story of Pygmalion and the ivory virgin projects an idealization of his own erotic fantasies onto narrative" and that "this is Orpheus's best shot at perfect love." But Janan does not make specific reference to the importance of the gaze and

Orpheus's desire to look without danger of destroying. It is important, further, that Orpheus can only achieve a free gaze over Eurydice and vice versa after death: *nunc praecedentem sequitur, nunc praevius anteit/ Eurydicenque suam iam tuto respicit Orpheus/* "Now Orpheus follows her as she precedes, now he goes before her, and looks back safely at his Eurydice" (*Met*.11.65–66).

38. In Virgil (*Georg.* 4.487) it is merely said that Eurydice should follow behind Orpheus, but this is mentioned only at the moment of Orpheus's failure and not before. Nothing is said in Virgil about the prohibition of looking back, although we can assume that the readers were familiar with this mandate from the myth. On this issue see Spencer (1997), 106.

39. See Barkan (1986), 53.

40. See Keith (1999), 221. On Perseus as "master of motion" see Barkan (1986), 53.

41. The lowering of the eyes can be perhaps equated with the blush. The whole episode of Perseus and Andromeda has been paralleled with Aeneas' quest for Lavinia. See Otis (1970), 159–65. In this sense, Lavinia's blush corresponds to Andromeda's lowering of the eyes.

42. Segal (1998), 19, 20, and quote on 21.

43. The text insinuates a similar effect on the lover in the episode of Herse and Mercury in book 2 where Mercury sees her from above when he is flying through the Munychian fields: *obstipuit forma Iove natus et aethere pendens/ non secus exarsit /* "The son of Jove was stupefied at her beauty and hanging in mid-air caught the fire of love" (*Met.* 2.726–27). See also how Circe is paralyzed at the sight of Picus: *qua simul ac iuvenem virgultis abdita vidit,/ obstipuit/* "As soon as, hidden in the bushes, she saw the youth, she was stupefied" (*Met.* 14.349–50).

44. For rape and entrapment see Segal (1998), 21

45. See McGrath (1992).

46. In an obscure version the setting is Joppa in Phoenicia. Pliny (*HN.* 9.4.11) comments that the skeleton of the monster that terrorized Andromeda was brought to Rome from Joppa. Note that in many ancient pictures Andromeda is represented as white. See McGrath (1992).

47. Cf. *OLD* (1997), *marmoreus* 2: "resembling marble, esp. whiteness (*of the human body*)" (original emphasis).

48. Anderson (1997), on *Met.* 4.675.

49. McGrath (1992), 7.

50. See Isaac (2004).

51. See Snowden (1970) and (1983).

52. There seems to be no evidence of Medusa petrifying women in classical versions. See Zeitlin in Vernant (1991), 138 n48.

53. On beheading and the suppression of women's identity, see Eilberg-Schwartz (1995).

54. Keith (1999), 222.

55. The fact that Elegy 'limps' rather than 'runs' could be seen as a problem here. However, in Propertius's implicit comparison of the elegiac mistress with Atalanta in 1.1, there is a connection between the running virgin and the elegiac *puella*. The problem of limping could perhaps be solved by thinking that Atalanta and other running virgins are 'written girls'/erotic poems, but with no strict reference to elegiac meter.

56. See the discussion in Anderson (1966).

57. For the erotic connotations of apples see Segal (1969), 46, and Gentilcore (1995).

58. On MORA, its wordplays with AMOR and their erotic implications, especially in elegy, see Pucci (1978), especially 52–54 with nn1–3.

59. Anderson (1972), on Met.10.629–30.

60. Anderson (1997), 669–72,

61. For Proteus's 'ambiguity' see Met. 2.9.

62. The birthplace of Artemis is controversial. The Homeric Hymn to Apollo states that Apollo was born on Delos and Diana on Ortygia, but Ortygia may itself be an earlier name of Delos. For the different versions of Artemis' birthplace, see Bell (1991), 70–74.

63. Note that just as by looking at things we fix them; equally by fixing things we make them visible: Δῆλος = 'visible.'

64. Solomon (1993), 104–5.

65. Ibid., 104. Cf. e.g. Plato, Timaeus 91c; Ellis Hanson (1991), 81–87; and Lefkowitz and Fant (1982), 90–91, 93–95, 225–26, 258.

66. Segal (1998), 27, thinks that Thetis' main function is to be a vessel for Peleus's seed and then she is forgotten, but there is surely more to her character.

67. For matrimonial images in the episode of Apollo and Daphne, see Laguna Mariscal (1989).

68. Hardie (1999), 264–67, and Janan (1988), 117–24, on Hyacinthus.

69. See n.19 of chapter 2. Specifically on Roman homosexuality see Williams (1999).

70. The idea that Narcissus has actually seen himself before could be enforced by the fact that, when he woos his beloved he says that *certe nec forma nec aetas/ est mea, quam fugias, et amarunt me quoque nymphae!/* "Certainly my beauty and age are not such that you may want to flee from me. Even nymphs have loved me!" (Met. 455–56). An easy way out of this is to say that he is only judging according to the opinion of the nymphs, but it is just as likely that he has actually seen himself before but, blinded now, he cannot form a clear recollection of it. In this sense, the moment of his 'self-recognition' is easier to understand: *iste ego sum: sensi, nec me mea fallit imago/* "It is me. I have recognized myself, and my own image does not deceive me" (Met. 3.463). All of a sudden, he recognizes the image of himself that he has seen before.

71. On the likeness as *imago* see Solodow (1988), 255 n43.

72. Spencer (1997), 40.

73. Ibid.

74. See n. 67 of this chapter.

75. Barthes (1979), 13–14.

76. See Beye (1974), 93.

77. This observation is taken from Beye (1974), 95.

78. This does not mean that women are completely static. Especially in fiction, their characters suffer changes; the circumstances of their lives are modified. In fact, Felson-Rubin (1994) even sees Penelope as a multifaceted figure, and proposes that Homer challenges traditional assumptions about 'good women' in her character. Nonetheless, if these women are truly 'ideal,' their status of 'good wives' and mothers tends to remain unchanged.

79. Things in the Aeneid are not simple because Dido is an exile and a traveler her-

self, but in the world of the Virgilian epic she remains on land. Paradoxically, she is the one called *mutabile: varium et mutabile semper/ femina/* "A manifold and ever-changing thing is Woman" (*Aen.* 4.569–70). Cf. Calpurnius Siculus, *Bucolic* 3.10: *mobilior ventis o femina!/* "Oh, woman, more changeable than the winds!" See Austin (1955), on *Aen.* 4.569. But it is clear that Mercury is lying here because Dido has been nothing but constant in her devotion to Aeneas. There are also etymological connections between *muto* and *moveo* (perhaps *mutare* comes from **movitare*). See Ernout and Meillet (1985), *muto*.

80. Examples of this in Latin elegy are Ovid, *Heroides* 1 (Penelope), 2 (Phyllis), 7 (Dido), and 10 (Ariadne), and Propertius' elegy 4.3 where Arethusa writes a letter to her husband. Lycotas, absent at war. In Roman elegy one can see a telling inversion of these epic parameters when the man remains immobile and the girl travels by sea (especially in Propertius). See Prop.1.6.1–6, 1.8A.1–8, 1.17.13–14, 2.26A.1–3; Ovid, *Am.* 3.2.48, 2.11.7–12; Tib.1.1.49–58 and 1.3.21–22. Note also the lover's rejection of seafaring in Ovid, *Am.* 3.2.48: *"nil mihi cum pelago, me mea terra capit"/* "'I have nothing to do with the sea, my land holds me.'"

81. See Hinds (1987), 32.

82. Anderson (1997), on *Met.* 4.237–40.

83. Segal (1969), 33.

84. For intertextual connections, see Bömer (1976a), on *Met.* 4.21.

85. The formula also recalls the idea that barbarians like Medea did not have the great Platonic virtue of *sophrosyne*, thus demonstrating *akolasia*, the opposite to the philosopher's *sophrosyne*, of which Medea seems to be a perfect example. See Hall (1991), 125.

86. See Newlands (1997), 186–92. According to Segal (2002), 11–19, the change in the use of magic also accompanies Medea's transformation.

87. *Heroides* 12 envisions Medea's passion in the same way: *"tunc ego te vidi, tunc coepi scire, quid esses;/ illa fuit mentis prima ruina meae./ et vidi et perii; nec notis ignibus arsi,/ ardet ut ad magnos pinea taeda deos./ et formosus eras, et me mea fata trahebant;/ abstulerant oculi lumina nostra tui"/* "'Then I saw you, then I began to know who you were; that was the beginning of my soul's ruin. I saw you and that was my end, and I burned with an unknown fire, as pinewood burns for the great gods. And not only were you beautiful but my own fates were dragging me. Your eyes had taken mine away'" (*Her.*12.31–36).

88. The same capacity to act appears in *Heroides* 12.39ff.

89. These types of scenes of fighting recall the gladiatorial spectacles in Rome.

90. See Tissol (1997), 143ff., for a detailed discussion. For parallel stories see Hollis (1970), 34–35. In Propertius, Tarpeia actually mentions Scylla as a precedent of herself (4.4.39–40) and then Ovid recovers her from Tarpeia's memory.

91. It is interesting that Ovid chose the version in which Caunus and Byblis are twins, though there were other versions circulating in which they were simply siblings. Nagle (1983), 305, believes that he does not play out the possibilities of this in *Metamorphoses*. For two recent studies of Byblis see Jenkins (2001) and Raval (2001).

92. Cf. Pausanias 9.31.7–9, with Elsner (1996), 256. The love for the same may also be suggested in the episode of Iphis and Ianthe in Book 9. Not only are they both girls, despite Ianthe not being aware of it, but they are also 'alike' and have the same education: *par aetas, par forma fuit, primasque magistris/ accepere artes, elementa aetatis, ab isdem/* "They were equal in age and beauty, and learned the first arts, their age's

education, from the same teachers'" (*Met.*9.718–19). But the conflict is resolved by Isis, who turns Iphis into a young man.

93. See Murgatroyd (1995) for nautical metaphors in love matters.

94. For a resisting reading of the episode see Sharrock (1991b), 177, who questions why Myrrha and her nurse are solely to blame here.

Chapter Four

1. Forrester (1980), 34.

2. Shlain (1998).

3. Whether this was an actual historical event or whether it only belongs to the realm of myth, is a matter of discussion, but Shlain bases his theory on the assumption that this was an actual change in human organization. For an overview of the various theories of why the 'Goddess' was overthrown, see Shlain (1998), 35–39.

4. On the distinction between the hemispheres of the brain see Shlain (1998), chapter 3. Shlain (1998), chapter 2, suggests, for example, that the hunter uses a more fixed, tubular vision that disregards the context to focus on a prey, while the female that usually stayed in the community and gathered fruits had also to keep an eye on the context for she usually also looked after young children while performing these tasks. See also Shlain (1998), 26–27.

5. Ibid., 1.

6. There are other criticisms to be raised to Shlain's theory, namely, that the "world of the Goddess" may not have been as "egalitarian" as he would like and that the gaze of the hunter may have and needs some sort of peripheral and holistic gaze—although one can suppose that in this case he would be using his 'feminine' side—in the same way as the gatherer needs the sharp focusing gaze precisely to select what to pick—as in the case of Medea. Constructionists would also object to his belief in certain 'natural' or inherent qualities pertaining to the male and the female. Finally, one could argue that Shlain seems to treat every female instinct or quality as more 'primitive' than those of males.

7. Miller (1986), 271.

8. Nymphs like Callisto, who are alternative in some way and do not represent the type of the ideal wife, do not weave but hunt instead.

9. Cohen (1989), especially 6–7, warns against the trap of identifying normative and cultural ideals with real life. In our case, weaving and also silence are not certain marks of 'real women' but part of a construction that serves as a model.

10. For further references to literal and metaphorical weaving in Homer and the Greek lyric poets see McIntosh Snyder (1981) and Scheid and Svenbro (1996), chapter 5. On weaving in Homer, see also Wace and Stubbings (1962), 531.

11. McIntosh Snyder (1981), 194.

12. On weaving as a masculine activity see Thompson (1982) and references in Scheid and Svenbro (1996), 181 n75.

13. See Paoli (1963), 117.

14. On the loom in the *atrium*, see Blümner (1911), 30 n3. Another telling example of virtuous women weaving in the *atrium* is the story of the wife of M. Aemilius Lepidus told by Asconius in *Pro. Mil.* 43.

15. Pomeroy (1995), 149 and 199.

16. Joplin (1984), 26.

17. This is an extremely complicated issue. Certainly some would object that it is not so easy to define art and that abstract patterns in a fabric can also be 'communicative.' Although it is not the aim of this discussion to go too far into this polemic, it is our view that while everything is at some level expressive and communicative, art that involves recognizable images and implies an action and a story is not the same as a decorative pattern.

18. Bergren (1983), 79 and Kennedy (1986), 1. For the links between Helen the weaver and the image of the poet, see Kennedy (1986).

19. Pantelia (1993), 495.

20. Circe is another great weaver in Homer. In the *Odyssey* (Hom., *Od.* 10. 220–23, 226–28, and 254–55), even though we don't know exactly what she weaves or whether she weaves figures or not, we know for sure that it is beautiful. While one may suppose that she weaves figures, not much can be inferred from the text. In *Metamorphoses* Circe is a more one-dimensional character than in Homer and her negative aspects are highlighted. There is no mention of her legendary loom in the poem.

21. Pantelia (1993), 495.

22. This fantasy is reflected in Aristotle's quote of Sophocles *Ajax* 293 in *Politics* 1.5.8. Cf. Aristophanes, *Lysistrata* 515, 530 with Henderson's commentary (1987) on 529–38. For the silence of women in Rome see Plutarch's comparison between Lycurgus and Numa (*Lycurgus and Numa* 3.5) and Pliny the Younger in *Panegyricus* 83. For voice as a marker of gender boundaries see Gleason (1995), 98. On the unnameability of women, see Thucydides' funeral speech of Pericles (2.45) and Pliny the Younger, *Panegyricus* 84. See also Fantham et al. (1994), 79, and Schaps (1977).

23. McIntosh Snyder (1981), 193.

24. The structural similarities of the loom and the lyre can be observed most clearly in Attic vase representations. See McIntosh Snyder (1981), 195. One may even suppose that women who weave and sing at the same time, like Circe and Calypso, for example, are deviant because they merge masculine and feminine tasks instead of confining themselves solely to womanly weaving.

25. See Galinsky (1975), 82–83; Curran (1972), especially 83–85; Feeney (1991), 190–95; Shaw Hardy (1995); von Albrecht (1979); Harries (1990); Vincent (1994); Rosati (1999); Miller (1986); Lateiner (1984), especially 15–17; and Winsor Leach (1974), especially 117–20. For iconography of the myth, see Weinberg and Weinberg (1956).

26. Otis (1970).

27. See Laird (1993), 19. Laird's point that an "obedient" ekphrasis is a description that could be easily represented as a picture or frieze, and "disobedient" is one that it would not be possible to represent pictorially is useful. But this distinction is still peculiar. Disobedient to what? Who is the authority that imposes limits to what is appropriate or not to describe?

28. Galinsky (1975), 82–83.

29. See Curran (1972), 83–85. On the whole problem of Augustanism and anti-Augustanism, see Due (1974), 66–89.

30. Harries (1990), 64–82, quote on 65.

31. Miller (1986), 273.

32. Joplin (1984), 48.

33. See Shaw Hardy (1995), 143.

34. Curiously, the cloak that Athena weaves for Jason in Apollonius's *Argonautica* 1 is very different in that it focuses neither on the divine order nor on the self-centered representation of the goddess, but rather resembles more closely Arachne's fluidity of composition.

35. Anderson (1972), on *Met.* 6.78.

36. On the 'stage-direction' see Anderson (1972), on *Met.* 6.82.

37. Ibid., on *Met.* 6.90.

38. This is Anderson's (1972) supposition, on *Met.* 6.98.

39. Joplin (1984), 49, considers the possibility that Medusa was actually sacrificed in the temple of Athena "as an offering to an 'angry' goddess," which would connect her to sacrificed virgins like Iphigenia.

40. See Towneley Parker (1996) and Arafat (1996).

41. Minerva's 'masculinity' is also seen in her definition as virago in *Met.* 6.130.

42. A different, more obscure version of the myth of Arachne relates that while Athena taught the heroine the art of weaving, Phalanx, her brother learned the arts of arms:

ὁ δὲ Ζηνοδότειος θεόφιλος ἱστορεῖ ὡς ἄρα ἐν τῇ Ἀττικῇ δύο
ἐγένοντο ἀδελφοί, Φάλαγξ μὲν ἄρσεν, θήλεια δὲ Ἀράχνη
τοὔνομα. καὶ ὁ μὲν Φάλαγξ ἔμαθε παρὰ τῆς Ἀθηνᾶς τὰ περὶ
τὴν ὁπλομαχίαν, ἡ δὲ Ἀράχνη τὰ περὶ τὴν ἱστοποιίαν·
μιγέντας δὲ ἀλλήλοις στυγηθῆναι ὑπὸ τῆς θεοῦ καὶ μετ-
αβληθῆναι εἰς ἑρπετά, ἃ δὴ καὶ συμβαίνει ὑπὸ τῶν ἰδίων
τέκνων κατεσθίεσθαι·

And Theophilus, of the School of Zenodotus, records that in Attica there were two siblings, Phalanx, the man, and the woman, named Arachne. But while Phalanx learned from Athena the martial arts and Arachne the art of weaving, they were abhorred by the goddess because they had intercourse with each other. They were transformed into animals who were eaten by their own offspring. (Schol. in Nic., *Ther.* 12.a)

The trigger in Nicander for this reference is a simple mention of φαλλάγια / "spiders," as Nicander does not use the word ἀράχνια (cf. Arist. *H.A.*622b28–29). The example recounted by the scholiast is quite paradigmatic and the opposition between weaving (the feminine) and war (the masculine) is clearly appreciated. Ovid certainly knew Nicander, but the version narrated by the scholiast may not have been familiar to a Roman audience. This variant adds a more deviant twist to the character of Arachne, which Ovid, if he had heard of it, preferred to omit. One possible moral to be drawn from the scholia is that the arts of men and women should remain separate and not be confused—at least by mortals.

43. Two other instances of textiles used as weapons can be observed in Deianeira and Medea. Both women send a poisoned robe which has the power to consume and kill. In the case of Deianeira, the tragedy of Heracles' death is the outcome of error. His wife sends him a tunic soaked in Nessus's poison believing that it was a love potion. Ovid (*Met.* 9.152–54) is not explicit about the origin of the robe, but Seneca imagines that Deianeira herself made it: *"cape hos amictus, nostra quos nevit manus"* /

"'Take this robe, which my own hands have woven'" (*Herc. Oet.* 571). Medea also uses a robe to destroy Jason's new bride Creusa (E., *Medea* 949 and Sen., *Med.* 817). Although it is unclear whether she wove the garment, the act can still be seen as a use of textiles as feminine weapons. In the literary treatments of these two myths, the language of fire and burning is dominating. An uncontrollable flame consuming the victims may even make one think of a certain transmission of the woman's own deadly passion into the woven product.

44. Kris and Kurz (1979), 17–19.

45. It is difficult to see in the very different styles how Minerva could have been Arachne's teacher.

46. Cf. *TLL,* vol. 3 fasc. 4, *certamen,* coll. 882–85, *de proeliis et bellis.*

47. Miller (1986), 273.

48. This ode is dedicated to the power of Augustus, who is in the poem and in the Augustan ideology in general identified with Jupiter. Note in particular *parentis* in line 13.

49. Recent feminist research has centered on the symbolism of the head as a locus of voice and identity. As Howard Eilberg-Schwartz suggests in the introduction to *Off with Her Head!* (1995), 1, the head is "the anatomical part of the female body that gives women a voice and an identity and that thereby threatens to unmake and disrupt the classic gender distinctions that have linked men to speech, power, identity and the mind. . . . Removing the female head relieves woman of both identity and voice and reduces her to a mere sexual and reproductive body." But there are other less obvious forms of beheading as the articles in this volume explore. In the case of Arachne the reduction of her head sits well with these theoretical views; we can clearly see it as another form of symbolic decapitation.

50. There are some recognized problems in considering Arachne, Minerva, or Philomela as 'narrators' and their tapestries as 'embedded stories' because it is Ovid who narrates what is expressed in their textiles. See Shaw Hardy (1995), 142. However, in a releasing reading this would not matter much.

51. See especially Joplin (1984), Marder (1992), de Luce (1993), Segal (1994), and Liveley (1999b).

52. Joplin's (1984) argument in particular uses the episode to foster a feminist agenda.

53. See discussion in Anderson (1972), on *Met.* 6.441.

54. Ibid., on *Met.* 6.453 and Wheeler (1999), 104.

55. Wheeler (1999), 104 and Anderson (1972), on *Met.* 6.451–54.

56. Segal (1994), 260.

57. Ibid., 271, and Barchiesi (1989), 72.

58. On Tereus's desire to be in the father's place, see Richlin (1992), 176, and Segal (1994), 260.

59. Note that Marder (1992), 159, observes that the comparisons with animals may actually indicate a "stutter in the narrative voice. The rape of Philomela's body is represented as unspeakable in human terms. . . . The animal comparisons serve to figure the symbolic silencing that is initiated by the rape."

60. Ibid., 160.

61. Ibid., 161, and Joplin (1984), 52: "her body was the original page on which a tale was written in blood."

62. Cf. Bömer (1976b), on *Met.* 6.582.

63. Nagle (1988a), 92.

64. Wheeler (1999), 51–53.

65. Segal (1994), 265.

66. Ibid.

67. See Slater (1927), on *Met*. 6.582.

68. Although *fatum* has in origin to do with "saying," it still provides some ambiguity in the sense of "fate."

69. *Aeneid* 6.34 is particularly important because *perlegerent oculis* refers to Aeneas' viewing of the images on the doors of the temple of Apollo.

Chapter Five

1. The distinction between poetic persona and author is a working assumption in much of Ovidian criticism, especially regarding the love poetry. See Durling (1958) and Fyler (1971). For a good discussion of the 'narrator-persona' and its relationship with the 'author,' see Wheeler (1999), 66–74. Wheeler (1999), 71–74, examines the difference between persona and author through a comparison of the narrators of *Fasti* and *Metamorphoses*. Other critics like Solodow (1988), 41, though aware of the distinction between author and poetic persona, see no point in making a difference in the *Metamorphoses*. Galinsky (1975), 173, also identifies the author with the narrator. Wheeler (1999), 70, however, believes in a distinction between the *poeta amator* and the 'epic' narrator and that Ovid was very much aware of the possibility of creating different personae; Graf (1988), 63, concurs with this.

2. Some important discussions of the internal narrators in *Metamorphoses* are Keith (1992), 4–5; Segal (1971) and (1978); Nagle (1983), (1988a), (1988b), (1988c), and (1989); Gamel (1984); Knox (1986), 48–64; Ahl (1985), 202–4; Hinds (1987), 91–93, and 121–32; Janan (1988); Barchiesi (1989); Konstan (1991); and Myers (1994a), 61–132.

3. See Appendix A in Wheeler (1999), 207–10.

4. For a listing of male narrators in *Metamorphoses*, see Wheeler (1999), Appendix A.

5. See Sharrock (1999) and Spentzou (2003) .

6. Rosati (1999). Laird (1993) exposes a similar textual strategy in Catullus 64.

7. Galinsky (1975), 92, believes that the tale of the Minyeides is an example of how the Cadmus "cycle is interspersed . . . with stories that have little or nothing to do with the theme and exist in their own right, thus providing diversions and digressions. . . . Similarly, the stories of the Minyeides (4.167–388), though they are connected well among each other, are independent of the theme of the misfortune of the Cadmeans and of the Bacchus theme to which Ovid gives great prominence." Segal (1971), 333, insinuates the connection of the narrative framework and the imbedded stories, referring especially to the Minyeides and the tale of Pyramus and Thisbe. Galinsky's view does not seem right. With Segal, one sees a strong connection between the narrative circumstances and the stories that the daughters of Minyas tell. In fact, these tales have much to do with Dionysus.

8. See Anderson (1997), 411, where he also states that in the tales of the

Minyeides "their narratives suggest what the Ovidian narrator has also been suggesting: that human beings have a richer, more responsible sense of emotion (especially love) and of ethics than the gods have. Thus their stories perform a more telling challenge of divinity in general than the women themselves can mount."

9. Campbell Rhorer (1980).

10. Ibid., 83–84, sees the lioness as a symbol of the violent wooing lover, embodied in the transformation of Atalanta and Hippomenes. "Thisbe's close brush with the lioness is like a brush with sexuality itself."

11. Ibid., 84.

12. Adams (1982), 30 with n. 3.

13. Segal (1969), 50.

14. See Anderson (1997), on *Met.* 4.122–24.

15. Hinds (1987), 31. For *ictus* of the male sexual act see Adams (1982), 148–49. Shorrock (2003) also sees sexual connotations in the image and suggests that it echoes another version where Thisbe is transformed into a spring and Pyramus into a river. The bursting of the pipe, then, represents a rupture in the narrative where the other version emerges.

16. Barkan (1986), 57.

17. Fowler (2000), 160, recognizes the erotic implications of the tale and remarks that "the story begins with a vulva-like crack and ends with a double penetration by a sword whose phallic symbolism is heightened by the intertext of Dido's suicide with Aeneas' sword."

18. Contrast with Due, who sees the feelings between the lovers as "the love of children," a love that is not yet sexual. Due (1974), 127. On maturity and immaturity see Segal (1969), 50.

19. Note how Dionysus the liberator is one who opens and unchains as seen with Acoetes in *Met.* 3.699–700. Unbinding is also perceived in the hairdo of the Bacchants (*Met.*4.6).

20. Segal (1971), 333.

21. Kris and Kurz (1979), 39, quoting Zilsel (1926). The other reason why artists were not regarded in such high esteem in antiquity, according to Kris and Kurz (1979), 39–40, and were not credited with "singular or special genius," "derives from the tenets of art itself and has, in Plato's formulation, achieved enduring significance: art as *mimesis*, as the imitation of nature, can provide only a distant reflection of true being, of ideas, which art attempts to reproduce at second hand, as it were, by imitating their earthly embodiments."

22. Curiously, Due (1974), 128, in a masculinist perspective that aligns with the Sun's gaze, seems to suggest that Leucothoe acts sensibly by surrendering to inevitable rape: "Leucothoe is neither an Io nor a Lucretia but a reasonable girl."

23. Canidia and her cronies at the end of Horace's *Satire* 1.8 lose their herbs, Proserpina loses her flowers, and Circe drops her herbs in Book 14. Callisto's quiver also falls from her hands after rape in Book 2.

24. See Labate (1992), 52–53. Compare Martial's emphasis on the mother and father in epigram 14.174: *Masculus intravit fontis: emersit utrumque:/ pars est una patris, cetera matris habet/* "He entered the spring as a male and came out as a mixture of male and female: a part of him was like his father, the rest like his mother."

25. Ibid., 53.

26. Spencer (1997), 49.

27. Labate (1992), 54, makes the interesting observation that Ovid displays a set of inversions and surprises. While the virgin Salmacis has none of the virginal purity of the usual nymphs who hunt with Diana and is obsessed with her own beauty, Hermaphroditus, the son of Venus, displays a virginal rejection of love.

28. Anderson (1997), 396–98, takes it as a tapestry with possible images: "the tapestry, which Ovid has not described, turns partly into a grape vine."

29. Ibid., on *Met.* 4.394–95.

30. Ibid., 456. Anderson believes that Dionysus 'weaves' grapes and ivy on the Minyeides' loom.

31. As Janan (1994) suggests, the failure of the Minyeides may be due to their inability completely to suppress desire enacted in the enjoyment of erotic tales. But possibly, their crime is not—in Bacchus's eyes—the delight in pleasure and eroticism, but the fact that it is a pleasure created and chosen by women for themselves, not heeding the type of organized pleasure directed by a male god.

32. See Wheeler (1999), 182: "The emphasis upon novelty recalls Ovid's own programmatic opening statement, "*In nova fert animus.*"

33. This is a difficult issue, because while Ovid in the exile poetry insists on the fact that he has lost his poetic capacity, he can still produce poems. However, he does not 'narrate stories' in the manner of *Metamorphoses* any more, and in this sense he is similar to the Minyeides.

34. On the episode see Cahoon (1996) and (1990), and Johnson and Malamud (1988).

35. For the complexity of narrative levels in the episode, see Wheeler (1999), 81–84.

36. On the Heliconian fount see Hinds's (1987) discussion, 3–24.

37. On the importance of virginity in the episode, see Segal (1969), 53.

38. On the Pierides' song see Winsor Leach (1974), 115–16.

39. Segal (1969), 33, and Parry (1964), especially 276–77.

40. Segal (1969), 34 with n. 65. See also Barkan (1986), 16 with the Homeric *Hymn to Demeter* 1–23. Compare also Milton's line about the grove "where Proserpin gathering flowers,/ herself a fairer flower, by gloomy Dis/ was gathered" (*Paradise Lost* 4.269–71).

41. Thomas (1979) advances the idea that the color combination white and red has implications of death. Perhaps something similar can be said for the combination white and purple.

42. Hinds (1987), 35.

43. See Cahoon (1996), 53.

44. The sisters of Phaethon and Cyparissus are also transformed through their tears. As a man, however, Cyparissus is not mollified by tears, but rather 'hardened' as he is transformed into a cypress in Book 10. Other stories of transformation into water in the *Metamorphoses* are: Arethusa (Book 5), the tears of the friends of Marsyas (Book 6), Hyrie (Book 7), Byblis (Book 9), Acis (Book 13), Canens (Book 14), and Egeria (Book 15). Most of them begin with a body liquid, namely tears, except for Arethusa whose 'melting' starts with her *sudor*, and Acis, who is transformed by Galatea. In most cases, dissolution seems to be the only possible escape from a problematic situation for women.

45. Ahl (1985), 59, sees a similar word play in the beginning of *Metamorphoses: mutatas dicere formas*. "Between MUTAtas (changed) and FORMas, he inserts the word *dicere* (speak of): this addition suggests the Latin MUTus (silent) as well as the idea of change. Ovid gives voice to forms that cannot speak for themselves." As Segal (1969), 54, notes, however, there is some inconsistency in Cyane's inability to speak, for other rivers and fountains in the poem have this power.

46. See Gowers (1993), 238–39; Adams (1982), 138–41; and Henderson (1975), 47–48, 52, 60–61, 129, and 142–44. Cf. Barkan's (1986), 51, metaphorical use of language when talking about Narcissus's desire: "Like Echo earlier, Narcissus wastes away; he perishes by his eyes. Ovid's description draws a close connection between the literal alimentary undernourishment that diminishes and destroys the boy's flesh and the spiritual undernourishment implicit in imaginary love. He tries to eat with his eyes and finding no food there, he neglects the feeding of his stomach." Cf. also Ovid's description of Tereus's passion at the sight of Philomela: *omnia pro stimulis facibusque ciboque furoris/ accipit/* "All these things are fuel and food for his passion" (*Met.* 6.480–81).

47. Cf. *stetit* (*Met.* 4.678) for Perseus, who stops and looks.

48. On the nature of the lizard see Ronnick (1993) and Myers (1992).

49. Segal (1969), 57, believes that there is no sexual content in the story of the boy transformed into a lizard. But this is questionable.

50. Hinds (1987), 89.

51. In Apollodorus's version (1.5.3) it is actually Demeter who punishes the boy.

52. Davis (1983), 52–53, believes that Arethusa, like other nymphs, rejects her very nature. He even defines her experience as "alienation from the self" and suggests that in the very name *nympha*, there is an etymological play with the archaic Greek meaning of the word 'bride' or 'nubile woman'—cf. Ernout-Meillet (1979), *nub*—and thus by rejecting sex they reject their own nature.

53. On Daphne's and Arethusa's nudity see Richlin (1992), 162, who believes that the "narrator stresses how visually attractive the disarray of flight and fear made the victims." Curran (1978), to whom Richlin responds, sees these types of descriptions as a mark of Ovid's sympathy toward raped women.

54. Johnson (1996), 139.

55. Winsor Leach (1974), 117.

56. Stehle (1990), 107. On goddesses and young men see also Reed (1995), 332–33; Winkler (1990), 202–26; and Gordon's (1997), 284–86 discussions of Sappho and Phaon in *Heroides* 15.

57. See Tissol (1997), 113. For an excellent discussion of the Theocritan intertext, see Farrell (1992).

58. Compare the comic effect of Mercury making himself pretty for Herse in *Met.* 2.733–36. There was a comic tradition of representing the Cyclops, as seen especially in Euripides' satyr-play *The Cyclops*, and Philoxenus's dithyramb *Cyclops* or *Galatea*.

59. On excessive grooming as a trait of effeminacy, see Williams (1999), 127–32.

60. See Wyke (1994), 134–38.

61. Tissol (1997), 20. One must of course note the amatory variant of captivation with the eyes in Propertius 1.1.1: *Cynthia . . . me cepit ocellis/* "Cynthia possessed me with her eyes."

62. Galinsky (1975), 218, already saw a parodic form of the paraclausithyron in the episode.

63. One should note that, as usual in Ovid, stories do not finish but are 'transformed.' This is what happens after Galatea finishes her narration. All the nymphs return to swim in the sea, but Scylla prefers safer waters closer to the shores. Thereafter, she is wooed by Glaucus, the fisherman turned sea deity. In this courtship, there is a reversed disposition of lover and beloved. The woman runs on earth and takes refuge on the top of a high mountain (*Met.*13.909–12), while the man stays at sea. As Segal (1969), 17, suggests, mountains seem to be safer than forests or woods.

64. For the episode of Polyphemus and Galatea as a 'dialogue of genres,' which includes elements of pastoral poetry, epic, and elegy against more traditionally monologic views that see the story as belonging to one genre only, see Farrell (1992).

65. Pomona is another interesting example of a woman assimilated to landscape, as Gentilcore (1995) shows.

66. On the use of different sources in the speech and in particular on the allusion to Horace, *Odes* 3.13, see Gross (2000).

67. Tissol (1997), 105–24. For a comparison between Virgil's *Eclogue* 2 and Ovid's episode see Galinsky (1975), 192–93.

68. Farrell (1992), 244.

69. For possible sources of Acis, see Tissol (1997), 114.

70. Barkan (1986), 80, stresses Acis' fluidity and Polyphemus's solidity and mass, but these terms are slightly deconstructed and transformed in the episode, as Acis becomes a stable identity.

71. For rivers having horns like bulls, see Achelous in *Met.* 9.80ff., whose loss of one horn at the hands of Hercules also points at his diminished masculinity.

72. Wheeler (1999), 136.

73. Definitions of childbirth deities are somewhat blurry. Ilythia (mentioned in *Met.* 9.283) is the goddess of childbirth, apparently a daughter of Zeus and Hera in Greek mythology, but sometimes she is identified with Juno herself as goddess of matrimony and family. Yet in Rome, Ilythia is linked to Lucina, who is also identified with Juno as a childbirth deity. See Grant and Hazel (1973), "Lucina." But what is curious is that in all this Diana also plays a role, as Artemis seems to have been blended with the figure of Lucina as a protector of young children and small things, a sense that is observed in Horace's *Carmen Saeculare*. See "Lucina" in *OLD* (1997) and Grimal (1986).

74. The Hippocratic doctors imagined the uterus of a woman as an upside-down jug, which is proved by the anatomical terms employed by both Hippocratics and sophisticated anatomists. They speak of the σταϑμός or πυϑμήν, *fundus*, "bottom," on top, while the στόμα, *os*, "mouth," lies at the bottom. The αὐχήν, cervix, "neck," opens in a downward direction. See Ellis Hanson (1990), 317, 321–25. These Greek terms and their Latin correspondents appear variously in the medical texts of Rome. See Adams (1982), 108–9. On the parallels between mouth and female genitalia see also Sissa (1990), 53–66 and 166–67. Mouth and womb are viewed as the upper and lower *stomata* of a woman and passages in the medical treatises show similar responses in both of them. Medication is aimed at both 'mouths.' See Ellis Hanson (1990), 328. Although doctors speak of the neck of the uterus, the link between the cervix and sex is rather stressed by poets. Most striking, however, is the idea that the neck becomes enlarged after a virgin has been deflowered. The distension of the girl's 'lower mouth and neck' is reflected in the widening of her upper neck. See Ellis Hanson (1990), 328–29.

75. For the weasel see Myers (1994b), 32–33. The idea that the weasel gives birth through her mouth is probably based on the experience of "seeing the weasel carry its children about in its mouth" (Pliny, *HN* 29.60).

76. Segal (1998), 28.

77. The model of the flower dripping blood here is probably Virgil, *Aeneid* 3.26ff.

78. See Segal (1969), 36.

79. Ovid narrates the attempted rape of Lotis at greater length in *Fasti* 1.415–40.

80. Note that the Hamadryads, also called dryads, were nymphs whose lives depended on that of the oak trees they lived in. The name "Dryops" itself (father of Dryope), means "oak-face." For Antoninus Liberalis' version with commentaries, see Celoria (1992).

81. For Adonis see Reed (1995), Detienne (1977), Ribichini (1981), and Piccaluga (1977).

82. As the poem suggests (*Met.*10.524), by falling in love with Myrrha's child, the text embodies a sort of vengeance for Myrrha's passion.

83. We should note that the love of Venus for Adonis also shows maternal feelings of care and protection for a child. There are some incestual overtones in the fact that Adonis is identified with Cupid, which is developed at the moment of Adonis' birth (*laudaret faciem Livor quoque; qualia namque/ corpora nudorum tabula pinguntur Amorum, talis erat, sed, ne faciat discrimina cultus,/ aut huic adde leves, aut illis deme pharetras/* "Even Envy would praise his beauty, for his body was like the body of naked Loves painted in canvas, but so that attire may make no distinction, you should give him a light quiver or remove it from them" (*Met.*10.515–18). Therefore, Venus reflects as in an inverted mirror Myrrha's incestuous love affair. See Galinsky (1975), 89–90 and 101–2.

84. The only stories involving women as central characters that come after the Sibyl are Circe in book 14 and the tale of Iphis and Anaxarete in the context of Vertumnus's wooing of Pomona, but this tale is narrated by a male in female disguise.

85. Segal (1971).

86. See Galinsky (1975), 228. For a discussion of Ovid's Sibyl in the light of Virgil's version, see Galinsky (1975), 225–29.

87. See Sharrock (2002c). Sharrock draws an interesting link between the prophetess and the figure of the epic poet acting as 'mouth' of the muse.

88. See Fitzgerald (1995), 10–11 and 80–81 for further discussions of mouths and their poetic and sexual functions.

89. For an account of inspiration, penetration, openings, and wordplay in the Virgilian version, see Paschalis (1997), 209–11.

90. Nikolopoulos (2003), 52, believes that the Sibyl is in her old age as vain as she was in her youth because what seems to hurt her most is that she will no longer be attractive. On old age in *Metamorphoses,* see Nikolopoulos (2003).

91. Ibid., 58.

Postscript

1. Hardie (1999), 270.

BIBLIOGRAPHY

✥

Abbreviations of Journals

AJPh: American Journal of Philology
BASP: Bulletin of the American Society of Papyrologists
ClAnt: Classical Antiquity
CJ: Classical Journal
CQ: Classical Quarterly
CW: Classical World
GB: Grazer Beiträge
G&R: Greece and Rome
HSPh: Harvard Studies in Classical Philology
JRS: Journal of Roman Studies
JWI: Journal of the Warburg and Courtland Institutes
MD: Materiali e discussioni per l'analisi dei testi classici
PCPhS: Proceedings of the Cambridge Philological Association
REL: Revue des études latines
RhM: Reinisches Museum für Philologie
Syll Class: Syllecta Classica
TAPhA: Transactions of the American Philological Association

The text of *Metamorphoses* is that of the Loeb edition: Goold, G.P, ed. (1984). *Ovid. Metamorphoses*. Cambridge, Mass.: Harvard University Press.

Adams J. N. (1982). *The Latin Sexual Vocabulary*. London: Johns Hopkins University Press.

Ahl. F. (1985). *Metaformations. Sound-play and Word-play in Ovid and Other Classical Poets*. Ithaca, N.Y.: Cornell University Press.

Alberti, Leon Battista (1972). *De Pictura*. Edited and translated by C. Grayson. London: Phaidon.

Altieri, C. (1973). "Ovid and the New Mythologists." *Novel: A Forum on Fiction* 7.1: 31–40.

Anderson, W. S. (1966). "*Talaria* and Ovid *Met*.10.591." *TAPhA* 97: 1–13.

_____. (1972). *Ovid's Metamorphoses. Books 6–10*. Norman: University of Oklahoma Press.

_____. (1982). "The Orpheus of Virgil and Ovid: *flebile nescio quid*." In J. Warden, ed., *Orpheus: The Metamorphosis of a Myth*, 25–50. Toronto: University of Toronto Press.

_____. (1997). *Ovid's Metamorphoses. Books 1–5*. Norman: University of Oklahoma Press.

Arafat, K.W. (1996). "Nike." In S. Hornblower and A. Spawforth, eds., *Oxford Classical Dictionary*, 1044. Oxford: Oxford University Press.

Armstrong, C. (1989). "The Reflexive and the Possessive View: Thoughts on Kertesz, Brandt, and the Photographic Nude." *Representations* 25: 57–70.

Austin, R. G. (1955). *Aeneidos Liber IV*. Oxford: Oxford University Press.

Bal, M. (1997). *Narratology. Introduction to the Theory of Narrative*. Translated by C. van Boheemen. Toronto: University of Toronto Press.

Barchiesi, A. (1989). "Voci e istanze narrative nelle Metamorfosi di Ovidio." *MD* 23: 55–97.

_____. (1999). "Venus' Masterplot: Ovid and the Homeric *Hymns*." In P. Hardie, A. Barchiesi, and S. Hinds, eds., *Ovidian Transformations*, 112–26. Cambridge: Cambridge University Press. .

Barkan, L. (1986). *The Gods Made Flesh. Metamorphoses and the Pursuit of Paganism*. New Haven: Yale University Press.

Barolsky, P. (1995). "A Very Brief History of Art from Narcissus to Picasso." *CJ* 90.3: 255–59.

Barthes, R. (1975). *The Pleasure of the Text*. Translated by R. Howard. New York: Hill and Wang. .

_____. (1979). *A Lover's Discourse. Fragments*. Translated by R. Miller. Hill and Wang. New York.

Bartsch, S. (1989). *Decoding the Ancient Novel, the Reader and the Role of Description in Heliodorus and Achilles Tatius*. Princeton: Princeton University Press.

Bauer, D. F. (1962). "The Function of Pygmalion in Ovid's *Metamorphoses*." *TAPhA* 99: 1–21.

Bell, R. E. (1991). *Women of Classical Mythology*. Oxford: Oxford University Press.

Bergren, A. (1983). "Language and the Female in Early Greek Thought." *Arethusa* 16: 69–95.

Beye, C. R. (1974). "Male and Female in the Homeric Poems." *Ramus* 3: 87–101.

Bing, P. (1999). "Review of S. M. Wheeler, *A Discourse of Wonders: Audience and Performance in Ovid's Metamorphoses* (1999). *Bryn Mawr Classical Review* 99.10.26 (online).

Blümner, H. (1911). *Die römische Privataltertümer*. Munich: Beck.

Bömer, F. (1969). *P. Ovidius Naso Metamorphosen: Kommentar, Buch I-III*. Heidelberg: Carl Winter Universitätsverlag.

_____. (1976a). *P. Ovidius Naso Metamorphosen: Kommentar, Buch IV-V*. Heidelberg: Carl Winter Universitätsverlag.

_____. (1976b). *P. Ovidius Naso Metamorphosen: Kommentar, Buch VI-VII*. Heidelberg: Carl Winter Universitätsverlag.

Borghini, A. (1979). "Riflessioni antropologiche sopra un mito di proibizione: la ragazza alla finestra (Ovidio *met*.14.795–861 e Antonino Liberale *met*.39)." *MD* 2:

137–61.

Brenkman, J. (1976). "Echo and Narcissus in the Text." *Georgia Review* 30: 293–327.

Brown, R. D. (1987). "The Palace of the Sun in Ovid's *Metamorphoses*." In Mi. Whitby, P. Hardie, and Ma. Whitby, eds., *Homo Viator. Classical Essays for John Bramble*, 211–20. Bristol: Bolchazy-Carducci Publishers.

———. (1988). *Lucretius on Love and Sex*. London: Brill Academic Publisher.

Buchheit, V. (1966). "Mythos und Geschichte in Ovids *Metamorphosen* I." *Hermes* 94: 80–108.

Butler, J. (1990). *Gender Trouble: Feminism and the Subversion of Identity*. London. Routledge.

Cahoon, L. (1990). "Let the Muse Sing On: Poetry, Criticism, Feminism, and the Case of Ovid." *Helios* 17: 197–211.

———. (1996). "Calliope's Song: Shifting Narrators in Ovid, *Metamorphoses* 5." *Helios* 23.1: 43–66.

Cairns, F. (1975). *Further Adventures of a Locked-out Lover: Propertius 1.17*. Liverpool: Liverpool University Press.

Campbell Rhorer, C. (1980). "Red and White in Ovid's *Metamorphoses:* The Mulberry Tree in the Tale of Pyramus and Thisbe." *Ramus* 9.2: 79–88.

Caws, M. A. (1985). "Ladies Shot and Painted: Female Embodiment in Surrealist Art." In S. R. Suleiman, ed., *The Female Body in Western Culture: Contemporary Perspectives*, 262–87. Cambridge, Mass: Harvard University Press.

Celoria, F. (1992). *The Metamorphoses of Antoninus Liberalis. A Translation with Commentary*. London: Routledge.

Cohen, D. (1989). "Seclusion, Separation, and the Status of Women." *G&R* 36.1: 3–15.

Copley, F. O. (1978). *Exclusus Amator. A Study in Latin Love Poetry*. Madison, Wis.: American Philological Association.

Culler, J. (1982). *On Deconstruction: Theory and Criticism after Structuralism*. London: Routledge and Kegan Paul.

Curran, L. C. (1972). "Transformation and anti-Augustanism in Ovid's *Metamorphoses*." *Arethusa* 5: 71–91.

———. (1978). "Rape and Rape Victims in the *Metamorphoses*." *Arethusa* 11: 213–41.

Davis, G. (1983). *The Death of Procris. Amor and the Hunt in Ovid's Metamorphoses*. Rome: Edizioni dell' Ateneo.

Deacy, S., and K. F. Pierce. (1997). *Rape in Antiquity*. London: Duckworth in Association with the Classical Press of Wales.

De Lauretis, T. (1984). *Alice Doesn't: Feminism, Semiotics, Cinema*. Bloomington: Indiana University Press.

De Luce, J. (1993). "'O For a Thousand Tongues to Sing': A Footnote on *Metamorphoses*, Silence and Power." In M. deForest, ed., *Women's Power, Man's Game: Essays on Classical Antiquity in Honor of Joy King*, 305–21. Wauconda, Ill.: Bolchazy-Carducci.

Detienne, M. (1977) *The Gardens of Adonis: Spices in Greek Mythology*. Translated by J. Lloyd. Princeton: Princeton University Press.

Devereaux, M. (1990). "Oppressive Texts, Resisting Readers and the Gendered Spectator: The New Aesthetics." *The Journal of Aesthetics and Art Criticism* 48.4: 337–47.

Dickie, M. W. (1993a). "Dioscurus and the Impotence of Envy." *BASP* 1–2: 63–66.

———. (1993b). "Baskania, probaskania and prosbaskania." *Glotta* 7.1 3–4: 1174–77.

Doane, M. A. (1987). *The Desire to Desire: The Woman's Film of the 1940s*. Blooming-ton: Indiana University Press.

Donaldson, I. (1982). *The Rapes of Lucretia. A Myth and Its Transformations*. Oxford: Oxford University Press.

Due, O. S. (1974). *Changing Forms. Studies in the Metamorphoses of Ovid*. Copenhagen: Gyldendal.

Durling, R. M. (1958). "Ovid as Praeceptor Amoris." *CJ* 53: 157–67.

Eagleton, M. (1996). *Feminist Literary Theory: A Reader*. Oxford: Blackwell.

Eilberg-Schwartz, H. (1995). *Off with Her Head!* Berkeley: University of California Press.

Ellis Hanson, A. (1990). "The Medical Writer's Woman." In D. Halperin, J. Winkler, and F. Zeitlin, *Before Sexuality. The Construction of Erotic Experience in the Ancient World*, 309–37. Princeton: Princeton University Press.

———. (1991). "Continuity and Change: Three Case Studies in Hippocratic Gynecological Therapy and Theory." In S. B. Pomeroy, ed., *Women's History and Ancient History*, 73–110. Chapel Hill: University of North Carolina Press.

Elsner, J. (1991). "Visual Mimesis and the Myth of the Real: Ovid's Pygmalion as Viewer." *Ramus* 20.2: 154–68.

———. (1995). *Art and the Roman Viewer*. Cambridge: Cambridge University Press.

———. (1996). "Naturalism and the Erotics of the Gaze." In N. Boymel Kampen, ed., *Sexuality in Ancient Art. Near East, Egypt, Greece and Italy*, 247–61. New York: Cambridge University Press.

Elsner, J., and A. R. Sharrock. (1991). "Re-Viewing Pygmalion." *Ramus* 20.2: 148–82.

Elsom, H. E. (1992). "Callirhoe: Displaying the Phallic Woman." In A. Richlin, ed., *Pornography and Representation in Greece and Rome*, 247–61. Oxford: Oxford University Press.

Ernout, A., and A. Meillet (1985). *Dictionaire etymologique de la langue latine*. Paris: Klincksiek.

Evans, D. (1996). *An Introductory Dictionary of Lacanian Psychoanalysis*. London: Routledge. Fantham, E., et al. (1994). *Women in the Classical World. Image and Text*. Oxford: Oxford University Press.

Farrell, J. (1992). "Dialogue of Genres in Ovid's 'Lovesong of Polyphemus' (*Metamorphoses* 13.719–897)." *AJPh* 113: 235–68.

———. (1999) "The Ovidian *Corpus*: Poetic Body and Poetic Text." in P. Hardie, S. Hinds, and A. Barchiesi, eds., *Ovidian Transformations*, 127–41. Cambridge: Cambridge University Press.

Feeney, D. C. (1991). *The Gods in Epic*. Oxford: Oxford University Press.

Feldherr, A. (1997). "Metamorphosis and Sacrifice in Ovid's Theban Narrative." *MD* 38: 25–55.

Felson Rubin, N. (1994). *Regarding Penelope. From Character to Poetics*. Princeton: Princeton University Press.

Fetterly, J. (1978). *The Resisting Reader: A Feminist Approach to American Literature*. Bloomington: Indiana University Press.

Fish, S. E. (1980a). "Literature in the Reader: Affective Stylistics." In J. P. Tompkins, ed., *Reader-Response Criticism. From Formalism to Post-Structuralism*, 70–100. Baltimore: Johns Hopkins University Press.

_____. (1980b). "Interpreting the *Variorum*." In J. P. Tompkins, ed., *Reader-Response Criticism. From Formalism to Post-Structuralism*, 164–84. Baltimore: John Hopkins University Press.

Fitzgerald, W. (1995). *Catullan Provocations: Lyric Poetry and the Drama of Position*. Berkeley: University of California Press.

Forrester, V. (1980). "What Women's Eyes See." In E. Marks and I. de Courtivron, eds., *New French Feminisms. An Anthology*, 181–82. Amherst: University of Massachusetts Press.

Fowler, D.P. (1991). "Narrate and Describe: The Problem of Ekphrasis." *JRS* 81: 25–36.

_____. (1990). "Deviant Focalisation in Virgil's *Aeneid*." *PCPhS* 36: 42–63. Reprinted in D. P. Fowler (2000), *Roman Constructions. Readings in Postmodern Latin*. Oxford: Oxford University Press.

_____. (2000). "Pyramus, Thisbe, King Kong: Ovid and the Presence of Poetry." In D. P. Fowler, *Roman Constructions. Readings in Postmodern Latin*. Oxford: Oxford University Press.

Fränkel, H. (1945). *Ovid. A Poet between Two Worlds*. Berkeley: University of California Press.

Fredrick, D. (1995). "Beyond the Atrium to Ariadne: Erotic Painting and Visual Pleasure in the Roman House." *ClAnt* 14.2: 266–87.

_____. (2002). "Introduction. Invisible Rome." In D. Fredrick, ed., *The Roman Gaze. Vision, Power and the Body*. Baltimore: Johns Hopkins University Press.

Freud, S. (1986a). "Female Sexuality." In *The Standard Edition of the Complete Psychological Works of Sigmund Freud, Volume XXI*, edited and translated by J. Strachey, 223–43. London: Hogarth Press and the Institute of Psycho-Analysis.

_____. (1986b). "Femininity." In *New Introductory Lectures on Psycho-Analysis 33*. In *The Standard Edition of the Complete Psychological Works of Sigmund Freud, Volume XXII*, edited and translated by J. Strachey, 112–35. London: Hogarth Press and the Institute of Psycho-Analysis.

Fuss, D. (1989). *Essentially Speaking*. New York: Routledge.

Fyler, J. M. (1971). "*Omnia vincit amor*: Incongruity and the Limitations of Structure in Ovid's Elegiac Poetry." *CJ* 66: 196–203.

Galinsky, K. (1975). *Ovid's Metamorphoses. An Introduction to the Basic Aspects*. Oxford: Blackwell.

Gamel, M. K. (1984). "Baucis and Philemon: Paradigm or Paradox?" *Helios* 11: 117–31.

Gamman, L., and M. Marshment, eds. (1988). *The Female Gaze: Women as Viewers of Popular Culture*. London: Women's Press.

Gandelman, C. (1991). *Reading Pictures, Viewing Texts*. Bloomington: Indiana University Press.

Genette, G. (1982). "Frontiers of Narrative." In *Figures of Literary Discourse*, translated by A. Sheridan, 127–44. New York: Columbia University Press.

Gentilcore, R. (1995). "The Landscape of Desire: The Tale of Pomona and Vertumnus in Ovid's *Metamorphoses*." *Phoenix* 49.2: 110–20.

Glare, P. G. W., ed. 1997). *The Oxford Latin Dictionary*. Oxford: Oxford University Press.

Gleason, M. W. (1995). *Making Men. Sophists and Self-representation in Ancient Rome*. Princeton: Princeton University Press.

Glenn, E. M. (1986). *The Metamorphoses: Ovid's Roman Games.* Lanham, Md.: University Press of America.

Goldhill, S., and R. Osborne, eds. (1994). *Art and Text in Ancient Greek Culture.* Cambridge: Cambridge University Press.

Gordon, P. (1997). "The Lover's Voice in *Heroides* 15: Or, Why Is Sappho a Man?" In J. P. Hallet and M. B. Skinner, eds., *Roman Sexualities,* 274–91. Princeton: Princeton University Press.

Gowers, E. (1993). *The Loaded Table. Representations of Food in Roman Literature.* Oxford: Oxford University Press.

Graf, F. (1988). "Ovide, les *Métamorphoses* et la veracité du mythe." In C. Calame, ed., *Metamorphoses du mythe en Grece antique,* 57–70. Geneva: Labor et Fides.

Grant, M., and J. Hazel, J. (1973). *Who's Who in Classical Mythology.* Oxford: Oxford University Press.

Grimal, P. (1986). *The Dictionary of Classical Mythology.* Translated by A. R. Maxwell-Hyslop. Oxford: Blackwell. .

Gross, K. (1992). *The Dream of the Moving Statue.* Ithaca: Cornell University Press.

Gross, N. (2000). "Allusion and Rhetorical Wit in Ovid, *Metamorphoses* 13." *Scholia* 9: 54–65.

Gubar, S. (1982). "'The Blank Page' and the Issues of Female Creativity." In E. Abel, ed., *Writing and Sexual Difference,* 73–93. Brighton: Harvester Press.

Hall, E. (1991). *Inventing the Barbarian. Greek Self-Definition through Tragedy.* Oxford: Oxford University Press.

Halperin, D. (1990). *One Hundred Years of Homosexuality.* New York: Routledge.

———, J. Winkler, and F. Zeitlin, (1990). *Before Sexuality. The Construction of Erotic Experience in the Ancient Greek World.* Princeton: Princeton University Press.

Hardie, P. (1990). "Ovid's Theban History: The First 'Anti-*Aeneid*'?" *CQ* n.s.40: 225–35.

———. (1999). "Ovid into Laura: Absent Presences in the *Metamorphoses* and Petrarch's *Rime Sparse.*" In P. Hardie, A. Barchiesi, and S. Hinds, eds., *Ovidian Transformations,* 255–70. Cambridge: Cambridge University Press.

———. (2002a). *Ovid's Poetics of Illusion.* Cambridge: Cambridge University Press.

———. (2002b). *The Cambridge Companion to Ovid.* Cambridge: Cambridge University Press.

———, A. Barchiesi, and S. Hinds, eds. (1999). *Ovidian Transformations.* Cambridge: Cambridge University Press.

Harries, B. (1990). "The Spinner and the Poet: Arachne in Ovid's *Metamorphoses.*" *PCPhS* 34: 64–82.

Havelock Mitchell, C. (1995). *The Aphrodite of Knidos and Her Successors. A Historical Review of the Female Nude in Greek Art.* Ann Arbor: University of Michigan Press.

Heath, J. (1992). *Actaeon, the Unmannerly Intruder.* New York: Peter Lang.

———. (1996). "The Stupor of Orpheus: Ovid's *Metamorphoses* 10.64–71." *CJ* 91.4: 353–70.

———. (1991). "Diana's Understanding of Ovid's *Metamorphoses.*" *CJ* 86: 233–43.

Henderson, J. (1975). *The Maculate Muse.* New Haven: Yale University Press.

———. (1987). *Aristophanes Lysistrata.* Oxford: Oxford University Press.

Hinds, S. E. (1987). *The Metamorphoses of Persephone. Ovid and the Self-conscious Muse.* Cambridge: Cambridge University Press.

———. (2002). "Landscape with Figures: Aesthetics of Place in *Metamorphoses* and

Its Tradition." In P. Hardie, ed., *The Cambridge Companion to Ovid*. Cambridge: Cambridge University Press.

Hollis, A. (1970). *Ovid, Metamorphoses. Book VIII*. Oxford: Oxford University Press.

Homer. (1999). *Iliad*. Trans. A. T. Murray. Rev. by W. F. Wyatt. Cambridge, Mass.: Harvard University Press.

———. (1995). *Odyssey*. Trans. A. T. Murray. Rev. by G. E. Dimock. Cambridge, Mass.: Harvard University Press.

Isaac, B. (2004). *The Invention of Racism in Classical Antiquity*. Princeton: Princeton University Press.

Iser, W. (1980). "The Reading Process: A Phenomenological Approach." In J. P. Tompkins, ed., *Reader-Response Criticism. From Formalism to Post-Structuralism*, 50–69. Baltimore: Johns Hopkins University Press.

Janan, M. (1988). "The Book of Good Love? Design versus Desire in *Metamorphoses* 10." *Ramus* 17: 110–37.

———. (1994). "There beneath the Roman Ruin Where the Purple Flowers Grow: The Minyeides and the Feminine Imagination." *AJPh*: 115.3: 427–48.

Jay, M. (1993). *Downcast Eyes: The Denigration of Vision in Twentieth-Century French Thought*. Berkeley: University of California Press.

Jed, S. H. (1989). *Chaste Thinking. The Rape of Lucretia and the Birth of Humanism*. Bloomington: Indiana University Press.

Jenkins, T. (2001). "The Writing in (and of) Ovid's Byblis Episode." *HSPh* 100: 439–51.

Johnson, P. J. (1996). "Constructions of Venus in *Metamorphoses* V." *Arethusa* 29.1: 125–49.

Johnson, P., and M. Malamud. (1988). "Ovid's Musomachia." *PCPhS* 23.1–2: 30–38.

Johnson, W. R. (1996). "The Rapes of Callisto." *CJ* 92.1: 9–24.

Joplin, P. (1984). "The Voice of the Shuttle Is Ours." *Stanford Literature Review* 1.1: 25–53.

Jouteur, I. (2001). *Jeux de genres dans les Métamorphoses d'Ovide*. Louvain: Peeters.

Kaplan, E. A. (1983). "Is the Gaze Male?" In A. Snitow., C. Stansell, and S. Thompson, eds., *Powers of Desire: The Politics of Sexuality*, 309–27. New York: Monthly Review Press.

Keith, A. (1992). *A Play of Fictions: Studies in Ovid's Metamorphoses Book 2*. Ann Arbor: University of Michigan Press.

———. "Versions of Epic Masculinity in Ovid's *Metamorphoses*." In P. Hardie, A. Barchiesi, and S. Hinds, eds., *Ovidian Transformations*, 214–39. Cambridge: Cambridge University Press.

Kennedy, D. F. (2000). "Making a Text of the Universe: Perspectives on Discursive Order in the *De Rerum Natura* of Lucretius." In A. R. Sharrock. and H. Morales, eds., *Intratextuality. Greek and Roman Textual Relations*, 205–26. Oxford: Oxford University Press.

Kennedy, G. A. (1986). "Helen's Web Unraveled." *Arethusa* 19: 5–14.

Keynes, G, ed. (1966). *Blake. Complete Writings*. Oxford: Oxford University Press.

Kirk, G. S. (1985). *The Iliad: A Commentary, Vol. I, Books 1–4*. Cambridge: Cambridge University Press.

Knoespel, K. (1985). *Narcissus and the Invention of Personal History*. New York: Taylor and Francis.

Knox, P. E. (1986). "The Song of Orpheus." In P. E. Knox, *Ovid's Metamorphoses and the Traditions of Augustan Poetry*. Cambridge: Cambridge Philological Society.

————. (1990). "In Pursuit of Daphne." *TAPhA* 120: 183–202.

Konstan, D. (1991). "The Death of Argus, or What Stories Do. Audience Response in Ancient Fiction and Theory." *Helios* 18: 15–30.

Kris, E., and O. Kurz. (1979). *Legend, Myth and Magic in the Image of the Artist*. Translated by A. Laing. New Haven: Yale University Press.

Labate, M. (1992). "Storie di instabilitá: l'episodio di Ermafrodito nelle *Metamorphosi di Ovidio*." *MD* 30: 49–62.

Lacan, J. (1998). *The Four Fundamental Concepts of Psychoanalysis*. Translated by A. Sheridan. New York: W.W. Norton & Company.

Laguna Mariscal, G. (1989). "Dos imágenes matrimoniales en el episodio de Dafne y Apollo (Ov. *Met.*1.452–567)." *Anuario de Estudios Filológicos* 12: 133–43.

Laird, A. (1993). "Sounding Out Ekphrasis: Art and Text in Catullus 64." *JRS* 83: 18–30.

Laslo, N. (1935). "Reflessi d'arte figurata nelle *Metamorfosi di Ovidio*." In *Ephemeris Dacoromana* 6: 368–441.

Lateiner, D. (1984). "Mythic and Non-mythic Artists in Ovid's *Metamorphoses*." *Ramus* 13.1: 1–30.

Lefkowitz, M.R., and M. B. Fant. (1982). *Women's Lives in Greece and Rome: A Source Book in Translation*. Baltimore: Johns Hopkins University Press.

Liveley, G. (1999a). "Reading Resistance in Ovid's *Metamorphoses*." In P. Hardie, A. Barchiesi, and S. Hinds, eds. *Ovidian Transformations*, 197–213. Cambridge: Cambridge University Press.

————. (1999b). "Re-visions." Unpublished Ph.D. dissertation. University of Bristol.

Lucian. (1993). *Amores*. 3rd ed. Trans. A. M. Harmon and ed. M. D. Macleod. Cambridge, Mass.: Harvard University Press.

Ludwig, W. (1965). *Struktur und Einheit der Metamorphosen Ovids*. Berlin: De Gruyter.

Maltby, R. (1991). *A Lexicon of Ancient Latin Etymologies*. Leeds: Cairns.

Marder, E. (1992). "Disarticulated Voices: Feminism and Philomela." *Hypatia* 7.2: 148–66.

Mariotti, S. (1957). "La carriera poetica di Ovidio." *Belfagor* 12: 609–33.

McGrath, E. (1992). "The Black Andromeda." *JWI* 55: 1–77.

McIntosh Snyder, J. (1981). "The Web of Song: Weaving Imagery in Homer and the Lyric Poets." *CJ* 76: 193–94.

Miller, N. K. (1986). "Arachnologies: The Woman, the Text and the Critic." In N. K. Miller, ed., *The Poetics of Gender*, 288–90. New York: Columbia University Press.

Mills, S. (1994). *Gendering the Reader*. New York: Harvester Wheatsheaf.

Milton, J. (1924). *Paradise Lost*. In Vaughn Moody, ed., *The Complete Poetical Works of John Milton*. Cambridge: Houghton Mifflin Company.

Mulvey, L. (1975). "Visual Pleasure and Narrative Cinema." *Screen* 16.3: 8–18.

————. (1989). "Afterthoughts on 'Visual Pleasure and Narrative Cinema." In L. Mulvey, *Visual and Other Pleasures (Theories of Representation and Difference)*. Bloomington: Indiana University Press.

————. (1996). "Pandora's Box: Topographies of Curiosity." In L. Mulvey, *Fetishism and Curiosity*, 53–64. Bloomington: Indiana University Press. .

Murgatroyd, P. (1995). "The Sea of Love." *CQ* 45.1: 9–25.

Myers, K. S. (1992). "The Lizard and the Owl: An Etymological Pair in Ovid: Metamorphoses Book 5." *AJPh* 113.1: 63–68.

_____. (1994a). "*Ultimus Ardor:* Pomona and Vertumnus in Ovid's *Met*.14. 623–771." *CJ* 89: 225–50.

_____. (1994b). *Ovid's Causes. Cosmogony and Aetiology in the Metamorphoses.* Ann Arbor: University of Michigan Press.

Nagle, B. R. (1983). "Byblis and Myrrha: Two Incest Narratives in the *Metamorphoses*." *CJ* 78: 301–15.

_____. (1988a). "A Trio of Love-Triangles in Ovid's *Metamorphoses*." *Arethusa* 21: 75–98.

_____. (1988b). "Erotic Pursuit and narrative Seduction in Ovid's *Metamorphoses*." *Ramus* 17: 32–51.

_____. (1988c). "Two Miniature Carmina Perpetua in the *Metamorphoses:* Calliope and Orpheus." *GB* 15: 99–125.

_____. (1989). "Ovid's *Metamorphoses:* A Narratological Catalogue." *Syll Class* 1: 97–125.

Newlands, C. E. (1997). "The Metamorphosis of Ovid's Medea." In J. J. Claus and S. Iles Johnston, eds., *Medea*, 178–208. Princeton: Princeton University Press.

Nicoll, W. S. M. (1980). "Cupid, Apollo and Daphne (Ovid, *Met*.1.452ff.)." *CQ* 30: 174–82.

Nikolopoulos, A. D. (2003). "Tremuloque gradu venit aegra senectus: Old Age in Ovid's *Metamorphoses*." *Mnemosyne* 56.1: 48–60.

Nugent, G. (1990). "The Sex Which Is Not One: De-Constructing Ovid's Hermaphrodite." *Differences* 2.1: 160–85.

O'Bryhim, S. (1990). "Ovid's Version of Callisto's Punishment." *Hermes* 18: 75–80.

Otis, B. (1970). *Ovid as an Epic Poet.* Cambridge: Cambridge University Press.

Panofsky, E. (1968). *Idea. A Concept in Art History.* Translated by J. S. Peake. Columbia: University of South Carolina Press.

_____, and D. Panofsky. (1956). *Pandora's Box: Changing Aspects of a Mythical Symbol.* London: Pantheon Books for Bollingen Foundation.

Pantelia, M. (1993). "Spinning and Weaving: Ideas of Domestic Order in Homer." *AJPh* 114.4: 493–501.

Paoli, U. E. (1963). *Rome. Its People, Life and Customs.* Translated by R. D. Macnaghten. New York: Longman.

Parry, H. (1964). "Ovid's *Metamorphoses:* Violence in a Pastoral Landscape." *TAPhA* 95: 268–82.

Paschalis, M. (1997). *Virgil's Aeneid. Semantic Relations and Proper Names.* Oxford: Oxford University Press.

Penley, C. (1989). *The Future of an Illusion: Film, Feminism and Psychoanalysis.* London: Routledge.

Perutelli, A. (1978). "L'inversione speculare. Per una retorica dell' ecphrasis." *MD* 1: 87–98.

Piccaluga, G. (1977). "Adonis, i cacciatori falliti e l' avvento dell' agricoltura." In B. Gentili and G. Paioni, eds., *Il mito greco*, 33–48. Rome: Ateneo-Bizzari.

Pinkster, H. (1990). *Latin Syntax and Semantics.* London: Routledge.

Pohlenz, M. (1913). "Die Abfassungzeit von Ovids Metamorphosen." *Hermes* 48: 1–13.

Pomeroy, S. B. (1995). *Goddesses, Whores, Wives and Slaves. Women in Classical Antiquity.* New York: Schocken Books.

Pribram, E. D. (1988). *Female Spectators. Looking at Film and Television.* London: Verso.

Pucci, P. (1978). "Lingering on the Threshold." *Glyph* 3: 52–73.

Raval, S. (2001). "'A Lover's Discourse': Byblis in *Metamorphoses* 9." *Arethusa* 34.3: 285–311.

Reed, I. (1978). *Mumbo Jumbo.* New York: Scribner.

Reed, J. D. (1995). "The Sexuality of Adonis." *ClAnt* 14.2: 317–47.

Ribichini, S. (1981). *Adonis: Aspetti 'orientali' di un mito greco.* Rome: Consiglio nazionali delle ricerche.

Richlin, A. (1992). "Reading Ovid's Rapes." In A. Richlin, ed., *Pornography and Representation in Greece and Rome,* 158–79. Oxford: Oxford University Press.

Ronnick, M. V. (1993). "*Stellio non lacerta et bubo non strix:* Ovid *Metamorphoses* 5.446–61 and 534–50." *AJPh* 114.3: 419–20.

Rosand, D. (1990). "Ekphrasis and the Generation of Images." *Arion* n.s.1: 61–105.

Rosati G. (1983). *Narciso e Pigmalione: illusione e spectacolo nelle Metamorfosi di Ovidio.* Florence: Sansoni.

_____. (1999). "Form in Motion: Weaving the Text in the *Metamorphoses.*" In P. Hardie, A. Barchiesi, and S. Hinds, eds., *Ovidian Transformations,* 240–53. Cambridge: Cambridge University Press

Schaps, D. (1977). "The Woman Least Mentioned: Etiquette and Women's Names." *CQ* 27: 323–32.

Scheid, J., and J. Svenbro. (1996). *The Craft of Zeus. Myths of Weaving and Fabric.* Cambridge, Mass.: Harvard University Press.

Schmidt, E. A. (1991). *Ovids poetische Menschwelt. Die Metamorphosen als Metapher und Symphonie.* Heidelberg: Winter.

Schweizer, B. (1934) "Mimesis und Phantasia." *Philologus* 89: 286–300.

Segal, C. (1969). *Landscape in Ovid's Metamorphoses. A Study in the Transformation of a Literary Symbol.* Wiesbaden: Hermes Einzelschriften 23.

_____. (1971). "Narrative Art in the *Metamorphoses.*" *CJ* 66: 331–37.

_____. (1978). "Ovid's Cephalus and Procris: Myth and Tragedy." *GB* 7: 175–205.

_____. (1982). *Dionysiac Poetics and Euripides' Bacchae.* Princeton: Princeton University Press.

_____. (1989). *Orpheus: The Myth of the Poet.* Baltimore: Johns Hopkins University Press.

_____. (1994). "Philomela's Web and the Pleasures of the Text." In I. J. F. de Jorg and J. P. Sullivan, eds., *Modern Critical Theory and Classical Literature,* 258–80. Leiden: Brill.

_____. (1998). "Ovid's Metamorphic Bodies: Art, Gender, and Violence in the *Metamorphoses.*" *Arion* 5: 9–41.

_____. (2001). "Jupiter in Ovid's *Metamorphoses.*" *Arion* 9.1: 78–99.

_____. (2002). "Black and White Magic in Ovid's *Metamorphoses:* Passion, Love and Art." *Arion* 9.3: 1–34.

Sharrock, A. R. (1991a). "Womanufacture." *JRS* 81: 36–49.

_____. (1991b). "The Love of Creation." *Ramus* 20.2: 169–82.

_____. (1996). "Representing Metamorphoses." In J. Elsner, ed., *Art and Text in Roman Culture,* 103–30. Cambridge: Cambridge University Press.

_____. (1999). "Resisting, Releasing, and Other Models of Gendered Reading." Unpublished lecture, University of London.

_____. (2000). "Intratextuality: Texts, Parts, and (W)holes in Theory." In A. R. Sharrock and H. Morales, eds., *Intratextuality. Greek and Roman Textual Relations,* 1–39. Oxford: Oxford University Press.

_____. (2002a). "Looking at Looking. Can you resist a Reading?" In D. Fredrick, ed., *The Roman Gaze*. Baltimore: Johns Hopkins University Press.

_____. (2002b). "Gender and Sexuality." In P. Hardie, ed., *The Cambridge Companion to Ovid*. Cambridge: Cambridge University Press.

_____. (2002c). "An A-musing Tale: Gender and Ovid's Battles with Inspiration in *Metamorphoses*." In E. Spentzou. and D. P. Fowler, eds., *Cultivating the Muse: Struggles for Power and Inspiration in Classical Literature*. Oxford: Oxford University Press.

Shaw Hardy, C. (1995). "Ekphrasis and the Male Narrator in Ovid's Arachne." *Helios* 22.2: 104–44.

Shlain, L. (1998). *The Alphabet versus the Goddess. The Conflict between Word and Image*. New York: Viking Penguin.

Shorrock, R. (2003). "Ovidian Plumbing in *Metamorphoses* 4." *CQ* 53.2: 624–27.

Showalter, E. (1971). "Women and the Literary Curriculum." *College English* 32: 855–62.

Simpson, J. A., and E. S. C. Weiner, eds. (1989). *The Oxford English Dictionary*. Oxford: Oxford University Press.

Sissa, G. (1990). *Greek Virginity*. Cambridge, Mass.: Harvard University Press.

Skinner, M. (1997). "Introduction: *Quod multo fit aliter in Graecia*." In J. P. Hallet and M. Skinner, eds., *Roman Sexualities*, 3–25. Princeton: Princeton University Press.

Slater, D.A. (1927). *Towards a Text of the Metamorphosis of Ovid*. Oxford: Oxford University Press.

Snow, E. (1989). "Theorising the Male Gaze: Some Problems." *Representations* 25.1: 30–41.

Snowden, F. M., Jr. (1970). *Blacks in Antiquity: Ethiopians in the Greco-Roman Experience*. Cambridge, Mass.: Belknap Press of Harvard University Press.

_____. (1983). *Before Color Prejudice. The Ancient View of Blacks*. Cambridge, Mass.: Harvard University Press.

Solodow, J. B. (1988). *The World of Ovid's Metamorphoses*. Chapel Hill: University of North Carolina Press.

Solomon, J. (1993). "The Wandering Womb of Delos." In M. deForest, ed., *Woman's Power, Man's Game. Essays on Classical Antiquity in Honor of Joy K. King*, 91–108. Wauconda, Ill.: Bolchazy-Carducci.

Spencer. R. A. (1997). *Contrast as Narrative Technique in Ovid's Metamorphoses*. Lewiston, N.Y.: Edwin Mellen Press.

Spentzou, E. (2003). *Readers and Writers in Ovid's Heroides: Transgressions of Gender and Genre*. Oxford: Oxford University Press.

Stehle, E. (1990). "Sappho's Gaze: Fantasies of a Goddess and a Young Man." *Differences* 2.1: 86–125.

Stephens, W. (1958). "Cupid and Venus in Ovid's *Metamorphoses*." *TAPhA* 89: 218–36.

Studlar, G. (1988). *In the Realm of Pleasure: Von Sternberg, Dietrich and the Masochistic Aesthetic*. Urbana: University of Illinois Press.

Tarrant, R. J. (2000). "The Soldier in the Garden and Other Intruders in Ovid's *Metamorphoses*." *HSPh* 100: 425–37.

Thibault, J. C. (1964). *The Mystery of Ovid's Exile*. Berkeley: University of California Press.

Thomas, P. L. (1979). "Red and White: A Roman Color Symbolism." *RhM* 122: 310–16.

Thompson, W. (1982). "Weaving: A Man's Work." *CW* 75: 217–22.

Tissol, G. (1997). *The Face of Nature. Wit, Narrative, and Cosmic Origins in Ovid's Metamorphoses*. Princeton: Princeton University Press.

Tompkins, J. P., ed. (1980). *Reader-Response Criticism. From Formalism to Post-Structuralism*. Baltimore: Johns Hopkins University Press.

Towneley Parker, R. C. (1996). "Athena." In S. Hornblower and A. Spawforth, eds., *The Oxford Classical Dictionary*, 201–2. Oxford: Oxford University Press.

Vernant, J-P. (1991). *Mortals and Immortals. Collected Essays*, F. I. Zeitlin, ed. Princeton: Princeton University Press.

Veyne, P. (1985). "Homosexuality in Ancient Rome." Translated by A. Foster. In P. Ariès and A. Béjin, eds., *Western Sexuality. Practice and Precept in Past and Present Times*, 26–35. Oxford: Blackwell.

Viarre, S. (1964). *L'image et la pensée dans les Métamorphoses d'Ovide*. Paris: Presses Universitaires.

Vincent, M. (1994). "Between Ovid and Barthes: Ekphrasis, Orality, Textuality in Ovid's Arachne." *Arethusa* 27.3: 361–86.

von Albrecht, M. (1979). "L' Episode d' Arachné dans les *Métamorphoses* d' Ovide." *REL* 57 (1979): 266–77.

Voigt, E. M., ed. (1979). *Sappho et Alcaeus*. Amsterdam: Hakkert.

Wace, J. B., and F. H. Stubbings, eds., (1962). *A Companion to Homer*. London: Macmillan.

Wall, K. (1988). *The Callisto Myth from Ovid to Atwood: Initiation and Rape in Literature*. Lingston, Ontario: McGill-Queen's University Press.

Weinberg, G. D., and S. S. Weinberg. (1956). "Arachne of Lydia at Corinth." In S. S. Weinberg, ed., *The Aegean and the Near East. Studies Presented to Hetty Goldman on the Occasion of her Seventy-fifth Birthday*, 262–67. Locust Valley, N.Y.: J. J. Augustin.

Wheeler, S. M. (1999). *A Discourse of Wonders. Audience and Performance in Ovid's Metamorphoses*. Philadelphia: University of Pennsylvania Press.

_____. (2000). *Narrative Dynamics in Ovid's Metamorphoses*. Tübingen: Gunter Narr Verlag.

Wilkinson, L. P. (1955). *Ovid Recalled*. Cambridge: Cambridge University Press.

Williams, C. (1999). *Roman Homosexuality. Ideologies of Masculinity in Classical Antiquity*. Oxford: Oxford University Press.

Wills, J. (1990). "Callimachean Models for Ovid's 'Apollo-Daphne.'" *MD* 24: 143–53.

Wilson, W. M. (1964). *Metamorphoses Book Fourteen*. London: Macmillan.

Winkler, J. J. (1990). *The Constraints of Desire*. New York: Routledge.

Winsor Leach, E. (1988). *The Rhetoric of Space: Literary and Artistic Representations of Landscape in Republican and Augustan Rome*. Princeton: Princeton University Press.

_____. (1974). "Ekphrasis and the Theme of Artistic Failure in Ovid's *Metamorphoses*." *Ramus* 3: 102–42.

Wyke, M. (1987). "Scripta Puella." *JRS* 77: 47–61.

_____. (1994). "Women in the Mirror: The Rhetoric of Adornment in the Roman World." In L. J. Archer and S. Fischer, eds., *Women in Ancient Societies. An Illusion of the Night*, 134–51. London: Routledge.

Yardley, J. C. (1978). "The Elegiac Paraclausithyron." *Eranos* 76: 19–34.

Zeitlin, F. I. (1994a). "Gardens of Desire in Longus's Daphnis and Chloe: Nature, Art and Imitation." In J. Tatum, ed., *The Search for the Ancient Novel*. Baltimore: Johns

Hopkins University Press.

_____. (1994b). "The Artful Eye: Vision, Ekphrasis and Spectacle in Euripidean Theatre." In S. Goldhill and R. Osborne, eds., *Art and Text in Ancient Greek Culture*, 138–96. Cambridge: Cambridge University Press.

_____. (1996). "Signifying Difference: The Case of Hesiod's Pandora." In F. Zeitlin, *Playing the Other. Gender and Society in Greek Literature*, 53–86. Chicago: University of Chicago Press.

Zilsel, E. (1926). *Die Entstehung des Geniebegriffes: Ein Beitrag zur Ideengeschichte der Antike und des Frühkapitalismus*. Tübingen.

INDEX LOCORUM

General Index

❦

absence, as feminine, 96, 111

Acis, 31, 184–92; as boy, 184–85, 187, 191–92; effeminacy of, 192, 193

Acoetes, 53

Actaeon, 14, 15, 40, 45, 46–53, 73, 85, 167, 170, 172, 175, 176, 181, 184, 197; gaze of, 46, 48, 49, 52; and Narcissus, 57–58; as narrator, 50; objectification of, 52; penetration by, 48–49; and Pentheus, 55–56; silencing of, 219n89

activity, as masculine, 67

Adams, J. N., 220n108, 222n31

Adonis, 31, 85–86, 95–96, 185, 201–3; as boy, 201–2; fixation of, 95–96; masculinity of, 203

adultery, 158–59

Aeneas, 97, 203–4, 206

Aeson, 107, 108

Agave, 54

Aglauros, 2, 26, 38–42, 216n49; gaze of, 42

Ahl, F., 233n45

Alberti, Leon Battista, 211n54

Alcithoe, 32

Alcmene, 8, 193–97; as narrator, 194, 196

Alcyone, 97

Alexandrianism. *See* poetics, Callimachean

Alpheus, 180, 181, 184

Altieri, C., 210n7

Anaxarete, 62, 64, 66, 220n110; gaze of, 62–63

Anchises, 50, 73, 175, 222n29

Anderson, W. S., 81, 89, 100, 129, 130, 140, 154, 155, 164, 215n30, 230–31n8, 232n28

Andraemon, 199–200

Andromache, as weaver, 122–23

Andromeda, 17, 77–84, 130, 188, 208; immobility of, 78; as lacking gaze, 78–79; metaphorical blindness of, 79, 83; object of the gaze, 79, 82; as statue, 79, 80

Aphrodite. *See* Knidian Aphrodite; Venus

Apollo, 6–7, 8, 13, 29–31, 36, 56, 81, 108, 140, 200, 203–4, 205; as rapist, 30, 199–200, 205; birth of, 91; compared to Echo, 36–37; fixation by, 91–93; gaze of, 30–31; identified with the sun, 98

appearance, contrasted with essence, 51, 52, 55–56

apples, symbolism of, 88, 94–95, 175

Arachne, 11, 13, 14, 20, 59–61, 118, 123, 125–39, 146, 174, 183; and envy, 42; gaze of, 128, 133, 139; as masculine, 136, 137, 138–39; as resisting male authority, 126; symbolic rape of, 138; as warrior, 135; as witness to rapes, 125, 126, 128, 132, 169

Arethusa, 8, 123–24, 175, 177–82, 184,

253